MY CHILDHOOD

Maxim Gorky is the pen-name of Alexei Maximovich Peshkov, who was born in 1868 in the city of Nizhny Novgorod, now renamed after him. After his father's death he spent his childhood with his mother and grandparents in an atmosphere of hostility. He was turned out of the house when his mother died and left to work in various jobs – in a bakery, in an icon-maker's shop, on barges – until his unsuccessful attempt at suicide. For three years he wandered in the south like a tramp before publishing his first story, 'Makar Chudra', in a Tiflis newspaper. After his return to Nizhny he worked on another newspaper, in which many of his stories appeared; he quickly achieved fame and soon afterwards his play *The Lower Depths* was a triumphant success at the Moscow Arts Theatre. By now active in the revolutionary movement, he was arrested in 1905 by the Tsarist government but released following a petition signed by eminent statesmen and writers. While in America in 1906 he savagely attacked American capitalism, and wrote his best-selling novel, *Mother*. During the First World War he was associated with the Marxist Internationalist Group, and in 1917 he founded *New Life*, a daily devoted to left-wing socialism but which outspokenly attacked Kerensky and Lenin's 'Communist hysteria'. In 1921 he went to Italy, where he wrote *My Universities*, the third part of his great autobiographical trilogy; the other parts are *My Childhood* and *My Apprenticeship*. He returned to Moscow in 1928, and from then on he was a champion of the Soviet cause. In 1936 he died – allegedly poisoned by his political enemies – and was given a hero's funeral in Red Square.

Ronald Wilks studied Russian language and literature at Trinity College, Cambridge, and later Russian literature at London University where he received his Ph.D. in 1972. He has also translated 'The Little Demon' by Sologub, and, for Penguin, *My Apprenticeship* and *My Universities* by Gorky, *Diary of a Madman* by Gogol, *The Golovlyov Family* by Saltykov-Shchedrin and four volumes of stories by Chekhov, *The Kiss and Other Stories*, *The Duel and Other Stories*, *The Party and Other Stories* and *The Fiancée and Other Stories*.

MAXIM GORKY

MY CHILDHOOD

TRANSLATED
WITH AN INTRODUCTION BY
RONALD WILKS

PENGUIN BOOKS

PENGUIN BOOKS

Published by the Penguin Group
Penguin Books Ltd, 27 Wrights Lane, London W8 5TZ, England
Penguin Books USA Inc., 375 Hudson Street, New York, New York 10014, USA
Penguin Books Australia Ltd, Ringwood, Victoria, Australia
Penguin Books Canada Ltd, 10 Alcorn Avenue, Toronto, Ontario, Canada M4V 3B2
Penguin Books (NZ) Ltd, 182–190 Wairau Road, Auckland 10, New Zealand

Penguin Books Ltd, Registered Offices: Harmondsworth, Middlesex, England

First published 1913
This translation first published 1966
20

Copyright © Ronald Wilde, 1966
All rights reserved

Printed in England by Clays Ltd, St Ives plc
Set in Monotype Garamond

Introduction

ALEXEI MAXIMOVICH PESHKOV, better known by his pen-name, Maxim Gorky, was born in 1868 in the City of Nizhny Novgorod, now renamed after him. During his life Gorky – significantly meaning 'bitter' – acquired a greater reputation than any other Russian writer, and more copies of his works are sold today in Soviet Russia than of even Tolstoy's or Dostoyevsky's. He is the great, central figure in twentieth-century Russian literature, and has become a Soviet 'institution', his authority and reputation unassailable. *My Childhood* is amongst his finest works, and is one of the most moving descriptions of boyhood ever written.

Gorky's early writings were like a fresh current of air in the stuffy literary atmosphere which prevailed at the turn of the century. His first stories, such as *Makar Chudra* (1892) and *Chelkash* (1895), are romanticized tales of gipsies, legendary heroes and wandering fishermen. Later he turned to tramps, social outcasts and the men who 'dwell along the fringe'. These stories were rapturously welcomed by a reading public whose appetite was somewhat jaded by the humdrum, pedestrian, naturalistic writings of the Populist School, and which was tiring even of the delicate and subtle nuances of Chekhov. With the rise of industry, writers were now describing town life instead of vegetable existence in the country. Gorky took as his subject downtrodden tramps and factory workers and the terrible squalor in which they lived. With this preoccupation with the common man, the town artisan, it was natural that Gorky should also become the great spokesman for the rising industrial proletariat and, for a major part of his life, a leading figure in the revolutionary movement, championing the cause, and often getting himself into serious trouble when he spoke out strongly against its excesses.

Few writers can have had such a wide experience of life – and this was indeed life in the raw. *Childhood*, which describes the first eight years of the author's life, begins with the funeral of Gorky's father, who had been a paperhanger and upholsterer, and had contracted cholera while working in Astrakhan. He had been unable to bear life with the mercenary, quarrelsome and depraved Kashirins (his wife's family), and had taken his wife and small son Maxim away from their terrible house in Nizhny. After his father's death Gorky returned with his mother and grandmother to his maternal grandfather's house, for much of the time a veritable living hell, where, in Gorky's words, everyone was 'choked by a fog of mutual hostility'. His grandfather had once been a fairly prosperous barge-hauler and had subsequently set up some dye-works in Nizhny. But he went bankrupt, rashly lending some money which was never returned. The young, impressionable Gorky was initiated into this world of cruelty, greed and bestiality at the tender age of five. He could not understand why people behaved like animals, and he tells us in *Childhood* that this hard life implanted in him a lasting preoccupation with the sufferings and misfortunes of others.

At the end of *Childhood*, after his mother's death, he is bluntly told by his grandfather that he must 'go out into the world', that there is no place for him in the house any more. Left to fend for himself, Gorky worked in barges and ships along the Volga, in a bakery, in an icon-maker's shop, enduring misery and poverty, but mixing with people who were trying desperately to eke out a living by doing the most degrading work. In his famous story *Twenty-Six Men and a Girl*, he describes what it was like working in a bakery for fourteen hours a day. In *Among the People*, he describes trying to study at night after a day of dreadful drudgery. Driven to despair by the hopelessness of life, he unsuccessfully tried to commit suicide and lay for weeks in hospital with a perforated lung.

In his early literary attempts, Gorky received encouragement and advice from a lawyer, Nicholas Lanin, and the established author Korolenko. After wandering like a tramp in the south for three years, he went to Tiflis, the capital of Georgia, where he wrote his first story, *Makar Chudra*, which appeared in a local daily, *The Caucasus*. After his return north to Nizhny, where Lanin and Korolenko had obtained a job for him on another newspaper, many of these early romantic stories appeared in the daily press, and fame was quick to come. Soon afterwards his play, *The Lower Depths*, was a triumphant success at the Moscow Arts Theatre, and was produced all over Europe.

He had now become active in the revolutionary movement, having met young Marxist socialists for the first time during his stay in Kazan, and in 1905 he was arrested by the Tsarist Government, but released following a petition signed by many famous statesmen and writers. The next year he made his disastrous visit to New York, where he was enthusiastically received until his enemies made it known that his female companion was not in fact his legal wife. He fled into the country from New York, which he called the City of the Yellow Devil, and wrote a series of savage attacks on American capitalism. While he was in the States he wrote his novel *Mother*, whose principal characters were based on the revolutionaries Zalomov and his mother, who had taken a large part in the strike and demonstrations at Sormovo in 1902. This novel, which became a best-seller, was really the first comprehensive portrait of the Russian socialist movement.

Gorky returned to Europe and settled in Capri, where his villa became the centre of a writers' colony. Visitors in later years included Trotsky and Lenin, and the villa became a training school for socialist-minded writers and politicians.

During the First World War, Gorky had become associated with the Marxist Internationalist Group and early in 1917 had founded *New Life*, a daily which was devoted to the interests of left-wing socialism but which was outspoken in its criticism of Kerensky and of what was called Lenin's 'Communist hysteria'. He had been shocked by the bloodshed that came with the Revolution and was growing ever more cynical of the often ruthless Communist leaders and the corrupting effect that ideologies had on men in power. In one of his newspaper articles he spoke of Lenin and Trotsky as having abandoned the concept of freedom of speech and of the individual. The Bolshevik press was quick to reply, and *Pravda* accused him of 'fawning on the *bourgeoisie*'.

Gorky was also hated by the moderate liberals for his support of the proletariat, although he fought untiringly not only for the preservation of cultural values in the swamping tide of Communism, but for the lives of writers, scholars and artists sentenced to death or exile for their ideas. He helped young writers and organized the enormous publishing enterprise known as International Literature. As a close friend of Stalin, he had an immense influence on the progress of literature and the arts in Soviet Russia and there is no doubt that he was the driving force behind the creation of a modern Soviet literature.

His attempted suicide was to affect his lungs permanently and in 1921, persuaded to go abroad by Lenin, he went to Italy, where he wrote the last part of his great autobiographical trilogy, *My Universities*, and *The Artamanov Affair*, a crime novel.

Seven years later he returned to Moscow and from then onwards he was a champion of the Soviet cause, both in his speeches and in his journalistic writings. He was proclaimed the father of Soviet literature. The cause of his death in 1936 was at first mysterious, but was later proved to have been brought about by his political enemies, with Yagoda, the former Chief of Secret Police, chiefly responsible. His doctor, Levin, was alleged to have given him camphor, and was subsequently executed, after the trial in Moscow.

Gorky was given a hero's funeral, in Red Square, where a vast crowd assembled. Stalin and other great figures of the day were there to pay homage and to lead the tributes.

Childhood, published in 1913, is the first part of an autobiographical trilogy – brilliantly filmed by Mark Donskoy – and is one of Gorky's greatest achievements. In the other two volumes, *Among the People* and *My Universities*, he describes his later youth.

Early on in the book Gorky tells us that painful though the truth may have been, he finds himself unable to gloss over the facts or to omit unpalatable episodes. In a famous outburst he says:

When I try to recall those vile abominations of that barbarous life in Russia, at times I find myself asking the question: is it worth while recording them? And with ever stronger conviction I find the answer is yes, because that was the real loathsome truth and to this day it is still valid.

It is that truth which must be known down to the very roots, so that by tearing them up it can be completely erased from the memory, from the soul of man, from our whole oppressive and shameful life.

Suffering for Gorky is not so much the spiritual dilemma of abstract issues that it was for Dostoyevsky: it is the 'here and now' of bestial, animal-like existence in industrial towns, where people go begging in the streets, taking their pickings from refuse heaps. (The adulation Gorky received for his portraits of tramps, beggars and social outcasts provoked Tolstoy into saying: 'I knew long before Gorky that tramps have souls.')

The young, impressionable Gorky is thrust into his grandfather's household, where, in the author's own words, life is one nightmare after the other. His two uncles Mikhail and Yakov quarrel openly about their father's will, fight like wild animals and, after drinking themselves silly in the town, return to the house to smash the furniture. For what are only petty crimes, his 'polecat-faced', sinewy, wily grandfather beats him until he is carried unconscious to bed, where he often lies for weeks, listening to the wind moaning in the chimney and the wolves howling in the distant fields. 'To such music,' he tells us, 'my soul matured.'

One source of relief from all this is Gorky's saintly grandmother. Meeting all the tribulations of life with a stoicism born from an unshakeable belief in God, she sees the Creator as a person sitting on a diamond throne in a meadow full of never-fading flowers, surrounded by his Saints. With a religious faith that is moving in its very naïvety, its childlike assurance that everything will turn out for the best and that the world is good and beautiful, she yet retains a primitive belief in 'spirits of the hearth', hobgoblins, and all sorts of traditional sprites. For this she is branded a heretic by Grandfather, who is fanatical in his adherence to the Orthodox catechism. Grandmother is also a rich source of folk legends and fairy tales, many of which are recited in full. Gorky must have found much material in them for his early romantic stories.

9

In contrast to this enormous woman with her incredibly long hair, there is small irascible Grandfather, who thinks nothing of savagely beating his wife, who inflicts monumental floggings on young Gorky, but who yet is capable of kindness and good humour. In calmer moments he tells his grandson of the hard old days when he worked along the Volga:

The sun scorched the back of your neck and your head seemed to boil like molten steel. And you, miserable wretch, bent double, your bones creaking, press on and on, till you don't see where you're going any more, you're blinded by sweat, and your soul weeps and a tear rolls down your cheek.

The pages of *Childhood* are filled with a vast array of living people, all drawn with remarkable powers of observation: the pathetic apprentice, Tsiganok; the eccentric lodger who experiments with copper filings and acid; the cemetery watchman with his philosophizing on death and corruption, and his hair-raising stories; and the loathsome, oily army officer who becomes Gorky's stepfather.

And all these are seen perceptively through a child's eyes. Remarkably, Gorky can recall the actual sensations and reactions to the external world he experienced *as a child*. One of the first passages in the book which clearly demonstrates Gorky's wonderful evocation of the sensations of a child is the funeral scene, when his father is being buried one rainy afternoon. His thoughts are not about his father (who has just died from cholera) but about some frogs knocked down into the grave by clods of earth as the pit is being filled in. He is terrified for their sakes: he is too young to realize the real tragedy. This is surely how a child *would* think, and it is this psychological truth that underlies the whole book. Taste, touch, smell – all these sensations are described in such vivid detail that we seem to be experiencing them ourselves. And, more important than these bodily sensations, Gorky portrays the terror and fear that a child can feel when alone, lying delirious in an attic bedroom, or before some cruel beating.

What is amazing in this book is the compassion and understanding Gorky shows to mankind at its lowest. We are left, not with an impression of bitterness and cynicism, but with the assurance that the author, much though he suffered as a boy, still retains strong hopes that men will grow out of their evil ways in the end.

In this respect it is very interesting to compare Tolstoy's work of the same name. Tolstoy was an aristocrat, was brought up by governesses and foreign tutors and was never tormented by poverty or hunger. He never knew the cruelty and suffering so vividly described by Gorky. 'Happy, happy, irrevocable days of my youth!' Tolstoy exclaims. 'It is impossible for me not to love and cherish all my memories. And these memories refresh, elevate my soul, and are a source for me of perfect delights.'

Tolstoy's own trilogy was a revelation to the Russian public when it first appeared (in the journal *The Contemporary* during the years 1852–5), and was one of the author's first works to attract attention. Tolstoy's *Childhood* shows considerable European influence and contains little that we in the West can call intrinsically 'Russian'. For this reason it is difficult to understand how Tolstoy could call Gorky 'not Russian', and claim that his thoughts 'were not Russian' and that everything in his writings was 'imagined, artificial, mighty sentiments, heroic and false'.

Childhood has its faults. The descriptive passages, especially about nature, tend to be rhetorical and cliché-ridden and Gorky never forgets his moral message – the dignity and rights of the working man and the downtrodden – which at times develops into tiresome preaching. But these are minor blemishes on a book which, for all the cruelty and horror it describes, leaves the reader with a feeling that, after all, there is some hope for humanity. 'Life is always surprising us,' he writes, 'not by its rich seething layer of bestial refuse – but by the bright, healthy and creative human powers of goodness that are for ever forcing their way up through it. It is those powers that awaken our indestructible hope that a brighter, better and more humane life will once again be reborn.' Significantly, the book is dedicated to his son. With its psychological insight and depth of characterization, Gorky's *Childhood* is one of the great masterpieces of its kind. It is a living autobiography of the spirit, a confession in a sense, through which

Gorky comes to terms with a squalid, cruel and depraved world, where justice has no place, and where men lust after money, and will spare nothing to get it. Reading it we enter into Russian life as it really was at the turn of the century, and this is an unforgettable experience.

R. W.

Chapter 1

FATHER lay on the floor, by the window of a small, darkened room, dressed in white, and looking terribly long. His feet were bare and his toes were strangely splayed out. His gentle fingers, now peacefully resting on his chest, were also distorted, and the black disks of copper coins firmly sealed his once shining eyes. His kind face had darkened and its nastily bared teeth frightened me.

Mother, half naked in a red skirt, was kneeling beside him, combing his long soft hair down from the forehead to the nape of his neck with the black comb I loved to use as a saw for melon rinds. She kept muttering something in a hoarse, deep voice. Her grey eyes were swollen and seemed to be dissolving in a flood of tears.

Grandmother was holding me by the hand. She was a fat, round woman with a large head, enormous eyes and a funny, puffy nose. All black and soft, she was terribly fascinating. She was crying as well, her voice pitched differently from Mother's but in a way that perfectly harmonized with it. Shaking all over, she pulled and pushed me over to Father. I stubbornly resisted and tried to hide behind her, for I felt frightened and out of place there.

I'd never seen grown-ups crying before and couldn't make head or tail of the words Grandmother repeated again and again:

'Say good-bye to your father. You won't ever see him again, dear. He died too young, before his time. . . .'

I'd been very ill and had only just started walking again. During my illness – and this I remember very clearly – Father had lightheartedly played games with me and kept me amused. And then he suddenly disappeared and a new person, Grandmother, took his place.

'Where did you walk down from?' I asked her.

She answered: 'From up the river, from Nizhny. But I didn't walk – I came by boat! You can't walk on water! Enough of your questions now!'

This I found both funny and puzzling. Upstairs in the house lived two bearded Persians, while the cellar was occupied by an old, sallow-faced Kalmuck who sold sheepskins. I could slide down the banisters or somersault down if I fell off – that was an accepted fact. But what did water have to do with it?

It all seemed wrong and ludicrously mixed up.

'And why should I be quiet?'

'Because you've always too much to say for yourself,' she said, laughing.

The way she spoke was warm, cheerful, rhythmical. We became firm friends from the very first day, and now I wanted both of us to get out of that room as soon as possible.

Mother's presence had a stifling effect on me and her tears and wailing awakened an unfamiliar feeling of anxiety in me. I'd never seen her like that before: she had always been stern with me and was given to few words. She was a clean, smooth, large person, like a horse. She had a firm body and extremely strong hands. And now she looked unpleasantly swollen and dishevelled. All her clothes were torn. Her hair, which was usually neatly combed into place like a large gay hat, was scattered over her bare shoulders, and hung over her face, and some of it, in the form of a large plait, dangled about, touching Father's sleeping face. For all the time I'd been standing in that room, not once did she so much as look at me, but just went on combing Father's hair, choking with tears and howling continually.

Some dark-skinned peasants and a local constable peered round the door. 'Hurry up and get him out of here!' the constable shouted angrily.

A dark shawl had been used as a curtain over the window and it swelled out like a sail. Once Father had taken me sailing and suddenly there was a thunderclap. Father had laughed, pressed me firmly between his knees and shouted: 'It's nothing, don't be frightened, Alex!'

Suddenly Mother lifted herself heavily from the floor, then fell down on her back, so that her hair brushed over the floor. Her unseeing, pale face had gone blue. Baring her teeth like

14

Father's, she said in a terrifying voice: 'Close the door. Get Alexei out of here!'

Grandmother pushed me aside as she made for the door.

'Friends, don't be afraid,' she cried. 'Don't touch her. And go away, for Christ's sake! It's not cholera. She's in labour – please go away!'

I hid in a dim corner behind a trunk and looked from there at Mother writhing over the floor, groaning and gnashing her teeth, while Grandmother crawled round her and said in a gentle, joyful voice:

'In the name of the Son and the Holy Ghost! Try and bear the pain, Varyusha! Holy Mother of God who prays for us....'

I was frightened out of my wits: there they were rolling over the floor, knocking up against Father's body, groaning and shouting; he didn't move and seemed to be laughing. This went on for a long time, and several times Mother got to her feet only to fall down again.

Grandmother kept rolling in and out of the room like a big black soft ball. Suddenly a baby cried in the darkness.

'God be praised!' said Grandmother. 'A boy!' And she lit a candle.

I must have dozed off in a corner as I don't remember anything more.

Another vivid experience that stands out in my memory is a rainy day in a deserted corner of a cemetery. I stood on a slippery heap of sticky mud and looked down into the pit where my father's coffin had been lowered. At the bottom was a lot of water, and a few frogs. Two of them had succeeded in climbing on to the yellow coffin lid. My grandmother, myself, a policeman who looked soaked to the skin, and two men with spades who were evidently in a very bad mood, had gathered round the grave. A warm rain, as fine as delicate beads, began to fall gently on us.

'Fill it in,' said the policeman as he walked away.

Grandmother burst into tears and hid her face in her shawl. The gravediggers, bent double, began piling the earth into the grave at great speed. Water squelched. The frogs jumped off the coffin and tried to escape up the sides, but were thrown back by clods of earth.

'Let's go now, Lenya,' said Grandmother as she put her hand on my shoulder. Reluctant to leave, I slipped out of her grasp.

'God help us,' she grumbled – not at me, or even at God, and she stood by the grave for a long time, quite silent. Even when the grave had been levelled off she still stood there.

The gravediggers smacked their spades against the mud, which made them ring out with a hollow sound. A sudden gust of wind drove away the rain.

Grandmother took my hand and led me to a distant church surrounded by a great number of dark crosses.

'Why don't you cry?' she asked when we left the cemetery. 'You *ought* to cry.'

'I don't want to,' I replied.

'Well, you'd better not if you don't want to,' she said softly.

I found this very strange. When I did cry, which wasn't often, it was usually because of some insult, and not from physical pain; my father always laughed at me, but Mother would shout:

'Don't you dare cry!'

Afterwards we rode in a droshky along a broad and very muddy street lined with houses painted deep red. I asked Grandmother:

'Will the frogs get out?'

'No, they don't stand a chance, God help them!'

Neither my mother nor my father ever mentioned the name of God so often and with such familiarity.

*

A few days later we were all travelling in a small cabin on board a steamboat. My newly-born brother Maxim had died and lay on a table in the corner, wrapped up in a white sheet tied round with red ribbon.

I clambered up on to the piles of luggage and trunks, and looked out of the porthole, which was round and bulging like a horse's eye. Beyond the wet glass the swirling foamy water stretched away endlessly. At times it seemed to rear up and lick the glass, making me jump back on to the floor.

'Don't be frightened,' said Grandmother as she gently lifted me in her soft arms and put me back on the pile of luggage.

A grey, damp mist hung over the water. Somewhere, in the distance, a dark mass of land would loom up, and then disappear. Everything around me was shaking. Only my mother, who was leaning against a wall, her hands behind her head, stood firm and steady.

Her face, clouded over, grimly set and with the eyes shut tight, was that of a blind person. Not once did she speak. She seemed to have changed into somebody else, strange and new. Even her dress was different.

Grandmother asked her over and over again, in the soft voice she had:

'Varya dear, try and eat something, won't you?'

My mother didn't reply and remained motionless.

Grandmother used to whisper to me; with my mother she raised her voice, but all the same approached her timidly and cautiously, saying very little. It struck me that she was afraid of her. This I could well understand, and I felt all the closer to my grandmother.

'Saratov!' my mother exclaimed in an unexpectedly loud and angry voice. 'Where's that sailor got to?'

The words 'Saratov' and 'sailor' were very strange and foreign-sounding.

A broad-shouldered, grey-haired man, dressed in blue, came into the cabin. He carried a small box. Grandmother took it from him and began to lay out my brother. When she had finished she took the box in her outstretched arms to the door. But she was far too fat to get through the narrow doorway – except sideways – and her confusion and embarrassment made me laugh.

'Oh Mother!' my mother cried, and took away the coffin. They both disappeared, leaving me staring at the man in blue.

'What, has your brother gone?' he said, leaning towards me.

'Who are you?'

'A sailor.'

'And who is Saratov?'

'Saratov's a town. Look out of the window . . . there!'

Through the window I could see the land slipping by. It was dark and steep, and the mist rose from it in smoky rings, reminding me of a large slice of bread freshly cut from the loaf.

'And where's Grandmother gone?'

'To bury her grandson.'

'Will they put him in the ground?'

'Of course. How else can they bury him?'

I told the sailor about the frogs buried alive with my father. He lifted me in his arms, gave me a firm hug and kissed me.

'You're too young to understand!' he said. 'You don't have to be sorry for the frogs, to hell with them! It's your mother you should pity. . . . See what life's done to *her*!'

Suddenly something hooted and roared above. I knew very well that it was the ship, and I wasn't at all afraid. But the sailor hurriedly put me down on the floor and rushed off saying:

'I've got to run!'

I wanted to run as well. I went out of the cabin. The dim narrow gangway was empty. Near the door, copper plates glinted on the ladder steps. I looked up and saw people with knapsacks and bundles. Clearly everybody was leaving the ship, and that meant I had to go too.

When I found myself in the middle of a crowd of men by the rail, just in front of the gangway, everyone started shouting at me:

'Who do you belong to?'

'Don't know.'

For a long time I was shoved around, shaken and poked. At last the grey-haired sailor appeared on the scene and seized me.

'He's the boy from one of the cabins, from Astrakhan,' he explained. He ran with me into the cabin, dumped me on a pile of luggage and pointed a menacing finger at me as he left.

'Don't you dare move!'

The noise up above gradually died down. The ship was steadily throbbing now and no longer pitched and tossed through the water. Something that looked like a wet wall shut out the light at the porthole. The cabin became dark and stuffy and the bundles of luggage seemed to swell up, crowding me out and making me feel cramped and ill at ease. Perhaps I'd been left alone on that empty ship for good?

I went to the door but couldn't budge the copper handle. I caught hold of a bottle of milk and smashed it against the handle as hard as I could. The milk drenched my legs and trickled right down to my shoes.

Angry at this failure, I lay down on the luggage and softly cried, after which I fell asleep with the tears still rolling down my cheeks.

When I woke up, the boat was shaking all over again and pounding through the water. Like the sun, the porthole seemed to be on fire. Grandmother was sitting near me, combing her hair and frowning as she muttered to herself. She had amazingly long hair – black streaked with blue – that reached right down to the floor, falling over her shoulders, breasts and knees. She would lift the long plaits with one hand and force a wooden comb, which only had a few teeth, through them with great difficulty. Her lips twisted and her dark eyes shone angrily, and her face, framed by that huge mass of hair, became small and comical.

Today she seemed in a bad temper, but when I asked her why she had such long hair, she told me in the same soft and warm voice as yesterday:

'It's one of God's ways of punishing me – it's the devil's own job combing the damned stuff out! Ever since I was a little girl I used to boast about my lion's mane. Now it's the curse of my life! Time you were asleep! It's still very early, the sun's only just risen.'

'But I don't want to sleep!'

'Then don't!' she agreed at once, plaiting her hair and looking at the divan where my mother lay, face upwards, taut as a violin string. 'Tell me how you broke that bottle yesterday. But quietly!'

When she spoke she seemed almost to sing her words and this made them take root firmly in my memory, like flowers – soft, bright and full of richness. When she smiled, the pupils of her dark cherry-coloured eyes opened wide blazing with a light that was too welcoming for words, and her strong white teeth were laid bare. In spite of the many wrinkles in the swarthy skin round her cheeks, her whole face suddenly became young and radiant again. What spoiled it was that puffy nose with its inflated nostrils and red tip – she took snuff which she kept in a black box decorated with silver. A dark figure, she shone from within with a warm, cheering light. Although she had a bad stoop and was almost hunchbacked, and fat into the bargain, she moved with a surprising ease and agility, like a large cat – and she was just as soft as that affectionate animal.

Before she came into my life I must have been lying asleep in a dark corner, but now she had woken me up, brought me out into the light, and bound up everything around me into a continuous thread which she wove into many-coloured lace. At once she became a friend for life, nearest to my heart, and the person I treasured and understood more than anyone else. It was her unselfish love of the world that enriched me and nourished me with the strength I would need for the hard life that lay ahead.

Forty years ago steamboats moved slowly. It took us ages to reach Nizhny, and I clearly remember that time when I first experienced nature's beauty to the full.

The weather had set in fair. From morning to night I would walk with Grandmother on the deck, under a cloudless sky, the banks of the Volga on either side looking like woven silk tinted with the gold of autumn. Without any hurry, slowly moving its rumbling paddles through the grey-blue water, a bright red-coloured steamboat swung up the river with a barge in tow, grey – just like a woodlouse. The sun moved up imperceptibly above the Volga. Every moment there was something new to look at, the scene was changing the whole time. The green hills looked like folds in the rich dress of the earth. Towns and villages lined the banks, and from a distance seemed to be made of gingerbread. Golden autumn leaves floated in the water.

'Look how beautiful it is!' Grandmother would exclaim as she went from one side of the boat to the other. Her face shone and her eyes were wide open with joy. She was so engrossed with looking at the bank, I might not have been there at all. She would stand at the rail, her hands folded across her breast. Then she would smile, not saying a word, and with tears in her eyes. I would pull at her dark flower-patterned skirt.

'What?' she would say with a start. 'I must have dozed off. It's all like a dream!'

'Why are you crying?'

'Because I'm so happy, dear – and so old,' she said, smiling. 'I'm an old woman. I've seen more than sixty years – just torn past they have.' After a pinch of snuff she would begin her wonderful stories about good robbers, saints, and all kinds of wild animals and evil spirits.

She would tell these stories in a soft, mysterious voice, her face turned towards me. Her wide-open eyes would stare into mine as if she were pouring strength straight into my heart, which uplifted me.

She seemed to sing the stories to me, and the longer she went on, the more harmonious and flowing the words became. Listening to her was the most marvellous experience. I would sit there, and then ask her: 'More!'

'It was like this: an old goblin was sitting by the fire when he got a splinter of vermicelli in his hand. He rocked to and fro with pain and whined: "Oh, little mice, I can't stand the pain!" ' She would lift her leg up high, grip it and shake it, comically wrinkling up her face as if she were in pain herself.

Some bearded sailors were standing by us. All of them looked very kind and they applauded and laughed as they listened to Grandmother's stories.

'Now, Grandma, let's have some more,' they kept on asking. Then they said: 'Come and have a bite with us.'

They gave Grandmother vodka and I was treated to water-melons and canteloupes. These had to be eaten secretly, for there was a man on board who forbade anyone to eat fruit and if he found any would take it away and throw it into the river. He was dressed like a policeman, with brass buttons on his uniform, and he was always drunk. Everyone hid when they saw him coming.

My mother rarely went on deck, and never came near us.

She said nothing all the time we were on the boat. Her large, shapely body, her dark emotionless face, her heavy crown of bright, plaited hair, her firmness and strength – all this I can picture now as though I were seeing her through a mist or a transparent cloud, from which her grey eyes, large as Grandmother's, peered out coldly and distantly.

Once she said sternly:

'People are always laughing at you, Mamma!'

'Let them!' answered Grandmother in an unconcerned voice. 'Let them laugh. It's good for them!'

I remember Grandmother's childlike joy when she first saw Nizhny. Holding me by the hand, she pulled me to the rail and cried:

'Just look! It's so beautiful! Nizhny! What a city! Can you see those churches there – they seem to be flying through the air!'

She was near to tears as she asked Mother:

'Varyusha, why don't you come and have a look? Just for a moment. Cheer up now!'

Mother produced a gloomy smile.

When the boat dropped anchor opposite the beautiful city, in the middle of a river crowded with boats and bristling with hundreds of pointed masts, a large rowing-boat full of people came alongside and hooked on to the lowered rope ladder. One by one the people climbed up. In front of everyone else was a small, shrivelled-looking old man in long black clothes and with a beard of tarnished gold. He had a nose like a bird's beak, and small green eyes, and he climbed rapidly to the top of the ladder.

'Father!' my mother cried in a loud deep voice and flung herself into his arms. He seized her head, swiftly stroked her cheeks with his small reddish hands and screeched:

'And how's my silly girl, eh? Now, now. You've come at last!'

Grandmother managed to embrace and kiss everyone at once and she spun round like a propeller. She pushed me forwards and said hurriedly:

'Move yourself now. This is Uncle Mikhail, and this is Uncle Yakov ... Auntie Natalya, and these are your cousins, both called Sasha, and your cousin Katerina ... it's a big family!'

Grandfather said to her: 'Are you well?' They kissed each other three times.

Grandfather hauled me away from the thick mob and asked me, holding me by the head:

'And who might you be?'

'I'm from Astrakhan, from the cabin. ...'

'What's he talking about?' Grandfather said to Mother.

Without giving me time to reply, he pushed me to one side and said: 'He's got his father's cheekbones. ... Get into the boat!'

We reached the shore and we all went up the hill along a road made of large cobbles, high embankments overgrown with rank trampled grass lining it on either side.

Grandfather and Mother led the way. Grandfather only came up to her shoulder and he took small, mincing steps while Mother glanced down at him and seemed to glide through the air. My uncles followed silently: Mikhail with his sleek black hair and the same withered look as Grandfather; and Yakov, his hair bright and curly. Then came some fat women in gay dresses, and six children, all older than me and all very subdued. I walked with Grandmother and my little Aunt Natalya. Pale-faced, blue-eyed, with an enormous belly, she stopped every now and again and panted for breath: 'I can't go any further,' she complained.

'Why did they have to bring *you* along?' Grandmother mumbled angrily. 'They've got no sense at all!'

I didn't like the grown-ups, nor the children, and I felt completely and utterly lost in their company. Even Grandmother seemed to recede into the background and became a stranger to me. I took a particular dislike to Grandfather, immediately sensing he was an enemy. For this reason I watched him closely, taking care lest my curiosity led me into danger.

We reached the end of the path. At the very top, leaning against the embankment on the right, and the very first house in the street, stood a squat, single-storeyed house painted dirty pink, with a roof hanging low over its bulging windows

23

like a hat pulled down. From the street it looked very big, but inside its dim little rooms it was very cramped. Angry people rushed about in all directions like passengers about to disembark from a ship, ragged children swarmed all over the place like thieving sparrows, and the whole house was filled with a strange pungent smell.

I stood outside in the yard, which was just as unpleasant: all around it hung huge wet rags and it was full of tubs containing oily-looking water, all different colours. Pieces of cloth were being dipped into them. In one corner, under a ramshackle lean-to, wood burnt fiercely in a stove. I could hear water boiling and bubbling and someone I couldn't see was shouting, very loudly, these strange words: 'Sandalwood, magenta, vitriol. . . .'

Chapter 2

AND there began a new life, infinitely strange and varied, in which the days rushed by at terrifying speed. Now I see it as a grim story, the creation of a sincere artist with a passionate devotion to the truth, however cruel. As I try to bring the past to life I find it hard to believe that it all really happened. That dreary life was so full of violence that I would even like to question or gloss over much of it.

But truth is nobler than self-pity and in fact I am not writing about myself alone, but about that close-knit, suffocating little world of pain and suffering where the ordinary Russian man in the street used to live, and where he lives to this day.

Grandfather's house was filled with a choking fog of mutual hostility. It poisoned the grown-ups and even infected the children. Later on, Grandmother told me that Mother had arrived just at the time her brothers were continually pestering her father to divide up the estate. Mother's unexpected return only sharpened their desire to get what they thought was their rightful share. They were afraid that Mother would ask for a dowry, to which she was entitled but which Grandfather had withheld because, as he put it, 'she had gone her own way' and married against his wishes. My uncles thought the dowry should go to them. For a long time they had been having long and violent arguments as to which of them should open a dye-works, in the town or across the Oka river in the Kunavino district.

Soon after our arrival a fierce quarrel started in the kitchen. The uncles, without any warning, suddenly leaped to their feet, leaned across the table, and started howling and roaring at Grandfather, shaking themselves and baring their teeth like dogs. Grandfather retaliated by banging his soup-spoon on the table. Then he went red in the face and screeched like a cock: 'I'll cut you all off without a penny!'

Her face twisted with pain, Grandmother said:

'Let them have the lot, then they'll leave you alone!'

'Shut up! I know you're on their side!' roared Grandfather,

his eyes flashing. I thought it very strange that someone so small could make such a deafening noise. Mother left the table slowly, went over to the window, and turned her back on everyone. Suddenly Uncle Mikhail gave his brother a backhander on the face. The injured brother howled with pain, started grappling with Uncle Mikhail, and they both rolled around the floor, groaning and swearing.

The children started crying. Aunt Natalya, who was pregnant at the time, gave a despairing moan. Mother took hold of her behind the arms and dragged her off somewhere. Yevgenia, our nanny, a cheerful pockfaced woman, chased the children out of the kitchen. Tables were sent flying. Tsiganok, a young broad-shouldered apprentice in the dyeworks, sat himself astride Uncle Mikhail's back while our foreman, Grigory Ivanovich, who was bald, had a beard and wore black glasses, calmly bound his arms with a towel.

Uncle Mikhail groaned terribly as he stuck his neck out and rubbed his black beard on the floor. Grandfather ran round the table miserably shrieking: 'Call yourself brothers! Your own flesh and blood. . . .'

Right at the beginning of the battle I had taken fright and leaped up on to the shelf over the stove. From this place of refuge I looked down with amazement at Grandmother washing the blood from Uncle Yakov's cut face with water from a copper basin. My uncle was crying and stamping his feet, while Grandmother said wearily: 'Savages, that's what you are. Take a grip on yourselves!'

Grandfather pulled his torn shirt over his shoulders and bellowed at her: 'Old bitch! It's wild animals you've given me, not sons!'

When Uncle Yakov had gone, Grandmother crept into a corner. She was shaking like a leaf and howling: 'Holy Mother of God, please make my children see reason!' Grandfather stood at her side, surveyed the table, which was littered with a mess of smashed crockery and overturned dishes, and said quietly: 'Mind they don't work Varvara to death. Anything that's decent they'll drag down into the dirt. . . .'

'For God's sake stop talking like that . . . let's have your shirt and I'll patch it up.'

26

She squeezed his head between her open palms and kissed him on the forehead. He looked so small next to her and his face bumped against her shoulder.

'That's all I can do now ... divide it between them. ...'

'Yes, that's what you've got to do.'

They went on talking for a long time. At first it was friendly, but then Grandfather started scraping his foot over the floor, like a cock impatient for the fight, and he poked his finger threateningly at Grandmother and whispered, loud enough for me to hear, 'Don't I know you by now! You feel more for them; that dear little Jesuit Mishka of yours; as for Yashka, he's nothing more than a Freemason! You'll see, they'll drink it all away. ...'

I turned clumsily on my perch on the stove and knocked an iron over. It clattered down the small ladder and fell into the sink with a loud splash. Grandfather sprang on to the ladder, hauled me down and stared me straight in the eyes as if he'd never seen me before.

'Who put you up there? Your mother?'

'I went up myself.'

'You're lying.'

'No, I'm not. I was frightened.'

He pushed me aside, giving me a gentle slap on the forehead.

'Just like his father! Clear off. ...'

I was only too glad to get out of that kitchen.

I could see all too clearly that Grandfather was in the habit of following me with his clever, sharp-sighted green eyes, and for this I was afraid of him. I can remember that I was for ever trying to hide from those all-devouring eyes. To me, Grandfather was a wicked person. He was sarcastic and offensive whenever he spoke to anyone, and always trying to provoke people.

'Oooh, what a lot!' he would often exclaim. That long drawn-out 'oooh' never failed to make me feel depressed and cold all over.

In the afternoon tea-break, when Grandfather, my uncles and the workmen came into the kitchen from the dyeing shop, tired out, with hands reddened by sandalwood and burned with vitriol, and their hair tied up in ribbons, so they all looked like the rather sinister icons in the kitchen corner – at that dangerous hour Grandfather would come and sit opposite me and make all the other children jealous by giving most of his attention to me. He had a sharp-edged angular appearance, finely moulded and well proportioned. His embroidered satin waistcoat was old and threadbare and his cotton shirt all crumpled. His trousers sported large patches at the knees, but in spite of this he looked well-dressed, cleaner, and smarter than his sons, with their jackets, false shirt-fronts and silk cravats.

Not long after our arrival he made me learn my prayers by heart. The other children were older and already learning how to read and write with the deacon from the Church of the Assumption – its golden dome could be seen from our windows. Aunt Natalya used to give me lessons at home. She was a timid, quietish woman with a face like a child's, and eyes so transparent I always imagined I could see right through them to the back of her head. I loved to gaze into her eyes for a long time without turning away or blinking. This made her screw up her eyes, move her head away and ask in a voice almost as soft as a whisper: 'Please repeat after me: "Our Father, Which art in Heaven" . . .'

If I asked: 'What does "art" mean?' she would look round in fright and say sternly: 'Don't you ask now – that only makes it worse. Just repeat after me: "Our Father." Well?' Why asking questions should make things worse worried me. The word 'art' took on a mysterious meaning, and I repeated it wrongly whenever I had the chance: 'which part', 'which heart', and so on. But my aunt, so pale she seemed to be fading away, would patiently correct me. 'Now just you say "which art".' She seemed as difficult to understand as the words she was trying to teach me. This annoyed me, and made it hard work for me to memorize my prayers.

One day Grandfather asked: 'Well, what you been up to today? Playing in the street, I bet. I can see from the bump on your forehead. It's not clever getting mixed up in fights! Can you recite the Lord's Prayer?'

My aunt said in her soft voice: 'He's got a bad memory.'

Grandfather laughed and cheerily raised his reddish eyebrows.

'In that case he deserves a good hiding.'

He turned to me again and asked: 'Did your father beat you?'

Not understanding what he was talking about, I didn't reply, and Mother intervened: 'No, Maxim never beat him and he didn't let me either.'

'Why not?'

'He used to say it never did any good.'

'What a fool he was, that Maxim, God forgive me for speaking ill of the dead!' These words were spoken in an angry, clipped voice. They deeply hurt me, and Grandfather noticed it.

'Stop sulking. You should see yourself. . . .'

He stroked his silvery-red hair and added:

'On Saturday I'm going to flog Sashka. Because of the thimble.'

'What's "flogging"?' I asked.

Everyone laughed and Grandfather said: 'Just you wait and see. . . .'

As I hid in my corner I thought! 'Flogging must mean the same as unstitching cloth before it's dyed. Whipping and beating mean the same. Horses, cats and dogs are beaten, and in Astrakhan policemen beat the Persians.' I'd seen it with my own eyes. But I'd never seen small children treated in this way, and although Grandfather used to smack the others on the head or neck, it never seemed to worry them at all, and all they did was scratch the place afterwards. More than once I asked them: 'Did it hurt?' and they always courageously replied: 'No, didn't feel nothing!'

I was acquainted with every detail of the tempestuous thimble story. One evening, about an hour before supper, the uncles and the foreman were sewing up pieces of dyed material into one length and pinning cardboard labels on it. Deciding to play a joke on Grigory who was half blind, Uncle Mikhail told his nine-year-old nephew to heat Grigory's thimble over a candle. Sasha gripped the thimble in some pincers used for snuffing the candles, waited until it was red-hot, put it down near Grigory's hand without him seeing, and hid behind the stove. At that moment who should come in but Grandfather, who sat down and put his finger in the red-hot thimble.

I remember escaping from the uproar into the kitchen and seeing Grandfather clutching his ear with his burnt fingers and comically hopping and shouting: 'What infidel did that?'

Uncle Mikhail, bent over the table, was chasing the thimble with his finger and blowing on it. Grigory went on sewing as if nothing had happened. Shadows from the fire flickered over his vast bald head. Uncle Yakov ran to see if he could help, then hid behind the stove, where he laughed quietly to himself. Grandmother took a moist potato and began grating it.

'It's Sasha's work,' Uncle Mikhail said suddenly.

'That's a lie,' retorted Uncle Yakov, springing out from his hiding-place.

In one corner his son could be heard crying and protesting: 'Papa, don't believe him. He told me to do it!'

The uncles started swearing at each other. All at once Grandfather calmed down, pressed the bits of potato to his finger, and left the room without saying a word, taking me with him by the scruff of the neck.

Everyone blamed Uncle Mikhail. My question, during tea, 'Would he get a flogging?' was perfectly natural in the circumstances.

'He deserves it,' snarled Grandfather, looking at me out of the corner of his eye.

Uncle Mikhail thumped the table and shouted to Mother:

'If you don't take that brat of yours out of here I'll bash his face in!'

'Just you lay a finger on him!' replied Mother.

No one said a word.

Mother had a knack of using short words as defensive weapons for warding off people, repelling them and making them feel powerless. It was obvious to me everyone was afraid of her. Even Grandfather spoke to her differently and in a more subdued voice. This pleased me and I used to boast about it to my cousins.

'My mother's strongest!'

And they didn't dispute it.

But an event that took place the following Saturday completely changed my attitude to Mother.

By then I had managed to get myself into serious trouble. The skill with which the grown-ups made the cloth change colour used to intrigue me very much. They would take a yellow piece of cloth and soak it in black water and it would come out deep blue, or 'indigo' as it was called. Then they would rinse out a grey piece in rusty coloured water, and it came out 'Bordeaux claret'. It was all so simple – and mystifying.

I wanted to try my hand at dyeing as well and told Uncle Yakov's Sasha about it. He was a serious boy, always tried to please the grown-ups, was polite to everyone and ready to do whatever anyone asked of him. The grown-ups praised his intelligence and obedience, but Grandfather would squint at him and say: 'You little crawler!'

Thin and swarthy-faced, and with eyes bulging like a crab's, Sasha spoke quickly, softly, and the words seemed to choke him. He was always looking around furtively, which made one think he was on the point of dashing off to hide somewhere. The hazel pupils of his eyes only moved when he got excited, and then they moved in unison with the whites. I didn't like him at all. I far preferred the lazy Sasha, Uncle Mikhail's son. He was a quiet boy with sad eyes and a pleasant smile whom I didn't see much of and who was the image of his sweet gentle mother. He had ugly protruding teeth that grew in a double row in the upper jaw. This worried him a great deal and he was perpetually fingering them and trying to pull out the back row. He would let anybody touch them. This was the only interesting thing about him. He lived alone in a house crammed from top to bottom with people. During the day he loved to sit in a dark corner, and in the evenings he moved over to the window. I liked to sit close to him, neither of us speaking for a whole hour, and watching the black crows circling and wheeling in the red evening sky around the golden cupolas of the Church of the Assumption, diving down to earth and draping the fading sky with a black net. Then off they would fly, leaving utter emptiness. A scene like this fills the heart with sweet sadness and leaves you content to say nothing.

On the other hand Uncle Yakov's Sasha could discourse at length and with the authority of an adult. When he discovered I wanted to become a dyer, he told me to get the white table-cloth, which was used for special occasions, and dye it blue.

'White's always easiest, and I should know,' he said in a very serious tone.

I pulled the tablecloth out, ran into the yard with it, but no sooner had I dropped it into the 'indigo' tub than Tsiganok pounced on me, hauled it out, squeezed it with his broad hands, and shouted to my cousin who had followed me out of the house to supervise the work:

'Call Grandmother at once!'

He shook his black, dishevelled hair ominously and said:

'You'll cop it for this!'

Grandmother came running, groaned, even burst into tears, and started to scold me with quaint, comical expressions.

'You no-good from Perm! Blockhead! I've a good mind to drop you in one of the tubs!'

Then she began exhorting Tsiganok:

'Vanya, don't dare tell Grandfather, whatever you do. I won't say anything and perhaps no one will find out.'

Vanya said anxiously, wiping his wet hands on his many-coloured apron: 'It's nothing to do with me, but I won't say anything.'

'I'll keep him quiet with a few coppers,' said Grandmother as she led me into the house.

On Saturday, just before evening prayers, someone took me to the kitchen, where it was dark and quiet. I clearly remember lots of doors shut tight, and beyond the windows, the misty greyness of an autumn night and the dull sound of rain. On a broad bench in front of the black-mouthed stove sat my friend Tsiganok, hardly recognizable. Grandfather stood in the corner by the sink, picking out long twigs from a bucket full of water. He measured them, bound them up, and made them whistle through the air.

Somewhere in the darkness Grandmother noisily took her snuff and grumbled: 'Leave him be, you butcher!'

32

Sasha Yakovov, who was sitting on a chair in the middle of the kitchen, rubbed his eyes with his fists and said in a drawling voice that sounded more like an old beggar's than his own:

'For Christ's sake, forgive him. . . .'

Shoulder to shoulder, like tree trunks, Uncle Mikhail's children – brother and sister – stood on the far side of the table.

'I'll forgive him when I've finished,' said Grandfather, laying a long wet twig across his hand. 'Right, take your trousers off.'

He said this calmly, and neither the sound of his voice, nor the noise of the children leaning on the creaky table, not even Grandmother scraping her feet along the floor, broke that memorable silence in the gloomy kitchen, beneath a smoke-blackened ceiling.

Sasha got up, undid his trousers, let them down to his knees and managed to keep them from falling right down with his hands. Bent double, he stumbled across to the bench. It wasn't a pleasant sight, and my legs shook in sympathy. But worse was to come, when he lay on the bench, like a lamb for the slaughter, face downwards. With a wide towel Vanka tied him to it round the armpits and neck, stooped over him and gripped his ankles with his black hands.

'Come a bit closer, Alexei,' Grandfather called. 'Did you hear me? Now you'll see what I mean by flogging! One. . . .'

He swung his hand, not very high, and brought the twigs down hard on bare flesh. Sasha gave a piercing scream.

'Liar,' said Grandfather. 'That didn't hurt! Try this for size!'

He struck him, so violently that the skin became inflamed at once and a red stripe appeared. My cousin howled continually.

'Isn't that delightful?' Grandfather inquired, raising and dropping his arm at regular intervals. 'Don't you like it? It's in payment for the thimble!'

When he swung his arm up or down, my heart rose and fell exactly in time.

Sasha screamed in a revolting, delicate little voice:

33

'I won't do it again. I told you about it, didn't I? I confessed. . . .'

Calmly, as though he were reading from the Psalter, Grandfather said:

'Telling tales is no excuse! Informers should be punished first. That's for the tablecloth!'

Grandmother rushed towards me and seized me in her arms. She cried:

'I won't let you take Alexei. I won't, you monster!'

She started kicking at the door and called out:

'Varya, Varvara!'

Grandfather fell upon her, knocked her off her feet, snatched me away from her and carried me to the bench. I struggled, pulled his red beard, bit his finger. He roared, squeezed me and finally threw me on the bench so that I cut my face open. I still remember his wild cry:

'Tie him up. I'll kill him!'

And I remember, too, Mother's pale face with its enormous eyes. She ran the length of the bench gasping:

'Papa! Let him go. Please don't. . . .'

Grandfather flogged me until I was unconscious and for several days I was very ill. I lay in a wide, stuffy bed, face downwards, in a little room with one window. In one corner, in front of a case crammed full of icons, burnt an everlasting lamp.

These days of sickness were very important for my future development, and during them I must have grown up a lot. I began to experience a totally new kind of feeling. From now onwards my concern for others never let me rest for a moment, and, just as if my heart had been laid bare, I became almost intolerably sensitive to any insult or physical pain, whether I, or someone else, was the victim.

A quarrel between Mother and Grandmother made more impression on me at this time than anything else. There was Grandmother, looking huge and black in that cramped room, angrily pushing Mother into the corner where the icons were.

'Why didn't you take him away?' she hissed.

'I was frightened.'

'A healthy woman like you! You should be ashamed of

yourself! I'm an old woman and I wouldn't have been afraid. Shame on you!'

'Leave me alone. I feel sick.'

'You don't love him. He's an orphan, and you don't feel any pity!'

Mother said in a loud, weary voice: 'What about me? I'll be an orphan for the rest of my life!'

For a long time they sat crying on the chest in the corner. Mother said:

'If it weren't for Alexei, I'd leave here! I can't live in this hell, I haven't the strength.'

'My own flesh and blood, my angel. . . .' whispered Grand-mother.

Mother wasn't very strong, and, like everyone else, was afraid of Grandfather. Because of me, she couldn't leave the house, where life was unbearable for her. It was all very depressing. But soon Mother did in fact disappear and she went to stay with some friends.

Suddenly, as if he'd jumped down from the ceiling, Grand-father appeared, sat on my bed and felt my head with a hand as cold as ice.

'Good morning, sir. ... Now, answer me, and don't be angry. How are you?'

All I wanted was to kick him but the least movement was painful. His hair looked redder than ever before. He shook his head restlessly, and his bright eyes seemed to be looking for something on the wall. He took out of his pocket a piece of gingerbread, two sugar cakes, an apple, a little branch with blue raisins, and put them all on the pillow, just by my nose.

'Look, I've brought you some presents!'

He leant over and kissed me on the forehead. Then he started talking to me, stroking my head with his small, rough hand covered all over in yellow dye, especially the deformed, birdlike nails.

'I've been very hard with you. But you lost your temper. You bit and scratched me and made me lose mine! It won't hurt you if you got more than you deserved. I'll count it as part payment for the future! You must remember that when someone of your own flesh and blood beats you, it's for your own good, and should never be considered an injustice. Do you think I was never thrashed? I got such beatings, the like you'd never see even in a nightmare. I was so badly treated that God would have wept to see it! And what good did it do me? I was an orphan, with a beggar for a mother, and in spite of that I got where I am now – a freeman, a member of the guild, a leader of men.'

He leaned up against me with his thin, finely built body, and began to tell me about his childhood in vigorous meaty words which he strung together with great skill and ease.

His green eyes burst into bright flames, his reddish-gold hair bristled as he deepened his voice and trumpeted right into my face:

'So you came on a boat with steam to help it along. When I was your age I fought against the Volga, pulling a barge which was in the water, and I had to struggle on my own along the bank, barefooted, walking over sharp stones, and rocks, right from dawn to dusk. The sun scorched the back of your neck and your head seemed to boil like molten steel. And you, miserable wretch, bent double, your bones creaking, press on and on, till you don't see where you're going any more, you're blinded by sweat, and your soul weeps and a tear rolls down your cheek. That was a life! On and on you'd go, then tumble free from the hauling rope, flat on your mug, and glad of it. Work like that sapped all your strength, and all you wanted was rest! That's how we lived, with Jesus Christ smiling down on us! . . . I measured out Mother Volga three times. From Simbirsk to Rybinsk, from Saratov to here, from Astrakhan to Makaryev, right to the fair . . . and that's a lot of miles. Four years later I was a water pumper, and I soon showed my boss how smart I was!'

He talked very quickly, and swelled like a cloud in front of me, changing from a small thin old man into someone of fabulous strength – just him against the river with his huge grey barge. . . .

Often he would jump from the bed and wave his hands about to show me how the barge haulers were harnessed with ropes, how they pumped the water out. In a bass voice he sang to me, then leaped on the bed like a young man and once more fascinated me with his racy, vigorous stories.

'And then, Olyesha, when we got to a resting place on a summer evening, in Zhiguli, somewhere at the foot of a green hill, we'd light fires and heat up some cabbage soup. Then one of us, crossed in love perhaps, would sing a heart-rending song that made you go cold all over and the Volga seemed to flow faster, just like a horse rearing up right to the clouds. And all our grief seemed like dust before the wind. We used to get so carried away that the pot would boil over and the cook would get it in the neck! Always keep your mind on the job, I say. . . .'

Several times someone poked his head round the door and called Grandfather, but I said imploringly:

'Don't go!'

He would laugh and wave everyone away:

'I won't be long. . . .'

He would go on telling his stories until the evening, and when he left, after an affectionate farewell, I realized Grandfather was not wicked or terrifying, and then it was terribly hard for me to remember that he had beaten me so cruelly; but all the same, I was never to forget it.

Grandfather's visit opened the door to the whole household, and from morning till evening there was usually someone sitting by the bed, doing all they could to amuse me. But their efforts weren't always successful. Grandmother was my most frequent visitor: she shared the same bed. But the one who left the most vivid impression on me was Tsiganok. With his huge square shoulders, broad chest and enormous curly head, he came to visit me one evening, gaily dressed, as if he were off to a party, in a golden, silky shirt, velvet trousers and boots that squeaked like a harmonica. His hair shone, his squinting eyes sparkled merrily under his thick eyebrows, and his white teeth gleamed beneath the black stripe of his young moustache. His shirt, gently reflecting the red flame of the icon lamp, seemed to be on fire.

'Just you look,' he said as he raised his sleeve to show me his bare arm which was covered up to the elbow in red scars. 'See how it's swollen! They've almost healed now – you should have seen them before! Like to know what happened? In comes your Grandfather in a blind rage and I see him start on you. So I put my arm between you and the whip, hoping it would break, so that Grandfather would have to go and get another one, and your Grandmother or Mother could have dragged you to safety. But no, the twigs didn't break, as the water made them too supple. Even so, I saved you from some of the strokes – you can see from the scars how many. I can be really crafty when it comes to it!'

He broke out into a silky laugh, looked again at his swollen arm and said, still laughing:

'You don't know how sorry I was for you! It fair choked me. But the way he lay about you with that whip!'

He snorted like a horse, tossed his head and started saying something about Grandfather that at once warmed me by its childlike simplicity.

I told him I was very fond of him and he gave me an answer I shall never forget:

'But I'm very fond of you – do you think I'd have taken all that punishment if I wasn't? Do you think I'd have done that for anyone else? To hell with anyone else!'

He lowered his voice, looked every now and again at the door, and gave me the following lesson:

'When you get another beating, mind you don't tense your body – understand? It hurts twice as much if you do that. Relax; let your muscles go, so you're all soft, like a piece of jelly! And don't hold your breath back – breathe out as hard as you can, shout blue murder. Now remember what I'm telling you.'

I asked: 'Will they flog me again?'

'What do you think?' Tsiganok said calmly. 'Of course they will. Hundreds of times more. . . .'

'What for?'

'Grandfather'll find some excuse.'

Then, with an anxious look in his eyes, he continued the lesson:

'When he brings the twigs straight down, lie quiet and relaxed. But if he hits you sideways on, to tear the skin off, wriggle towards him and try and follow the direction of the birch. Then it's much easier to bear!'

Winking with his dark, squinting eye he said: 'I know more about this kind of thing than a policeman! You could make a pair of leather gloves from all the skin I've lost!'

I peered into his cheerful face and called to mind Grandmother's stories about Prince Ivan, and Ivanushka the Idiot.

Chapter 3

WHEN I was well again it became clear that Tsiganok occupied a very special place in the household. Grandfather didn't shout at him so often and so angrily as he did at his sons, and when he wasn't there would screw up his eyes, shake his head and say: 'My Ivanka's got hands of gold. Mark my words: he's made of very fine stuff!'

The uncles were also very friendly and kind to Tsiganok, and never played jokes on him as they did with Grigory, devising some malicious, nasty trick to play on him every evening. They used to heat the handles of his scissors or stick a nail with the point upwards on his chair; or, taking advantage of his blindness, would give him bits of cloth, all differently coloured, to sew up into one length, which made Grandfather swear and curse at him.

Once, when he was having an after-supper nap in the kitchen, on the shelf over the stove, someone dyed his face red, and for a long time he could be seen walking around, a ludicrous and terrifying figure. The lenses of his dark spectacles showed up dully against his grey beard and his long purple nose drooped dejectedly, like a tongue. The ingenuity of my uncles in thinking up fresh torments was apparently inexhaustible, but Grigory bore it all silently, and only rarely did he show signs of pain by crying out weakly. Before he touched anything made of steel, like an iron, or a pair of scissors or a thimble, he would liberally smear his fingers with saliva. This became a habit with him and even at the supper table, before taking his knife or fork, he would slobber all over his fingers, much to the amusement of the children. When his fingers got burnt, his face became a sea of ripples that flowed over his forehead and eyebrows, and vanished mysteriously in his bare skull.

I don't remember how Grandfather felt about the way his sons amused themselves, but Grandmother would shake her fist at them and shout: 'Ought to be ashamed of yourselves, wicked beasts!'

The uncles would discuss Tsiganok angrily, behind his back, sneering at him, criticizing his work, calling him a thief and an idler.

I asked Grandmother why they carried on like this. Always ready and willing to make everything clear to me, she began to explain:

'Both of them want to have Ivan working for them when they open their own dye-works, that's why they're always pretending to find fault with him, and they make sure the other notices. They call him a bad workman, but they're lying, and it's all part of their cunning. They're afraid they'll lose Ivan to your grandfather. And your grandfather's very used to having his own way. He's thinking of opening a third dyeing-works with Ivanka, which wouldn't do the uncles any good. Do you see?'

She laughed softly.

'They're up to their tricks all the time. Why, they'd even make a fool of God! But Grandfather can see through their cunning and teases Yasha in front of Misha, on purpose. "I'm going to buy Ivan his military exemption," he says, "so he won't have to go into the army. *I* need him!" This makes them angry, as that's the last thing they want! And they're worried about the money – it costs a fortune to buy someone out of the army!'

Now I was living with Grandmother again, as I did on the boat, and every night before I went to sleep she told me stories about fairies, or about her life – which was just like a fairy story.

When it came to family matters, such as the sharing out of the inheritance, or Grandfather's wanting to buy a new house for himself, she spoke half mockingly, indifferently, as if she had no personal interest and were only a neighbour and not the second eldest in the family.

I found out from her that Tsiganok was a foundling: one rainy night, in early spring, they found him on a bench by the front door.

'There he was, tucked up in an apron,' Grandmother said in a pensive, mysterious voice. 'He was so numb with cold he could hardly raise a whimper.'

'Why did they leave him at the front door?'

'His mother had no milk and couldn't feed him. She happened to know that a newly-born child had died recently in the neighbourhood, so she left hers in its place.'

She stopped speaking, scratched her head, sighed at the ceiling and went on:

'Poverty is worse than anything, Alexei. And a lot of what I've seen I couldn't even describe to you! It's considered shameful for an unmarried girl to have a baby. Grandfather wanted to take Ivan to the police station, but I talked him out of it. I said, "Let's keep him." God has sent him to replace those we lost. And I had eighteen. If they'd all lived, there would have been enough to fill a whole street – imagine, eighteen houses! I was married at fourteen and had a baby when I was fifteen. But God took such a liking to my children, he kept taking them to be his angels. Oh, how happy it makes me feel – and how sad!'

As she sat on the edge of my bed, wearing nothing except a shift, her long black hair falling over her shoulders, she looked so huge and shaggy she reminded me of the bear the bearded forester from Sergach had brought into the yard a few days before.

When she crossed her snowy white breast she laughed softly and shook all over:

'The good Lord took the best for himself. Ivanka brought me much joy. How I love little children! Well, we took Tsiganok into the house and had him christened and he wanted for nothing. At first I called him Beetle, because he droned just like one, crawling around and droning so loud we could hear him all over the house. Try and give him some love – he's a simple soul!'

This required no effort, and I marvelled at everything he did with blind devotion.

Every Saturday, when Grandfather had meted out the floggings due to all the children who had committed some offence during the previous week, and had gone off to evening service, a new kind of life, entertaining beyond description, came into being in the kitchen. Tsiganok would catch some cockroaches behind the stove, quickly make a harness from cotton threads, cut some sleigh runners from a piece of paper, and there, across the yellow, clean scrubbed table a coach and four would gallop, Ivan guiding the black steeds with a thin sliver of wood and shouting excitedly:

'They're off to fetch the Archbishop!'

Then he would glue a tiny scrap of paper to the back of a cockroach and sent it in pursuit of the sleigh, explaining:

'They've forgotten the mail bag. The monk's got it and is trying to catch them up.'

He tied the legs of another cockroach with a thread so that it stumbled along, its head twitching. Vanka shouted at it, and clapped his hands.

'The deacon's just leaving the pub for evening prayers!'

He would show us his little mice, which he had trained to stand and walk on their hind legs, dragging their long tails behind them, and blinking their bright black beady eyes comically. He was very careful how he handled his mice, carried them inside his coat, and fed them with sugar from his own mouth. He used to kiss them and say persuasively:

'A mouse is a very clever and affectionate animal to have around, and hobgoblins are very fond of them. It brings you good luck if you're kind to them. . . .'

He could do tricks with cards and money, could shout louder than all the children, and in every way was one of us. Once, when the children were playing cards with him, he was 'donkey' several times running, became very depressed as a result, sat sulking to show how offended he was and threw his cards down. Afterwards he complained to me, his nose twitching angrily:

'You don't have to tell me it was all fixed! They winked signals to each other and passed cards under the table. Do you call that a game? I couldn't cheat better if I tried. . . .'

He was nineteen and was bigger than all four of us put together.

I particularly remember him from those festive evenings, when Grandfather and Uncle Mikhail went visiting. Uncle Yakov would appear in the kitchen with a guitar, his curly hair dishevelled. Grandmother would prepare some savouries and bring out the vodka bottle, which was all green, with red flowers cleverly worked from glass on the bottom. Dressed for the occasion, Tsiganok would spin around like a top. Grigory would creep in sideways, his dark glasses flashing. In would come our nanny, Yevgenia, a pock-marked girl, red-skinned and fat as a jug, with cunning eyes and a trumpet of a voice. Sometimes the hairy deacon from the Church of the Assumption would join us, and some other mysterious people, who looked slippery as eels or pikes.

They all breathed heavily from excessive eating and drinking. The children were given presents – a glass each of some sweet liquid – and gradually the merrymakers became inflamed with an uninhibited, but strange gaiety.

Uncle Yakov would start tuning his guitar with loving care and when this was done, would always say: 'Right, here goes!'

Tossing back his curly head, he would bend over the guitar and stretch out his neck like a goose. His tranquil face took on a sleepy look and his lively, elusive eyes would lose their fire in an oily haze. He would gently pluck the strings and play a tune so infectious that you couldn't help standing up. His music demanded complete silence; it flowed away somewhere in the distance like a rushing torrent, seeping through the floor and the walls, stirring the heart and arousing a strange sensation of melancholy and uneasiness, which I found hard to understand. The music made you feel sorry for yourself and everyone else. Under its influence the grown-ups became like children and everyone sat motionless, lost in thoughtful silence.

Sasha Mikhailov was a particularly attentive listener. The whole time he leant towards where his uncle was sitting, and looked at the guitar, his mouth wide open, so that saliva trickled down over his lip. Frequently he was so carried away that he slipped off his chair on to the floor, his hands thrust forward to break his fall. When this happened he would stay just where he landed, his eyes bulging with a lifeless stare.

And everyone grew stiff as if a spell had been cast on them. Only the samovar hummed softly, but didn't interfere with the guitar's lament. The square outlines of the two windows in the room peered out into the gloom of the autumn night and now and again someone knocked softly on them. The yellow flames of the two tallow candles, sharp-pointed like spears, flickered on the table.

Uncle Yakov fell deeper and deeper into a kind of stupor. With his teeth clenched he seemed to be sound asleep. Only his hands had any life in them. The bent fingers of his right hand trembled together over the dark plectrum, like a bird fluttering and beating its wings. The fingers of his left hand tore over the finger board almost too fast for the eye to see.

When he'd had a few drinks, he almost never failed to produce an endless song which he sang through his teeth with a nasty whistling sound:

> If Yakov were a dog
> He would howl from morning to night,
>> Oh, I'm so bored!
>> Oh, I'm so sad!
> The nun walks along the street
> And the cow sits on the fence.
>> Oh, I'm so bored.
>
> The cricket chirps behind the stove,
> And the cockroaches scurry about.
>> Oh, I'm so bored!
> The beggar hung his trousers to dry
> And along came another and stole them.
>> Oh, I'm so sad!
>> Oh, I'm so bored!

This was too much for me and when Uncle began to sing about tramps, I burst into a wild sobbing, unable to control my feelings.

Tsiganok listened to the music with the same rapt attention as the others, running his fingers through his thick black hair as he looked into a corner and sniffed. Now and again he would suddenly exclaim in a plaintive voice:

'Ah, if only I had a voice like that. How I should sing!'

Grandmother sighed and said:

'You'll break your heart one of these days, Yasha! Vanya, let's have a dance. . . .'

45

Her requests weren't always immediately carried out, but usually the guitarist would suddenly press the palm of his hand against the strings for one second, then clench his fist and with a wild sweep pretend to throw something invisible and soundless on to the floor, shouting vigorously:

'Away with sadness! Vanka, get up!'

Tsiganok would smarten himself up, straighten his shirt and very carefully, as if he were walking over nails, take up his place in the middle of the kitchen. His tanned cheeks were flushed and he asked with an awkward smile:

'A little faster, Yakov!'

Frenzied twangings came from the guitar, heels thumped on the floor, the plates and dishes on the table and in the cupboard clattered. There, in the middle of the kitchen, was the fiery Tsiganok, rushing madly like a kite, his arms swinging out as if they were wings, shifting his feet almost too fast for the eye to see. With a whoop he squatted on the floor and tossed himself about like a golden bird, lighting everything around him with the glow of silk, shimmering and flowing in a stream of fire.

Tsiganok danced tirelessly, oblivious of everything around him. If anyone had opened the front door then, I am sure he would have danced right out into the street, through the town, anywhere. . . .

'Give me some room!' shouted Uncle Yakov, stamping his feet. He gave a piercing whistle and cried in a voice that grated on the nerves:

> Ah, if I weren't sorry for my shoes
> I'd have left wife and children long ago.

The people at the table began to fidget and at times they too cried out, screeched, just as though they had been burnt. The bearded Grigory slapped his bald head and mumbled something. On one occasion he leant over to me, so my shoulders were covered with his soft beard, and said, right into my ear, as though he were addressing one of the grown-ups:

'If your father were here now, Alexei, he would have kindled a different sort of fire! He was a kind man, and so full of life. Do you remember him?'

'No.'

'No? Well, once he and Grandmother . . . wait a minute!'

He stood up, so tall and at the same time so thin that he looked like one of the saints in the icons, bowed to Grandmother and asked her in an unusually deep voice:

'Akulina Ivanovna, will you be good enough to dance for us. Like you used to with Maxim. Please!'

Grandmother laughed and shrank away: 'Go on with you, Grigory! At my time of life! I'd be a laughing-stock!'

But everyone started persuading her and suddenly she sprang up like a young girl, straightened her skirt, held herself erect, tossed her head back and walked round the kitchen shouting:

'Laugh if you want to, it's good for you! Yasha, let's have some music!'

My uncle braced himself, closed his eyes and played something a little slower. Tsiganok stopped for a moment, leaped over to where Grandmother was, squatted, and started dancing round her, while she sailed over the floor without a sound, as if she were flying, her hands flung outwards, eyebrows raised and her black eyes peering into the distance. She struck me as very funny and I burst out laughing.

Grigory pointed a sternly threatening finger at me and all the grown-ups looked at me disapprovingly.

'Give her room, Ivan!' laughed Grigory. Tsiganok obediently jumped to one side and sat by the door. Yevgenia, her Adam's apple popping up and down, began to sing in a deep, pleasant voice:

> All week long, until Saturday,
> A maiden wove her lace.
> The work tired her out,
> Now there's hardly any life in her.

Grandmother seemed to be telling a story rather than dancing. She moved quietly, deep in thought, swaying and looking out from under her arms, her whole enormous body hesitating as her feet carefully felt their way. Suddenly, as though startled by something, she stopped, her face trembled, became clouded over and then, just as suddenly, was lit up by

47

a friendly, welcoming smile. She tottered, as though she were letting someone pass and at the same time waving someone aside. She let her head drop, stood quite still and seemed to be listening to something. Her smile grew gayer and gayer and suddenly she whirled around impetuously, looking more graceful and taller than I had ever seen her before. It was impossible to take one's eyes off her, so wildly beautiful and enchanting had she become in those brief minutes when she had miraculously recovered her youth.

And our nurse Yevgenia kept up her deep trumpeting:

> On Sunday from early mass to midnight she danced.
> She was last to leave the street
> And then it was Monday.

When she had finished dancing Grandmother went to her seat by the samovar. Everyone applauded and she said, setting her hair in place:

'That's enough! Haven't you seen a real dancer before! When we lived in Balakna, there was a young girl – I forget her name now – who made people cry with joy when she danced. It really did you good just to look at her! And I was jealous of her!'

'Singers and dancers are the salt of the earth!' Yevgenia said seriously and began a song about King David. Uncle Yakov embraced Tsiganok and said:

'You should dance in the pubs – you'd be a roaring success!'

'But I want to be a singer!' complained Tsiganok. 'If God gave me a voice, I'd sing for ten years, and then go into a monastery.'

Everyone was drinking vodka – especially Grigory. Grandmother poured out glass after glass for him, and warned:

'With all that drink you'll go blind altogether!'

Not dismayed, he answered:

'What do I care? I don't need eyes any more – I've seen everything. . . .' The drink had little effect on him, except that it made him more and more talkative, and then he nearly always started telling me about my father.

'He had a big heart, my old friend Maxim. . . .'

Grandmother agreed with a sigh:

'Yes, God's own child. . . .'

These facts about my father were all terribly interesting, and kept me in a continuous state of excitement. They brought on a mild sadness that could never be exhausted. Sadness and joy lived side by side in people, almost inseparably, and one was always giving way to the other with a terrifying, mysterious speed.

Once, when he wasn't as drunk as usual, Uncle Yakov began ripping the shirt he was wearing to pieces, furiously tugging at his hair, his thin moustache, his nose and protruding lip.

'What's the good of it?' he howled, tears pouring down his cheeks. 'What's it all for?'

He struck himself across the cheek, forehead and chest, and sobbed:

'I'm a lazy good-for-nothing, a lost soul!'

Grigory snarled:

'At last you've spoken the truth!'

Grandmother, also under the vodka's influence, caught hold of her son by the hands and urged him:

'Enough of that kind of talk, Yasha. The Lord knows best!'

When she was drunk, she seemed all the finer for it. Her smiling, dark eyes spread a heart-warming light on everybody and as she fanned her flushed face with a handkerchief she said in a sing-song voice:

'Lord, how good everything is! Why can't you see that! You only have to look around you!'

This was spoken straight from the heart, and was her motto throughout life.

I was very shocked by my uncle's tears and shouting, as he normally took things as they came.

I asked Grandmother why he cried and swore and hit himself all over.

'You want to know everything,' she said, with a reluctance that was unusual for her. 'It's too early for you to be poking your nose into these things. . . .'

This aroused my curiosity all the more. I went to the workshop and started questioning Ivan, but I got nothing out of him. All he did was to laugh softly and look at Grigory out of the corner of his eye. Then he started shouting and pushing me out of the room.

'Clear off and don't come back, or I'll dip you in a vat and dye you a different colour!'

Grigory, who was standing in front of a low, wide stove with three vats cemented into it, was stirring the colours with a long black stick and every now and then took it out to inspect the colours dripping off the end. The fire burnt fiercely and its light was reflected on his leather apron, as brightly coloured as a priest's vestment.

Coloured water hissed in the vats, sending off billowing clouds of acrid steam almost as far as the door. A dry wind blew outside in the courtyard.

Grigory looked at me from under his glasses, with his turbid, bloodshot eyes, and said to Ivan gruffly:

'Get some wood; can't you see we're running short?'

When Tsiganok ran out into the yard, Grigory sat down on a bag of sandalwood, beckoned me over to him and said:

'Come and sit here!'

He put me on his knees, brushed his warm soft beard against my cheek and said in a way I shall never forget:

'Your uncle beat and tortured his wife to death, and now his conscience is troubling him! Understand? You must try and understand everything, or else you won't get very far in this world!'

Grigory spoke simply, like Grandmother, but at the same time he made me feel ill at ease, and he seemed to look right through everything from under his glasses.

'And how did he beat her to death?' he said slowly. 'Like this: he'd lie down in bed with her, cover her with a blanket from the head downwards, and start pummelling her. Why? He doesn't even know himself!'

Taking no notice of Ivan, who'd come back with an armful of firewood, he squatted in front of the fire to warm his hands, and continued:

'He may have beaten her because she was better than him, and he was jealous. The Kashirins, my boy, don't like any-thing that's good, they get envious and can't stand it, and

50

destroy it in the end! Just ask your grandmother how they wore your father to death. She'll tell you everything as it happened. She can't bear falsehood, and doesn't understand why people lie. She's like a saint, even if she does have a drop now and again, and her pinch of snuff. An angel of a woman. Mind you stick to her. . . .'

He pushed me away and I went into the yard feeling dejected and frightened. Just as I was going into the house Vanushka caught me up, seized me by the head and whispered:

'Don't be afraid of him, he's all right. Look him straight in the eyes – he likes that.'

Everything was strange and very disturbing. I knew no other life, but had a dim recollection of my mother and father leading a different sort of existence. They spoke a different language, didn't enjoy themselves as we did, and were always close together, side by side. In the evenings they used to sit by the window, singing at the tops of their voices and laughing loud and long, so that people in the street would gather and look up. Their upturned faces absurdly reminded me of unwashed dishes after dinner. But with these people there wasn't much laughter, and when they did laugh I didn't always understand what they were laughing at. Often they would threaten or shout at each other and whisper secretly in corners. The children were quiet and inconspicuous, and seemed to be plastered to the ground, like dust after a rainstorm. I felt a stranger in the house and my whole life there pricked me into being wide awake, suspicious, and very watchful of everything that went on.

My friendship with Ivan grew stronger and stronger. From sunrise until late at night Grandmother was busy with the housework, and I had the whole day to follow Tsiganok around. When Grandfather flogged me, he still put his arm in the way of the birch twigs and the next day would show me his swollen fingers and complain:

'I must be mad! It doesn't help and look what I get as a result! I'm not going to do it any more, so to hell with you!'

And with the next flogging he would again suffer unnecessarily.

'But you said you wouldn't do it any more!'

'That's right, but I put my hand there – I didn't even notice what I was doing.'

I soon discovered something about Tsiganok which made my interest in him all the greater and deepened by love.

Each Friday Tsiganok would harness to the wide sledge Sharap, our bay gelding, Grandmother's favourite, a cunning rogue, with a pronounced sweet tooth. Tsiganok dressed himself in a short fur coat which only reached his knees and a heavy-looking hat, and when he'd pulled his green belt tight, would drive off to the bazaar for the groceries. Sometimes he was a long time getting back. Everyone became worried, would keep walking up to the windows to look up the street, their breath melting the ice on the panes.

'Can you see him?'

'No!'

Grandmother used to worry more than anyone else.

'Oh God,' she would say to her sons and to Grandfather, 'you'll be the ruination of a good man and a horse. You should be ashamed of yourselves. Have you no sense of decency? Or not enough money for yourselves? A lot of grasping thieves! God will punish you one day!'

Grandfather would frown and mumble: 'All right then, this is the last time.'

Sometimes Tsiganok didn't return until midday. The uncles and Grandfather would rush outside, and behind them, furiously taking pinches of snuff and moving like a great she-bear, followed Grandmother. For some reason, at this time of day, she seemed very clumsy. Out ran the children, and then, amid rapturous scenes, sucking pigs, whole birds, fish and pieces of meat of every kind would be unloaded from the sledge.

'Did you buy everything you were told to?' asked Grandfather, gauging the contents of the sledge out of the corner of his sharp eyes.

'Everything you asked for,' Ivan replied gaily, leaping across the yard and loudly clapping his gloves together to warm himself.

'Don't bang your gloves like that – they cost money,' Grandfather sternly shouted. 'Any change?'

'No.'

Grandfather slowly walked round the sledge muttering:

'Looks like you've brought a lot of stuff back. Sure you've paid for it all? I won't have any dishonesty in this house.'

And he hurried away, his face wrinkled up.

The uncles joyfully leaned on the sledge and started weighing in their hands the birds, fish, goose's giblets, legs of veal and huge chunks of meat. They would whistle and shout approvingly:

'He's bought very well!'

Uncle Mikhail was more enraptured on these occasions than anyone else. Like a coiled spring, he would jump round the sledge, sniffing at everything with his woodpecker beak, smacking his lips with relish, blissfully screwing up his restless eyes. He was thin, like his father, but taller and dark. Hiding his frozen hands in his sleeves he started cross-examining Tsiganok.

'How much did Father give you?'

'Five copecks.'

'But there's about fifteen copecks' worth here! How much did you spend?'

'Four and a half.'

'Then you should have a half left. Notice how it all adds up, Yakov?'

Uncle Yakov, standing in the freezing cold with just his shirt on, quietly laughed and winked at the cold blue sky.

'How about standing us half a bottle of vodka each, Ivan?' he said lazily.

Grandmother unharnessed her horse.

'What is it then? Feel like a bit of fun? Go on then. God won't mind!'

The huge Sharap would shake his thick mane, scratch at her shoulder with his white teeth, pluck the silk kerchief from her hair, look right into her face with smiling eyes, gently neighing as he shook the frost from his eyelashes.

'Like a little piece of bread?'

She stuffed a large, well-salted crust between his teeth, held her apron out like a sack under his mouth and thoughtfully watched him eat.

Tsiganok, playful as a young horse himself, pranced up to her and said:

'That's a clever gelding you've got there, a fine horse.'

'Go away, and stop wagging your tail about!' cried Grandmother, stamping her foot. 'You're in my bad books today!'

She explained to me that he had stolen more than he bought at the market.

'If Grandfather gives him five roubles, he'll spend three roubles and steal ten roubles' worth. He likes stealing. He tried it once and wasn't found out, and everyone laughed and praised him for his success, and after that it became a habit with him. From the time he was a young boy Grandfather had his full taste of poverty, and now old age has made him greedy, and money means more to him than his own children. He's only too pleased to get something for nothing. As for Mikhail and Yakov. . . .'

She waved her hand and fell silent for a moment. Then she looked at her open snuffbox and grumbled:

'It's all as complicated as a piece of lace, Alexei, spun by a blind woman. You can't make out any pattern in it. If they catch Ivan stealing, he'll be beaten to death. . . .'

After a short silence she added in a soft voice:

'Ah well! There's a lot of rules, but there's no real truth in them. . . .'

Next day I pleaded with Tsiganok to stop stealing.

'If you don't, you'll get beaten to death. . . .'

'They'll never catch me: I'm too clever for them, and I've a fast horse!' he said laughing, and then suddenly frowned, with a sad expression on his face. 'Of course, stealing is wicked, and dangerous as well. I do it from boredom. I don't manage to save any money, with those uncles of yours about. In a week they cheat me out of it. But I don't care, they're welcome to it. I don't starve. . . .'

Suddenly he picked me up and gently shook me.

'You don't weigh much, but although you're thin you've got good bones. You'll grow up to be very strong. Why don't you learn the guitar? Go and ask Uncle Yakov! The

54

only thing is, you're still a bit on the small side, and for your size you've a nasty temper. Don't you like your grandfather?'

'I'm not sure.'

'Apart from Grandmother, I don't like any of the Kashirins. Only the Devil could like them!'

'What about me?'

'You're a Peshkov, not a Kashirin. You've got different blood, you're a different breed.'

Suddenly he squeezed me tight and said almost in a groan: 'If only I could sing! Then I would set the town alight. ... It's time I did some work. ...'

He dropped me on to the floor, put a handful of tacks into his mouth and started nailing a width of wet, dark material on to a large square board, pulling it tight as he banged the nails in.

Soon afterwards he was killed.

This is how it happened: by the gates in the yard, leaning against the fence, was a large oak cross with a thick, gnarled stump at one end. It had been there a long time.

I noticed it when I first came to the house. Then it was new and yellow, but the autumn rains had blackened it considerably. It had the acrid smell of fumed oak and there was really no use for it in that dirty, crowded yard.

Uncle Yakov had bought it for his wife's grave, and made a vow to carry it on his own shoulders to the cemetery on every anniversary of her death.

This year the anniversary fell on a Saturday, at the beginning of winter. It was frosty and the wind scattered the snow off the roof. Everyone had gone outside. Grandfather, Grandmother and the three grandchildren – before anyone else was up – had gone to the cemetery for the memorial service. I had been left at home as a punishment for being naughty. The uncles, both wearing identical knee-length black fur coats lifted the cross and stood under its arms. Grigory and some man I hadn't seen before lifted the heavy stump after a struggle, and placed it across Tsiganok's broad shoulders. He staggered and braced himself by setting his feet wide apart.

'Think you'll make it?' asked Grigory.

'I don't know. It's going to be hard. ...'

Uncle Mikhail shouted angrily:

'Open the gates, you blind devil!'

Uncle Yakov joined in:

'Shame on you, Vanka, we're both thinner than you!'

But Grigory, as he swung the gates open, sternly advised Ivan: 'Mind you don't do yourself an injury. God help you!'

'You bald nitwit!' shouted Uncle Mikhail from the street.

Everyone in the yard laughed and talked loudly to show how pleased they were that someone was taking the cross away.

Grigory led me into the workshop and said:

'If you're lucky, Grandfather won't beat you today. Looks as if he's in a good mood.'

Inside the workshop he made me sit down on a pile of wool ready for dyeing, wrapped it round me up to my shoulders and said pensively as he sniffed the steam rising from the vats: 'I've known your Grandfather for thirty-seven years. I was with him when we started, and I won't leave him now. We used to be friends, and started this business together, thought everything up ourselves. He's a clever man, your grandfather! He set himself up as boss. But I wasn't smart enough. God knows more than all of us, though. He only has to smile to make a fool of the wisest man on earth. You don't understand the why and wherefore of things yet, but before long you'll have to. It's rough being an orphan. Your father, Maxim, was a fine man – he understood everything and that's why Grandfather hated him and wouldn't recognize him as his son-in-law.'

I loved listening to those kind words and watching the red and gold fire flickering in the stove and milky white clouds of steam rising over the vats, leaving a dove-coloured crust, like hoar frost, on the sloping rafters of the roof, where jagged chinks let through blue patches of sky. The wind died down, the sun came out, and the whole yard seemed sprinkled with ground glass. The screeching of sleighs came from the street, light blue smoke curled up from chimneys, and soft shadows glided over the snow as if they too had a story to tell.

The tall, bony Grigory, hatless, with his long beard, and large ears, looked like a kind-hearted magician as he stood there mixing the bubbling dye and continued the lesson:

56

'Never be afraid to look a person straight in the face. Even the dog that attacks you will run away then. . . .'

His heavy spectacles pinched the bridge of his nose, making its tip turn blue, like my Grandmother's.

'What's that?' he said all of a sudden, listening hard. He pushed the stove door shut with his foot and bounded through the yard. I rushed after him.

In the middle of the kitchen floor Tsiganok was lying face upwards. Broad shafts of light came through the window, one falling on his chest, the other on his legs. His forehead shone with a strange light, and his eyebrows were raised high. Squinting eyes stared at something on the black ceiling. His dark lips trembled and blew out pinkish bubbles. Blood flowed from the corners of his mouth, across his cheeks, on to his neck and down to the ground. It flowed in thick streams from under his back. Ivan's legs lay in an awkward heap and his slippers, clearly soaked through, were stuck fast to the floor-boards. The floor had recently been scrubbed clean with sand and shone like the sun. Little rivers of blood ran towards the doorway, glinting fiercely where they crossed the rays of light from the window.

Tsiganok lay motionless and only his fingers, stretched out by the side of his body, moved and scratched at the floor, their dye-stained nails glittering in the sun.

Yevgenia, our nanny, squatted by Ivan and tried to put a thin candle in his hand, but he couldn't grasp hold of it and the candle fell into a pool of blood and went out. Nanny picked the candle up, wiped it on the corner of her apron and tried once more to place it between his restless fingers. The kitchen was filled with whispers, which rose and fell like waves. It was like a gale which tried to tear me from the door, but I clung hard to an iron clamp.

'He tripped on something,' Uncle Yakov said in a toneless voice, shuddering and twisting his head. All the colour was drained from him and he looked crumpled and dishevelled. His eyes had lost their fire and he blinked incessantly. 'He fell and it crushed him – right in the back. We would have caught it but we let go – just in time.'

'You killed him,' said Grigory in an empty voice.

57

'What you talking about?'

'You did it!'

The blood still flowed and by the door it had collected into a dark pool which somehow seemed to be growing higher. Foaming pink at the mouth, Tsiganok bellowed, as if he were having a bad dream and he became flatter and flatter. His body clung close to the floor and sank gradually into it.

'Mikhail's ridden off to the church for Father,' whispered Yakov. 'I piled him into a cab and got back here as soon as I could. A good thing I didn't carry the stump, or I'd be in the same mess. . . .'

Once more Nanny pressed the candle into Tsiganok's hand and the wax fell with her tears on to his palm.

Grigory said in a gruff, loud voice:

'Stick it to the floor, near his head, stupid!'

'Yes.'

'Take his cap off!'

Nanny took his cap off, and the back of his head hit the floor with a dull thud. Then it rolled over to one side, and the blood flowed more abundantly, but only from one corner of his mouth now. It flowed for a horribly long time. At first I expected Tsiganok to rest a little, sit up, spit something out and say:

'Whew! It's hot in here!'

He always used to say this on Sundays, when he woke up from his after-supper nap. Now he didn't get up, but he just lay there, his life ebbing away.

The sun had already moved away from him and the bright strips of light had shortened and fell on the window sills. Tsiganok had gone black all over, his fingers didn't move any more, and the foam had dried from his lips. Around his head burnt three candles, their flickering golden spears lighting up his dishevelled, blue-black hair, his blood-stained teeth and the tip of his sharp nose, throwing quivering yellow patches on his swarthy cheeks.

Nanny, who was kneeling by him and weeping, whispered: 'My angel, light of my life.'

It was cold in the room and I hid under the table in terror. Then my grandfather, in his raccoon-fur coat, burst into the kitchen, followed by Grandmother, who was wearing her cloak with the little tails hanging on the collar, Uncle Mikhail, and a lot of strangers.

Grandfather flung his coat on the floor and roared:

'Bastards! Feel satisfied now you've killed him? He would have been worth his weight in gold in five years' time!'

The heap of clothes which they'd flung down on the floor blocked my view of Ivan. I crawled out and stumbled against Grandfather's legs. He kicked me away and shook his red fist menacingly at the uncles.

'Wolves!'

He sat on the bench, propped himself up with his arms, and sobbed. In a grating voice he said:

'I knew well enough – he was a spoke in your wheel! Poor Ivan, you weren't clever enough. What are we going to do now . . . do you hear me? . . . What have we done to make God treat us like this? Can you tell me, Mother?'

Grandmother had flattened herself against the floor and was pinching Ivan's face, his head and his chest, breathing into his eyes and rubbing his hands. All the candles were knocked over. Then she wearily rose to her feet, in her shiny black dress, opened her eyes wide and softly said:

'Clear out, you bastards!'

Everyone except my grandfather left the kitchen.

Tsiganok had a miserable little funeral and there isn't much I can remember about it.

Chapter 4

I LAY on a wide bed, with a heavy blanket wrapped four times round me, listening to Grandmother praying. She was kneeling, pressing one hand to her breast, and now and again she slowly crossed herself with the other.

I could hear the frost crackling outside. Greenish moonbeams shone through windows covered with patterns of ice, lighting up her kind face and her large nose, kindling her dark eyes with phosphorescent fire. The silky shawl that covered her hair shone like forged steel. Her dark shifting dress flowed down from her shoulders and spread out over the floor.

When she had finished her prayers she began silently to undress, folded her dress with great care on the chest in the corner of the room and approached the bed, where I lay pretending to be asleep.

'I know you're awake,' she said ever so quietly. 'Stop pretending and let me have some of the blanket.'

Relishing the thought of what was to follow I could not help smiling. Then she snapped:

'How dare you play tricks on your poor old grandmother!'

She took hold of the edge of the blanket and tugged it with such force that I was catapulted up into the air, turning over several times before I landed back on the soft feather mattress. She roared with laughter:

'What's the matter, turnip-head? Swallowed a mosquito?'

Sometimes, however, she prayed so long that I really went off to sleep and didn't hear her get into bed at all.

She always prayed for a long time after a day full of quarrels and aggravation. Her prayers made fascinating listening. Grandmother told God about everything that had happened in the house, down to the last detail. Massive, just like a mountain, she would kneel down and start off very quickly and in an unintelligible whisper and then deepened her voice to a loud grumble.

'As you know too well, God, everyone wants the best of

things. Mikhail, the elder, should really stay in the town, and he wouldn't like it if he had to go across the river, where everything's new and hasn't been tried out yet. I've no idea what will happen. Father has more love for Yakov. Do you think it's a good thing to love one child more than the others? He's an obstinate old man. Please, God, make him see reason!'

As she looked at the dim icon with her large, shining eyes, she instructed God:

'Let him have a dream which will make him understand how to give himself to both his sons!'

She crossed herself, bowed down to the ground, banging her forehead against the floorboards. Then she stood upright again and said persuasively:

'Why don't you let my Varvara smile once more? What has she done to annoy you? Has she sinned more than the others? Why should a young healthy woman lead such a wretched life! And don't forget Grigory – his eyes are getting worse all the time. If he goes blind he'll have to go begging. He's worked himself to the bone for Grandfather, and do you think he'd help him? Oh God!'

For a long time she said nothing and let her head and her arms hang down, submissively, just as if she'd fallen fast asleep or suddenly frozen.

'What else?' she said, and, suddenly remembering, wrinkled her face and said: 'Save all Believers. Forgive me, stupid fool that I am. You know that I don't sin on purpose, but only because I'm stupid.'

After a deep sigh she said in a warm, contented voice:

'Dear God, you know everything that goes on.'

I liked Grandmother's God very much, as he was so near to her and I often used to ask her:

'Tell me about God!'

She had a particular way of talking about him: she would speak very softly, with a strange drawl and her eyes closed. She always sat down at first. Then she would get up, sit down again, cover her bare head with a shawl and carry on until I fell asleep.

'God sits on a hill, on a diamond throne in a heavenly pasture, shaded by silver lime trees that flower the whole year round. In heaven there's no winter, or autumn, and the flowers never fade, but go on blossoming the whole time, so the Saints can enjoy them. And around God fly hundreds of angels, like snowflakes or swarming bees, and they fly down to earth as white doves and then back to heaven to tell God all about us.

'There's my angel, and yours, and Grandfather's – everybody has one: God treats us all equally. Say, for example, your angel reported back to God: "Alexei poked his tongue at Grandfather!" God would order: "Let the old man give him a flogging." And he treats everyone according to what they deserve, whether it's joy or suffering. All is perfect harmony in heaven and the angels rejoice, flap their wings and sing, "Glory to you, God, Glory!" and He, dear, just smiles back at them!' And she smiled herself as she shook her head.

'Have you seen all this?'

'I haven't seen it, but I know all about it,' she answered pensively.

When she talked about God, heaven or the angels she grew smaller and more gentle, her face regained its youth and her moist eyes radiated a particularly warm light. I took the heavy locks of her hair in my hands and wound then round my neck. All ears, I would sit quite still as I listened to her endless stories that never once bored me.

'Man can't see God – if he did, he'd go blind. Only the Saints can look him full in the face. And I've seen angels too. You can only see them when your soul is pure. Once I was at early Mass and I saw two of them on the altar, like patches of mist, and you could see right through them. They were so shining bright and their wings were like muslin lace and reached down to the floor. They moved around the communion table and helped old Father Ilya. When he lifted up his weak arms to pray, they supported them by the elbows. He was very old, blind as well, and was always poking his nose in everywhere. He died soon after. When I saw the angels I nearly died from joy. My heart ached and the tears flowed down my cheeks. Oh, it was so wonderful! Oh, dearest Lenka, everything in heaven's so wonderful . . . and on earth too. . . .'

'Is it wonderful where *we* are?'

Grandmother crossed herself and answered:

'Praised be Our Lady. Everything is wonderful!'

This rather disturbed me: it was hard to admit that everything in that house was wonderful. It seemed to me that things were going from bad to worse. Once as I was passing Uncle Mikhail's room I saw Aunt Natalya, dressed all in white, her hand pressed to her breast, throwing herself about screaming, not very loud, but in a way that terrified me:

'God help me, take me away. . . .'

This prayer of hers I could understand, just as I understood Grigory when he grumbled:

'In the end I shall go blind and have to go begging; even that will be better than staying in this place.'

I wanted him to go blind as soon as possible – I would have asked to be his guide and together we should have gone begging.

I had already mentioned this to him. Laughing into his beard he replied:

'All right, then, we'll go off together. I'll tell them in the town that you are the grandson of Vassily Kashirin, master dyer. It should be very amusing.'

Often I could see blue swellings under Aunt Natalya's empty eyes, and the puffed-out lips on her yellow face. I used to ask Grandmother:

'Does Uncle beat her?'

'Yes, but on the quiet, the swine! Grandfather was against it so he does it secretly, at night. He's a wicked devil and she's like a piece of jelly.'

Then she would tell me, the enthusiasm creeping into her voice:

'All the same, beatings today don't compare with those we used to get. Now it's only a question of a clout on the ear or the teeth, or you get your hair pulled – but in my day we were tortured for hours! Once Grandfather beat me from the first day of Easter right from early mass until the evening. He'd lash out, have a rest, and then start again. With leather straps or anything he could lay his hands on.'

'What for?'

'I can't remember. And then a second time he nearly beat me to death and made me fast for five days. I was lucky to get over that. . . .'

I was numbed by this revelation: Grandmother was twice as big as Grandfather and I couldn't believe that he could overpower her.

'Was he really stronger than you?'

'Not stronger, but older. Besides, he's a man!'

To see her wipe the dust from the icons and clean the chasubles was both an interesting and a pleasant experience. The icons were very rich, with pearls, silver and coloured stones along their edges. She would nimbly pick an icon up, smile at it and say with great feeling:

'What a lovely little face!'

Then she would cross herself and kiss the icon.

'It's all dusty and covered in soot. Ah, Holy Mother, light of my life! Look, Lenya, the writing's so fine and the figures so tiny, but everything stands out clearly. It's called "The Twelve Holy Days" and there in the middle is the saintly Fyodorovna. And this one's "Don't mourn me in the grave, Holy Virgin".'

Often, it seemed, she played at icons like my crippled cousin Katerina played with her dolls, seriously and with deep emotion.

Many times she claimed to see devils in large numbers or one at a time:

'One night in Lent I was passing the Rudolfs' house. Everything was bathed in moonlight. Suddenly in front of me I saw something black sitting astride the roof, near the chimney. It was bending its horned head over the chimney and sniffing and snorting. So big and hairy it was, lashing away with its tail against the roof and scraping its feet over the tiles. I crossed myself and said: "Christ will rise again and his enemies will be scattered." At this he gave a little squeak and somersaulted down from the roof into the yard. – That got rid of him! The Rudolfs must have been cooking meat and of course he caught wind of it and came to enjoy the smell, so pleased he was that it was Lent and they were eating meat.'

The thought of the devil rolling head over heels down from the roof made me burst out laughing. Grandmother laughed too and said:

'They love getting up to mischief, like little children! I remember once I was doing the washing in the bath round about midnight. Suddenly the oven door blew open, and out they poured, smaller and smaller, red ones, green, black, just like cockroaches. I made for the door but couldn't reach it: I got stuck in the middle of thousands of devils. They filled the whole bathroom so tight that you couldn't move, crawling under my feet, tugging at me and pressing up against me so I couldn't even cross myself! Just like kittens they were, all furry-soft and warm, but they stood on their hind legs the whole time. They whirled and strutted about, showing their little teeth like mice. Their tiny eyes were green and their horns were just coming through and stuck out like small knobs. They had piglet's tails. Oh, Good Lord! I fainted clean away and when I came to, the candle had almost burnt out, the water in the tub had gone cold, and there was washing all over the floor. "You devils!" I thought, "Go back to hell!" '

When I closed my eyes I could see a dense stream of hairy creatures, all different colours, come pouring out of the mouth of the stove and from the little pebbles round it, filling the bathroom, blowing on the candle and cheekily sticking out their pinkish tongues.

It was both funny and horrifying. Grandmother shook her head and said nothing for a moment. Then she made another passionate outburst.

'I've seen lost souls as well. At night-time, too, in winter, when a storm was raging. I was crossing the ravine at Diukov where Yakov and Mikhail wanted to drown your father in one of the ice-holes in the pond – remember? Well, I was going my way and was just slithering down the path to the bottom of the gully when I heard such a whistling and whooping! There, in front of me, was a troika of black horses bearing right down on me with a fat devil in a red nightcap

65

standing out like a piece of wood on the driving-seat and driving them on with reins made from steel chains in his outstretched hands. There wasn't any path round the gully and the troika, hidden in a cloud of snow, went straight over the pond. All the passengers were devils, and they whistled and shouted and waved their caps. I counted seven troikas that flew past like fire engines. The horses were black as crows and all of them were people who'd at one time been cursed by their parents. They provide good sport for devils, who ride them and drive them through the night to their different celebrations. It must have been a devil's wedding I saw. . . .'

It was impossible not to believe Grandmother – she spoke so simply and convincingly.

But best of all were the verses she recited about how the Holy Virgin walked through this world of suffering, how she pleaded with the 'Robber Princess' Yengalycheva not to beat or rob the Russian people; about Alexei, man of God; about Ivan the Warrior; her verses about the all-wise Vasilisa, about the Goat-Pope and the divine Godson; and those terrifying legends about Martha the Mayoress, about Baba Usta, the bandit leader; about Maria the Egyptian Sinner; about the sorrows of the bandit's mother; there was no end to the fairy tales, legends and poetry she knew.

Quite fearless of people, or Grandfather, or devils or any kind of evil spirit, she was absolutely terrified of cockroaches, even when they were nowhere near her. She used to wake me up at night and whisper:

'Olyosha, dear, there's a cockroach crawling over the floor. Kill it, for heaven's sake!'

Half asleep, I would light the candle and creep over the floor in search of the enemy. It usually took me a long time to find it, and often I didn't find anything.

'I can't see it,' I would say. But Grandmother, lying motionless, would answer, hardly audible from under the bedclothes:

'Yes there is! Please, please find it! I know it's there. . . .' And she was never wrong – I would always find a cockroach somewhere not far from the bed.

'Did you kill it? God be praised! Thank you. . . .' With a

sigh of relief she would throw the blanket from her head and smile.

If I didn't manage to find the insect she couldn't sleep. I could feel her body trembling at the least rustling sound, there in the deathly silence of night, and I could hear her holding her breath and whispering:

'It's by the door . . . it's crawled under the chest. . . .'

'Why are you so frightened of cockroaches?' I said.

This made her reply sharply:

'I can't understand what use they are, for the life of me . . . they do nothing but crawl about, and they're all black. God gave the lowest creature some appointed task; the wood-louse shows a house is damp. A bedbug means the walls are dirty. A louse means that someone's going to be ill – it all makes sense! But these things – who knows what evil power lives in them or what they're here for?'

Once when she was kneeling, having one of her heart-to-hearts with God, Grandfather flung open the door and said hoarsely:

'God's really come to see us this time – we're on fire!'

'What are you talking about?' Grandmother cried, jumping to her feet. With heavy stamping they both rushed into the darkness of the front parlour.

'Yevgenia, take the icons out! Natalya, get the children dressed!' Grandmother gave these commands in a firm, stern voice while Grandfather softly howled:

'Oooo!'

I ran out to the kitchen; the window overlooking the yard shone as if it had been turned to gold. Yellow patches of light flickered and drifted over the floor. Uncle Yakov, in bare feet, was trying to put his shoes on. He jumped on them just as if the soles were alight and shouted:

'It's Mishka's work. He's set us alight and then left us to it!'

'Quiet, you dog,' said Grandmother, as she pushed him towards the door so hard he nearly fell over.

Through the frost on the windows the workshop roof could be seen burning. Inside its open door there was an inferno of curling flames. Its fiery red flowers blossomed without any smoke in the quietness of the night. Only a darkish cloud hung in the air without obscuring the silver flow of the Milky Way. The snow gleamed purple and the walls of the outhouses shuddered as though they were trying to reach the corner of the yard where the fire was blazing merrily, lighting up the broad gaps in the workshop walls and thrusting twisted flames through them like red-hot nails. Red and golden ribbons of fire swiftly ran along the dry planks of the roof and coiled round them. The thin clay, smoking chimney stuck out in the middle. A soft crackle and silky rustle could be heard at the window. The fire grew bigger and bigger and the workshop, now looking beautiful in the fire, resembled the iconostasis in a church and lured one on irresistibly.

I threw a heavy sheepskin coat over my head, shoved my feet into someone else's boots and dragged myself out into the passage and then on to the front steps, where I stood stock-still, blinded by the fierce light of the dancing flames, deafened by the shouts of Grandfather, Grigory and my uncle and the crashing noise from the fire, and frightened out of my wits by the way Grandmother carried on: with an empty sack thrown over her head and with a horse-blanket round her she ran straight into the fire and shouted: 'The vitriol, idiots! The vitriol will explode. . . .'

'Grigory, stop her!' howled Grandfather. 'She'll never get out of there alive. . . .'

But Grandmother, her hand shaking and the smoke coming from her clothes, had already emerged, bent under the weight of a flagon of oil of vitriol which she held in her outstretched hands. 'Father, get the horse out!' she said, with a wheezing cough. 'Take this thing off my shoulders – can't you see I'm on fire?'

Grigory snatched the smouldering blanket from her shoulders and, stooping low, began furiously shovelling huge lumps of snow at the workshop door. Near him my uncle jumped about with a chopper in his hands. Grandfather ran around Grandmother, hurling snow at her. She threw the flagon into a snowdrift, and rushed to the main gates, opened them and said as she ran to meet the neighbours who came pouring in:

'Save the barn! If the fire spreads to the barn and the hayloft everything will go up – your own houses as well. Cut the roof down and throw the hay into the garden! Grigory, throw the snow upwards. What's the use of chucking it on the ground! Yakov, stop fussing and give these people spades and choppers! Dear neighbours, all work together and God will help us.'

She fascinated me as much as the fire. Lit up by it, and appearing to be enveloped by the flames, she dashed around the yard, a figure in black, turning up everywhere at once, giving orders to everyone. Sharap ran out into the courtyard, reared up and knocked my grandfather over. The fire was reflected in his gleaming red eyes. The horse snorted and jibbed. Grandfather let go of the halter and leaped to one side.

He shouted: 'Hold him, Mother!'

She threw herself under the feet of the rearing horse and stood in front of him, looking like a cross with her arms outstretched. The horse gave a mournful neigh and craned its neck towards her, squinting from the fierce light.

'Now don't be frightened,' Grandmother said in a deep voice as she patted its neck and took the halter. 'Do you think I'd leave you in this! You little mouse. . . .'

The little mouse, three times her size, followed her meekly to the gates and snorted as it peered into her flushed face.

Yevgenia brought the children out of the house, all wrapped up in blankets and wailing. 'Vassily, I can't find Alexei,' she cried.

'Come on. Get out of here,' Grandfather answered, shaking his hand. I hid under the porch steps so Yevgenia couldn't take me as well.

The workshop roof had already collapsed. Thin, smoking rafter beams stuck out against the sky and glowed like golden red-hot coals. Inside the building green, blue and red whirlwinds roared and crackled as they exploded. The flames surged out into the yard in broad ribbons of fire, flung themselves at the crowd of people standing in front of the great conflagration and shovelling snow on to it. The vats boiled furiously in the fire and steam and smoke rose from them in a thick cloud. Strange smells wafted round the yard, making the eyes water. I climbed out from under the steps and stumbled right into my grandmother's legs.

'Get out of here!' she cried. 'You'll get crushed to death. Get out! . . .'

A horse-rider wearing a brass helmet rode into the yard. His rust-coloured horse was foaming at the mouth. He carried a whip in his hand and he lifted it high, shouting in a menacing voice:

'Make way!'

The bells rang out merrily, rapidly, and everything seemed bright and festive to me.

Grandmother pushed me on to the steps:

'Can't you hear? Get out of here!'

This time I had to obey her. I went into the kitchen, pressed my face to the window again, but could see no trace of the fire through the dark mass of people – only brass helmets among the black winter hats and peaked caps.

The fire was swiftly trampled into the ground, and put out with water. The police dispersed the crowd and Grandmother came into the kitchen.

'Who's that? Oh, you! Too frightened to sleep? Don't be afraid, it's all over. . . .'

She sat by me, silently rocking from side to side. The quiet night and darkness had returned once more and I felt pleased. But I was sorry about the fire. Grandfather came in, stood by the door and asked:

'Mother?'

'What?'

'Get burnt?'

'No.'

He struck a sulphur match and its blue flame lit up his pole-cat face, all dirty with soot. He found a place for the candle on the table and slowly seated himself beside Grandmother.

'You'd better have a wash,' she said, covered in soot herself and smelling acrid from the smoke.

Grandfather sighed:

'God's been kind to you. He's given you a lot of common sense!' He stroked her shoulder and added, showing his teeth in a broad smile, 'He only lets you have it for a short while, though. About an hour at a time!'

Grandmother also smiled and wanted to say something, but Grandfather frowned.

'We'll have to get rid of Grigory – he's to blame! There's no more work in him, he's finished. There's Yashka sitting on the steps crying, the little fool. You'd better go to him. . . .'

She got up and walked away holding her hand in front of her face and blowing on her fingers. Without looking at me, Grandfather asked:

'Did you see it all, from the beginning? What do you think of your grandmother now? An old woman . . . broken down and worn out. Yet you saw what she could do! As for the rest of them! . . .'

He bent down and said nothing for a long time. Then he stood up, snuffed the candle with his fingers and asked me again:

'Were you afraid?'

'No.'

'Of course, there was really nothing to be afraid of. . . .'

He angrily stripped his shirt off and went over to the washbasin in the corner. There, in the darkness, he stamped and shouted:

'Fancy having a fire! Anyone who loses everything he has in a fire should be flogged publicly in the square. He's either a fool or a thief! If people followed my advice there wouldn't be any fires. Off to bed with you now. What are you sitting there like that for?'

I went away to my room, but that night I couldn't sleep. I had just lain down when an unearthly howling made me spring out of the bed. I ran into the kitchen again, and there, in the middle, stood Grandfather, shirtless and holding a candle which trembled in his hands. Without moving he scraped his feet over the floor and said in a wheezing voice:

'Mother, Yakov, what's that?'

I jumped up over the stove and hid in the corner. The place was filled with the same uproar as when the fire started. The painful howling grew louder and louder, and broke in regular waves against the ceiling. Grandfather and Uncle ran around

as if they had gone out of their minds, Grandmother shouted
to them to go away. With a heavy, crashing sound Grigory
crammed some wood into the stove, poured water into some
cast-iron pots and walked around the kitchen nodding his
head like a camel from Astrakhan.

'First get the stove going!' ordered Grandmother.

Grigory hastily began to search for kindling on top of the
stove, brushed against my foot and cried out in a worried
voice:

'Who's there? Ooh, you gave me a fright. . . . You seem to
be everywhere you're not supposed to be! . . .'

'What's going on?'

'Aunt Natalya's in labour,' he said in an indifferent voice
as he jumped down on to the floor.

I remembered that Mother didn't shout like that when she
had a baby.

Grigory put the iron pots in a corner, climbed up to where
I was on the ledge above the stove, took a clay pipe out of
his pocket and showed it to me.

'I've started smoking. It's for my eyes! Grandmother told
me to take snuff but I think I'm better off smoking. . . .'

He sat on one side of the stove, his legs dangling, and
looked down at the feeble flame of the candle. One of his ears
and his cheek were smeared with soot and his shirt was torn
on one side; I could see his ribs through the tear. They were
broad, like barrel hoops. One of the lenses in his dark glasses
was broken and half of it hung out of the frame, revealing in
the gaping hole it left, a red, moist eye just like a wound. He
filled his pipe with leaf tobacco, listened to the pregnant
woman's groans and muttered incoherently to himself, like a
drunkard:

'Grandmother got burnt all the same. How will she be able
to deliver the baby now? Just listen to her groaning out there!
They forgot about her in the excitement. The pains came on
right at the beginning of the fire – the fright started her off.
Men don't realize what women have to go through when they
have a baby and they've no respect for them. Remember:
respect the weaker sex – mothers, I mean. . . .'

I dozed off but was soon woken up by the terrible din of

doors being slammed and the drunken shouts of Uncle Mikhail. Strange words came to my ears:

'Open the altar doors. . . .'

'Give her some lamp oil mixed with rum and soot: half a glass of oil, half of rum and a spoonful of soot.'

Uncle Mikhail kept on nagging.

'Let me have a look at her.'

He sat on the floor, his legs wide apart. He kept spitting on the floor in front of him and hitting it with the palms of his hands.

It became unbearably hot over the stove and I climbed down. When I came level with my uncle, however, he caught me by the leg and pulled me, making me fall and hit the back of my neck.

'Idiot,' I said to him.

He jumped to his feet and swung me in the air, bellowing like a wild beast: 'I'll smash you on the stove.'

I came to in a corner of the front room, near the icons. Grandfather had me on his knees, and he rocked me, and muttered:

'None of us will be forgiven, no one. . . .'

An icon lamp burned brightly above his head and a candle burnt on the table in the middle of the room. The dull winter morning was already looking in through the window.

Grandfather leant over and asked me:

'Where does it hurt?'

Everything hurt. My head felt wet, and my body was heavy, but I didn't want to tell him, as everything around me seemed so strange: people I had never seen before were sitting on nearly every chair in the room – a priest dressed in purple, a grey-haired old man in military uniform who wore glasses, and many more; they all sat motionless, like pieces of wood, frozen in expectation as they listened to water splashing somewhere quite near. Uncle Yakov stood by the door jamb, stiff and erect, with his hands hidden behind his back. Grandfather said to him:

'Take him off to bed.'

Uncle beckoned to me and we tiptoed to Grandmother's room. When I had climbed into bed he whispered:

73

'Aunt Natalya's dead . . .'

This didn't surprise me – for some time now she had cut herself off from everybody in the house and never came into the kitchen or ate with us at the table.

'And where's Grandmother?'

'There,' Uncle answered, waving his hand and tiptoeing off in his bare feet.

I lay in bed and looked around. Blind, grey, hairy faces pressed against the window panes. In one corner, over the chest, hung Grandmother's dress – I knew this very well, but now it seemed that something alive was there, waiting. . . . I hid my head under the pillow and peeped out at the door. I felt like jumping out of the feather bed and running away. It was stuffy and the room was full of an oppressive, rank smell, which reminded me of the time Tsiganok died, and his blood flowed in rivers over the floor.

Something seemed to be swelling larger and larger in my head – or was it my heart? Everything I had seen in that house ran through me like a sledge along a wintry street, choking and crushing me.

The door opened very slowly and into the room crept Grandmother. She shut the door with a nudge of her shoulder, leant with her back against it and, stretching out her hands towards the little blue icon light, said in a soft, plaintive, childlike voice:

'My poor hands, they hurt. . . .'

Chapter 5

TOWARDS spring the uncles split up. Yakov stayed in the
city, while Mikhail went across the river. Grandfather bought
himself a large, interesting house in Polyevoi Street, with a
tavern on the ground floor – built of stone – a tiny, cosy little
attic room, and a garden which sloped down to a ravine thickly
overgrown with bare, bristling willow shoots.

'Very good for whips!' said Grandfather, with a gay wink,
as we went together down the soft, thawing paths to inspect
the garden. 'I think I'll start teaching you the alphabet next –
something it's time you knew.'

The whole house was crammed with lodgers. Only the top
floor was kept free by Grandfather for himself and for when
he was entertaining. Grandmother took up residence in the
attic with me. The window overlooked the street and if you
leaned out over the sill you could see the drunkards in the
evening. When there was a holiday, they staggered out of the
tavern and tottered along the street, swearing as they fell.
Sometimes they were flung out into the street like sacks,
only to force their way back in again. The door would slam,
its screeching hinges would make a dreadful grating noise,
and a fight usually followed. All this was very amusing to
watch from my attic window. Every morning Grandfather
would ride off to his sons' workshops to help them get
things going. He used to return in the evening, tired out,
irritable and depressed.

Grandmother would sew, cook and potter round in the
herb and vegetable gardens, dash about the whole day long
just like an enormous top driven on by an invisible whip,
take her snuff, sneeze with evident relish and say as she
wiped her sweaty face:

'Praised be God for evermore, we've found peace and quiet
at last, 'Lexei! Thanks to the Holy Virgin everything's very
peaceful now!'

But our life there didn't strike me as very peaceful. From
morning till late at night the lodgers' wives bustled around

the yard and now and again neighbours would turn up. All of them were always rushing somewhere, complaining they were late, and were always getting themselves ready for something and calling out:

'Akulina Ivanovna!'

Greeting one and all with the same friendly smile and concern, Akulina would push the snuff up her nose with her thumb, meticulously wipe her nose and finger with a red check handkerchief and say:

'If you want to get rid of lice you should bath more often and steam yourself with mint vapour. If the lice are under the skin, take a spoonful of purest goose fat, three drops of mercury, pound it all up seven times in a small dish with a piece of china and smear it on. If you use a wooden spoon or a bone you'll lose the mercury. And never use copper or silver – it's very harmful!'

Sometimes she would think hard and say thoughtfully:

'My good woman, you'd better go and see Father Asaph at Pechory Monastery. I can't solve your problem.'

She was a midwife, sorted out family quarrels and arguments, treated the children when they were ill, could recite 'The Virgin's Dream' by heart so the women could learn it for 'good luck', and gave them advice on domestic matters.

'You can tell from the look of the cucumber when it's ready for pickling. As soon as they lose their earthy smell and get their natural smell back, take them and salt them. If you want good kvass, then you must insult it, make it angry. Kvass can't stand sweet things so throw in a few raisins, or some sugar – a small teaspoonful to a bucket will do. . . . There's different ways of clotting cream – there's the Danubian and Spanish and even the Caucasian way. . . .'

All day long I followed her around, whether she was in the garden, or in the yard, or went off to a neighbour's house, where she would drink tea for hours, telling her incessant stories. I felt as if I had been grafted on to her and can remember nothing else about that time of my life except the indefatigable old woman who never faltered in her kindness.

Sometimes my mother would put in a brief appearance.

She was proud, and stern, and looked upon everything with cold grey eyes, like the winter sun, and later she quickly disappeared, leaving nothing at all to be remembered by. Once I asked Grandmother:

'Are you a witch?'

'Whatever next!' she said, bursting out laughing and then suddenly adding in a serious voice:

'How could I be a witch? Witchcraft isn't learnt in five minutes. Besides, I can't even spell – don't know "a" from "b". Your grandfather is the one for book learning, but the Holy Virgin didn't bless me with brains.'

And then she unveiled another part of her life.

'I was an orphan as well. My mother had nothing, and was a cripple. When she was still a young girl her master did something to frighten her. One night she jumped out of the window from fear and hurt her side and shoulder, and from that time onwards her right hand, the one she used most, withered up – a fine thing for a marvellous lacemaker. Well, she was no use to her masters now and they let her go free. Then she had to fend for herself. But how can anyone live without their right hand? So she wandered about, living on charity. In those days people were better off, and kinder. There were the wonderful carpenters and lacemakers of Balakhna – they made you feel proud! Mother and I used to wander through the towns in autumn and winter, but when the archangel Gabriel waved his sword, winter was driven away and spring would come over the earth – then we would go on further, wherever the fancy took us. We went to Murom, and Yurievets, and up the Volga and along the peaceful Oka. It's marvellous to be in the open in the spring and summer. The ground's warm and soft, the grass like velvet! The Holy Virgin has sprinkled the fields with flowers. It fills you with joy and leaves room for the soul to breathe. Mother was in the habit of half closing her blue eyes and singing so she could be heard high in the heavens. Her voice wasn't strong, but it was clear as a bell, and everything around her would stop still and listen, entranced by her. Dear God, it was good to be alive! When I was nine Mother began to feel ashamed of taking me with her on her wanderings, and thought begging was such a disgrace that she settled down in Balakhna. She'd dash from house to house, except on Sundays, when she begged at the church gates. While she was gone I sat at home learning as fast as I could how to make lace – I wanted to be a help to Mother. And if something went wrong, the tears would roll down my cheeks. In just over two years, mind you, I learnt the art and became very famous over the whole town. If anyone wanted anything extra special, they'd come straight to us, and say: "Come on Akulya, get those bobbins moving!" And I was so glad, it wasn't like work to me at all! Of course, it wasn't that I was so good, so much as doing what Mother told me. With one hand she couldn't do very much, but she made up for it by being a very good teacher, and a good teacher is worth more than ten workmen. I was so proud and used to say: "You can stop going round begging now, because I can support you!" Mother would reply: "Enough of that talk, all the money's being saved up for your dowry." Soon after, Grandfather appeared on the scene, and a remarkable young man he was: twenty-two and already a foreman bargee. His mother had singled me out, and she could see I was a worker, and that I was a beggar's daughter, which meant I'd make an obedient wife. . . . Well, she used to sell bread and was a wicked old woman, God rest her soul! Why should we remember the wicked? God has his eye on them without our interfering. He sees what they're doing all right, and the Devil loves them.'

She would laugh with that warm laugh of hers and it was funny to see her nose twitch. But her eyes, shining and thoughtful, would caress me and tell me more than ever words could.

I remember one calm evening, I was drinking tea with Grandmother in Grandfather's room. He was out of sorts and sat on the bed without his shirt, his shoulders covered with a long towel. Every minute he wiped floods of sweat off his forehead and his breathing was rapid and hoarse. His green eyes had gone dim, his face was swollen, and purple – especially his small pointed ears. It was painful to see his hand shake when he reached for a cup of tea. He was in very low spirits and not at all his usual self.

'Why haven't I got any sugar?' he asked Grandmother in the capricious voice of a spoilt child.

She replied in a friendly, but firm voice:

'Honey'll do you more good!'

Heaving a breathless sigh he quickly swallowed his hot tea and said:

'Mind I don't die on you!'

'Don't worry, I'll look after you!'

'Yes: if I died now, it would be like I never lived at all – everything would be squandered.'

'Stop your chattering and lie still.'

For a minute he said nothing and lay with his eyes closed, smacking his dark lips. Suddenly, as if someone had stuck a pin in him, he shook himself and started pondering aloud:

'Yashka and Mishka must get married as soon as possible. Perhaps having a wife and children to look after will tame them a bit, eh?'

He began running over all the names of the people in the town who had eligible daughters. Grandmother didn't interrupt and kept drinking cup after cup. I sat by the window and watched the sun set glowing over the town, turning all the windows of the houses red – Grandfather had forbidden me to go out into the yard or the garden because I'd been up to some mischief.

Flying beetles hummed around the birches in the garden. The cooper was working away in the yard next door and somewhere someone was sharpening knives. From the gully, which lay beyond the garden, came the noise of children scrambling around in the dense bushes. I longed to be free and the sadness of evening poured into my heart.

Suddenly, with a loud noise, Grandfather slapped a newish-looking book he'd taken down from somewhere against his palm and called out to me in a lively voice:

'Well, now, cucumber ears, come here! Sit down, Kalmuck face. Can you see that letter? It's "a". Repeat now "a", "b", "c". What's this one?'

' "B".'

'Right! And this?'

' "C".'

79

'Wrong! It's "a". Look, this is "d", then "e". What's that?'

' "G".'

'Good! And this?'

' "D".'

'Right! And this?'

' "A".'

Grandmother interrupted.

'You should be lying down. . . .'

'Quiet! This is just what I need to take my mind off things. Carry on, Alexei!'

Grandfather put his warm, moist arm round my neck and poked at the letters across my shoulder, keeping the book under my nose. He smelt hot – of vinegar, sweat and baked onion, which nearly suffocated me. He flew into a temper, made a hoarse, wheezing noise and shouted into my ear: ' "People", "earth". . . .'

These words were well known to me, but the Slavonic letters didn't correspond to them: the letter 'e' looked like a worm, the letter 'g' made me think of the humpbacked Grigory, and the letter 'ya' reminded me of myself with Grandmother, while Grandfather had something in common with all the letters. He made me slave for a long time over the alphabet and forced me to repeat the letters in and out of sequence. His warm passion infected me and I broke out sweating as well and shouted as loud as I could. This made him laugh and he would cough, clutch at his chest, crumple up the book and say hoarsely: 'Mother, he's a clever boy, isn't he? You plague from Astrakhan, what are you shouting about?'

'You're the one who's shouting. . . .'

I loved to watch the two of them: Grandmother, her elbows on the table, and her cheeks propped up by her fists, would watch us, laugh softly and say:

'You'll do yourself an injury by all that shouting! . . .'

Grandfather would explain in a friendly tone, 'I'm shouting because I'm ill. What have you got to shout about then?'

He would shake his wet head and say to Grandmother:

'Natalya was wrong when she said he had a bad memory.

He's got a memory like a horse! Let's have some more, snubby-nose!'

Finally he would playfully push me off the bed.

'That's enough. You can keep the book. Tomorrow I want to hear the whole alphabet without any mistakes. If you get it right I'll give you five copecks. . . .'

When I reached for the book he drew me to him again and said gloomily:

'What did your mother have to leave you for?'

Grandmother gave a start.

'Don't say things like that!'

'I wouldn't have, but it makes me feel so bad, it has to come out sometimes. Ah, when I think of the mess that girl's got herself into. . . .'

He roughly pushed me away.

'Go and play! But not in the street – only in the yard or garden.'

As it happened I had a reason for wanting to go into the garden: as soon as I appeared on the little mound of earth, the boys from the street used to start throwing stones at me from the gulley and I loved to pay them back in the same way.

'Toffee-snout is here!' they would shout as they caught sight of me, quickly gathering handfuls of ammunition. 'Hit him!'

I had no idea what 'toffee-snout' meant and therefore the insult was wasted. I enjoyed being one against many and seeing a well-aimed stone make one of the enemy run for cover in the bushes. The battles were quite harmless and friendly, and they usually ended without any bad feeling.

Reading and writing came easily to me and as I progressed Grandfather paid more and more attention to me and flogged me less and less, although, in my own opinion, I deserved to be flogged more than ever. As I grew bigger, and bolder, I broke Grandfather's rules and regulations far more often, but all he did by way of retaliation was to heap abuse on me or shake his fist.

I thought that perhaps all the floggings I'd had before were undeserved and once I mentioned this.

Prodding me gently under the chin he raised my head, winked, and said in his drawling voice:

'Whaaaaat?'

Then he would add with a thunderous laugh:

'You little heretic! Who are you to say how many floggings you should have? Who can decide this except me? Clear off!'

But then he'd suddenly seize me by the shoulder and ask once more, looking me in the eyes:

'I can't make out if you're cunning or just simple!'

'I don't know. . . .'

'Don't know? Well, let me tell you: it's better to be cunning. Simple-mindedness is the same as stupidity, do you follow? A sheep's simple-minded. Remember that. Now go and play. . . .'

Soon I could read the letters of the Psalter. We usually got down to this after evening tea and each time I had to read a whole psalm.

'H-a-p-p-y i-s t-h-e m-a-n,' I spelled out, running the pointer across the page, and asking out of sheer boredom:

' "Happy is he . . .": do they mean Uncle Yakov?'

'I'll give you a clip round the ear in a minute, then you'll soon see who's happy!' Grandfather said with an angry snort. But I felt that he was only being angry from habit, for the sake of discipline.

And I was hardly ever wrong. A minute later Grandfather, who'd clearly quite forgotten I was there, would grumble:

'When it comes to singing or dancing, he's just like King David. But in business, he's a venomous Absalom. A song-writer, a rhymester, a joker. Ugh! Merrily merrily dancing and prancing . . . dancing won't get you far. Well, will it?'

I stopped reading to listen to him and peer into his frowning, worried face. His screwed-up eyes seemed to look right through me, at some distant object, and they shone with a sad warmth, which told me that his customary sternness was about to melt away. His golden eyebrows shone and the dye-stained nails of his thin fingers shone as he tapped on the table.

'Grandfather!'

'What is it?'

'Tell me a story.'

'You get on with your reading, lazy good-for-nothing,' he muttered, rubbing his eyes as if he had just woken up. 'It's fairy tales you like – not reading the Psalter. . . .'

I suspected that he himself preferred fairy tales to the Psalter, though he knew the Psalms almost by heart, having made a solemn vow to read a portion aloud every night before going to sleep, just like the church cantor chanting the breviary. After persistent pleading for him to tell me a story, the old man softened up and finally gave in.

'Oh, all right then! You've your whole life to learn the Psalms but I'll soon be at God's judgement seat. . . .'

He leant against the wool-embroidered back of the old-fashioned armchair and, pressing more and more heavily against it, he threw his head back, stared at the ceiling, and started telling me about the old days, about his father, in a soft, thoughtful voice. Once a band of robbers came to Balakhna to strip the merchant Zaev's shop. Grandfather's father had rushed to the bell-tower to sound the alarm, but the robbers caught up with him, cut him to pieces with their sabres and threw him down from the belfry.

'I was only a small boy at the time and I didn't see it and don't remember anything about it. I only began to remember things from the time the French came in 1812, when I was just twelve. About thirty prisoners had been brought into Balakhna. All of them were skinny and small and dressed in whatever they could find; worse than beggars they were, shivering, some of them frost-bitten and hardly able to stand. The villagers wanted to beat them to death, but the escort guard wouldn't let them. The garrison troops turned up and drove the villagers back to their homes. After that there was no trouble and everybody got used to each other. The French were a quick-witted, clever lot, even cheerful – they used to sing songs. The landowners used to come down from Nizhny on their troikas to look the prisoners over. Some would swear at them, threaten them with their fists, even beat them. Others would talk kindly to them in their own language, give them money and all sorts of warm clothes. One old gentleman covered his face with his hands and burst out crying. "That wicked Bonaparte," he used to say, "has completely destroyed the French." There's something for you: a Russian, even one of the gentry, but a good man. He took pity on a foreigner. . . .'

For a moment he would say nothing, his eyes shut, and would smooth his hair with the palms of his hands. Then he would take up the story again, taking care with every detail in his evocation of the past.

'In winter the snowstorms raged in the street, frost gripped the houses and the French used to run up to our window, where my mother stood baking loaves, and they would shout and jump around, banging on the glass and asking for warm loaves. Mother never let them into the house, but pushed the bread through the open window. The French would seize them, all hot and covered with flour dust, and stuff them inside their shirts, right against their bellies. How they survived that kind of life will always be a mystery. A lot of them died of cold – the ones who were used to a hot climate and had never known frost. Two of them lived in our bath house, in the garden, an officer and his batman, Miron. The officer was tall and thin, all skin and bones and went around in a woman's cloak which came down to his knees. He was very friendly, but he drank a lot. Mother used to brew beer on the quiet and sell it. He'd go and buy some, get drunk, and start singing. He picked up some Russian and used to jabber: "Your country not white – black, wicked!" He spoke Russian very badly, but you could understand what he was saying and he knew what he was talking about. He used to say the climate in the north of Russia was harsh, but that it got warmer down south along the Volga and beyond the Caspian you don't see any snow at all. And it seems to make sense to me. Nothing's said about snow or winter in the Gospels, nor in the Acts, not even in the Psalms, and that's where Christ lived, down there in the south. When we've finished the Psalms we'll go on to the Gospels.'

He would lapse into silence again, appearing to doze off. He seemed to have grown small again and sharp-edged as he squinted and looked out of the window, lost in thought.

'Tell me some more,' I would say softly, trying to bring him back to the story.

'Well,' he'd say with a start, 'I was telling you about the French, wasn't I? Well, they're human beings and no worse than us sinners. They used to shout out to my mother: "Madame, madame," which means "my lady". That "madame" would carry more than a hundred pounds of flour from the chandler's. She was too strong to be a woman and right up to the time I was twenty she could swing me round by the hair like nothing – and I was no feather-weight. Now this batman Miron loved horses. He would wander from yard to yard and ask if they'd let him groom the horses. This he had to do by making signs with his hands as he couldn't speak our language. At first everyone was afraid to let him touch them, as he was one of the enemy, after all, and he might make a mess of it, but afterwards the stable hands themselves used to call out to him: "Come and help us, Miron!" He would laugh, put his head down, and charge like a bull. His hair was almost as red as a carrot, and he had a big nose and thick lips. He was very good with horses and produced miraculous cures for them when they were ill. Later on he became a horse-doctor here in Nizhny, but he went mad in the end and the men from the fire brigade beat him to death. Towards spring the officer fell ill with consumption and on St Nicholas' day passed quietly away. He was sitting musing at the bath-house window and there he died, his head hanging out of the window. I felt sorry for him and even had a little cry. He was a gentle person, and very often caught hold of my ears to whisper something in his own language that I couldn't understand, but which I knew was kind. You can't buy affection in this world. Once he started teaching me French, but my mother stopped him and even took me along to the priest, who had me flogged and complained about the officer. People were cruel then, and that's something you won't have to suffer – others have suffered for you; never forget this. Look what I went through. . . .'

It was dark now. Grandfather seemed to have grown mysteriously bigger in the twilight and his eyes gleamed like a cat's. About everything except himself he spoke softly, thoughtfully, cautiously, but when he was the subject he grew excited and boastful, and talked feverishly and very quickly.

I didn't like it when he started talking about himself, and neither did I like his incessant orders: 'Remember that. Don't forget it now!'

Much of what he told me I didn't want to remember, but, without any instructions on Grandfather's part, many things stuck in my memory like painful splinters. He never told me any fairy stories, only about things that had really happened, and I noticed he didn't like questions. For this reason I kept asking questions like:

'Who's better, the French or the Russians?'

'How do I know? I've never seen what they're like in their own country,' he would snarl angrily and then add:

'Even a skunk is all right in its own burrow.'

'And are the Russians good?'

'In their own small way. They were better under the land-owners, strong as wrought iron they were. Now they're all free, and they've nothing to eat. The gentry, of course, are a hard lot, but then they've a good deal more common sense. You can't say that about all of them, but if you come across a good gentleman, then you have to admire him! But some are idiots, like sacks, and they'll hold whatever you stuff them with. There's a lot of empty shells around today. At first sight they look like human beings, but go a bit closer and you'll see they're not people but empty shells, with all the goodness inside eaten away. Nowadays we must try to learn as much as we can, sharpen our wits, but there's no real grindstone. . . .'

'Are the Russians strong?'

'A few, but it's a question of skill rather than strength. A horse is always more powerful than the strongest of us.'

'But why did the French fight us?'

'The war's the Tsar's business, and it's not for us to understand!' But I shall always remember how he answered when I asked him who Napoleon was:

'He was a bold man who wanted to conquer the whole world and he wanted everyone to be equal – no lords or civil servants but simply a world without classes. Names would be different, but everyone would have the same rights. And the same faith. I don't have to tell you what nonsense that is.

86

Only crabs are all alike, but fish are different. The sturgeon's no friend of the cat fish, and the sterlet doesn't mate with the herring. We've had our own Bonapartes – Razin, Pugachov – I'll tell you about them some other time. . . .'

Sometimes he would stare at me long and silently, his eyes opened wide as if he had just seen me for the first time. This I found very unpleasant. And he never spoke about my father or mother. . . .

Grandmother often used to join us in these conversations. She would sit quietly in one corner, out of sight, and after a long silence would suddenly ask Grandfather in that caressing voice of hers: 'Do you remember the good times we had when we went on a pilgrimage to Murom? What year was that?'

After a moment's reflection Grandfather replied, taking great pains to get his facts right: 'I don't know exactly, but it was before the cholera epidemic, when they were chasing those Olonchans in the forest.'

'That's right! I remember how frightened we were at the time.'

'Hm, yes. . . .'

I asked who the Olonchans were and why they were being chased through the forests. Grandfather reluctantly replied:

'The Olonchans were just peasants on the run from the hangman, or from factory work.'

'How did they catch them?'

'How do you think? It was like boys playing in the street: some of them ran away and others went after them. When they caught up with them they whipped and flogged them. They even had their nostrils slit and their foreheads branded to show they'd been punished.'

'What for?'

'It's hard to say who was in the wrong – those who did the running away, or the ones who were after them.'

'Do you remember,' Grandmother asked again, 'the time after the great fire?'

A stickler for accuracy, Grandfather would ask sternly: 'What great fire?'

As they reminisced I was completely forgotten. Their quiet voices blended so well, they seemed to be singing. And it was a sad song, about illness, fires, floggings, sudden deaths, clever swindles, holy idiots, cruel masters. . . .

'The things we've been through!' Grandfather muttered softly.

'Do you think it's been a bad life?' said Grandmother. 'Remember that wonderful spring after I had Varya!'

'That was in 'forty-eight, the year of the Hungarian campaign: the day after the christening her godfather Tikhon was taken away. . . .'

'And he never came back,' sighed Grandmother.

'Yes, never came back! Ever since then God's gifts began to flow into our house, like water over a raft. Ah, Varvara. . . .'

'That's enough, Father.'

He looked angry and frowned.

'Enough of what? Our children have turned out to be failures, whatever way you look at them. Where's all our strength and youth gone to? We thought we were putting everything into a strong basket, but God put a badly-made sieve into our hands instead. . . .' He cried out, just as if he'd burnt himself, ran round the room bitterly complaining, cursing his children and threatening Grandmother with his little bony fist.

'And you were always on their side, the robbers! You witch!'

Roused to wailing and tears by these painful memories he hid in the corner where the icons were kept, and he beat his thin, hollow-sounding chest with wild movements:

'God, am I worse than anybody else?'

He was shaking all over, and his moist eyes shone spitefully from a sense of outrage.

Grandmother, who was sitting in the darkness, silently crossed herself and then, approaching him cautiously, began her exhortations:

'Why torment yourself like this? God knows what he's doing. And are other people's children any better than ours? It's the same everywhere – quarrels, arguments, chaos and confusion. All parents wash away their sins with their own tears – you're not the only one. . . .'

Sometimes these speeches would calm him and he would

wearily fall on to the bed without saying a word, while Grandmother and I went quietly away to our attic.

Once, though, when she went up to him with her soft cajoleries, he quickly swung round and cracked her on the face with his fist, making a crunching sound. Grandmother staggered back, her hands pressed to her lips, then she straightened up and said softly and calmly:

'You fool. . . .'

She spat out blood at his feet, but all he did was to let out two piercing shrieks, raise his arms and shout:

'I'll kill you if you don't go away!'

'Fool,' she repeated as she went to the door. Grandfather flung himself on her but, without hurrying, Grandmother stepped through the doorway and slammed the door in his face.

'Old cow,' Grandfather hissed, his face red as a hot coal as he caught hold of the door jamb and scratched at it with his fingers.

More dead than alive, I sat on the bench, hardly able to believe what I had seen. It was the first time he had struck Grandmother in front of me and this for me was terribly degrading, and revealed a new facet of his character that I could never tolerate and which humiliated me beyond description. He kept standing there, his nails dug into the jamb, growing smaller and greyer, just as if he had been showered with ash. Suddenly he strode into the middle of the room, kneeled, and, unable to keep upright, slumped forward, brushing the floor with his arm. Then, suddenly, he straightened up, hit himself on the chest and cried out:

'Oh God!'

I slid off the warm tiles of the couch by the stove as though I'd been lying on ice, and fled.

Upstairs Grandmother was walking up and down the room rinsing her mouth out.

'Does it hurt?'

She went over to the corner, spat the water out into the slop-pail and calmly answered:

'It's nothing, the teeth aren't broken, only the lip's cut.'

'What did he do it for?'

Glancing out of the window she said:

'Lost his temper. It's hard for an old man like him with the failures he's had. ... Off to bed with you now and forget all about it. ...'

I began to ask her about something else but she shouted back at me with a sternness that was rare for her:

'Am I speaking to the wall? Go to bed. You never do what you're told!'

She sat down by the window and sucked her lip, spitting every few seconds into her handkerchief. As I undressed I watched her. The stars twinkled in the blue square of window above her head. In the street it was quiet, and the room was dark.

When I'd got into bed she came over, gently stroked my head, and said: 'Sleep tight, I'm going down to Grandfather now. Don't feel sorry for me, angel, I'm as much to blame. Go to sleep!'

After she had kissed me and left me I felt unbearably miserable. I jumped out of the wide, soft, warm bed, and went to the window. As I gazed down into the empty street I suddenly felt numb and helpless with a hopeless despair.

Chapter 6

AND once again something nightmarish happened. One evening, after we'd had tea, when Grandfather and myself were sitting reading the Psalms, and Grandmother was washing up, in rushed Uncle Yakov, dishevelled – as always – and looking like a worn-out broom. Without saying good evening, he flung his cap into the corner and started talking very rapidly, to the accompaniment of wild flourishes:

'Mishka's gone berserk, Father! He had dinner at my place, got drunk and then went completely off his rocker. He smashed the crockery, tore up a woollen dress that was all ready for a customer, broke the windows, swore at me and Grigory. He's on his way here breathing hell fire and shouting: "I'll pull Father's beard off, I'll kill him." You'd better look out. . . .'

Grandfather, his hands resting on the table, slowly rose to his feet, and his face became one big frown round the nose, so it looked terrifyingly like a hatchet.

'Do you hear that, Mother?' he screeched. 'Coming to kill his own father. My own son! Well, it's time. . . .'

He threw his shoulders back and started pacing up and down the room. Then he went to the door, shoved a heavy bolt into the lock and turned to Yakov:

'Do you still want to grab Varvara's dowry? Well, this is what you'll both get!'

He stuck his fingers under Uncle's nose, making him jump back from the insult.

'Father, what would I want with it?'

'You? I know you too well!'

Grandmother didn't say anything and hurriedly cleared away the tea things into the cupboard.

'I came to protect you. . . .'

'That's a good one,' sneered Grandfather. 'Thank you, son! Mother, give this cunning fox something to hold, a poker'll do, or an iron. And you, Yakov Vassilyev, as soon as your brother breaks the door down, give him one – on *my* head, of course!'

Uncle thrust his hands in his pocket and slunk off to a corner.

'If you don't trust me . . .'

'Trust?' shouted Grandfather, stamping on the floor. 'I'd trust any wild beast – a dog, hedgehog, but you! I know you got him drunk and put the whole idea in his head. Well, have a go with the poker. Anyone you like: him, me. . . .'

Grandmother softly whispered to me:

'Run upstairs and keep an eye open for Uncle Mikhail. As soon as you see him coming down the street, come and tell us, as quick as you can! Off with you now, and hurry.'

And upstairs I went, rather frightened at the thought that my drunken uncle was soon to arrive, but proud all the same at being entrusted with such a task. I craned my neck out of the window and looked down the street. It was wide and covered with a thick layer of dust, out of which large cobble-stones poked like great swellings. It stretched away to the left, crossed a gully and came out into Ostrozhnaya Square, where the grey buildings of the old prison with its four towers stood solidly on the clayey soil. For me this imposing build-ing had a certain melancholy beauty. To the right, three houses away from ours, was the broad expanse of Sennaya Square, surrounded on all sides by the yellow block of the convict barracks and the lead-coloured fire tower. At the top of the wide-eyed tower walked a watchman like a dog on a chain. The whole square was cut up by gullies, and at the bottom of one stood a greenish slime. Over to the right was the stagnant Dyukov pond, into which, according to the tale Grandmother told, the uncles had thrown my father one winter, right through a hole in the ice. Almost exactly opposite my window was an alley lined with little brightly painted houses; it finished up by the fat squat church of the Three Saints. If you looked straight in front of you, you could see roofs, just like overturned boats floating in the green waves of the gardens.

Worn by the storms of long winters, and washed by the

interminable autumn rain, the faded houses in our street were all covered with dust. They huddled close to each other, like beggars at the church door, and, like me, they seemed to be waiting for somebody, their eyes protruding suspiciously. There were few people about, and they walked slowly, just like pensive cockroaches in front of the fire. The stifling heat rose up to where I was sitting and the nasty smell of onion and carrot pies which made me terribly depressed was heavy in the air.

I felt weary, in some special way that I found almost unbearable. My breast seemed to be filled with hot, liquid lead and it crushed me from within, and threatened to burst through my chest and ribs. I felt as if I was swelling up like a blister and that little room with its coffin-like ceiling made me feel cramped, hemmed in.

And here he was, Uncle Mikhail. He was looking round the corner of an alley, outside a grey house. His cap was pulled down over his head so his ears stuck out. He was wearing a rust-coloured waistcoat, dusty boots that reached to his knee and held one hand in a pocket of his check trousers, clutching his beard with the other. I couldn't see his face from where I was, but from the way he was standing, he seemed to be about to leap across the street and beat against Grandfather's door with his black hairy hands. I should have run downstairs to tell everybody he'd arrived, but I could not tear myself away from the window at the sight of Uncle crossing the street, cautiously, as if he was frightened of getting dust on his grey boots. Now I could hear the door creak as he opened it, and the tinkling of glass. I dashed downstairs and banged on Grandfather's door.

'Who's that?' he asked gruffly, without opening up. 'You? Well? Been to the pub? Right. Back upstairs.'

'I'm frightened up there.'

'You'll have to lump it for a bit longer.'

Once more I went back to my window. It was getting dark. The dust in the street was piled deeper and blacker. Oily, yellow blotches of light appeared in the windows of the houses. From the house opposite came the sound of music – guitar strings singing sadly and sweetly. And there was singing in the pub as well. When the door opened I could hear the tired, broken voice of Nikitushkin, an old bearded beggar with a burning coal instead of a right eye, and whose left eye was always shut tight. His voice was cut off like an axe when the door slammed shut again.

Grandmother was envious of him, and whenever he sang she would say with a sigh, 'What luck knowing all those beautiful songs.' Sometimes she would call him into our yard. He would sit on the steps, leaning on a stick and singing and telling stories, while Grandmother would sit next to him, listening, and asking:

'What's that, the Holy Virgin was in Ryazan?' And the beggar would reply convincingly, in a deep voice:

'She was everywhere, in all the provinces.'

Imperceptibly a wave of heavy drowsiness seemed to flow down the street and weighed down on my heart and eyes. How wonderful if Grandmother would come! Or even Grandfather. What kind of person must my father have been for my uncles and Grandfather to have hated him? And for Grandmother, Grigory and Aunt Yevgenia to say such good things about him?' And where was my mother?

I had been thinking more and more about Mother, and made her the chief character of all the fairy tales and legends Grandmother used to tell me. The fact that Mother didn't wish to live in her own family made her loom larger and larger in my dreams. I imagined she lived at a highway inn with a band of robbers who stole from rich travellers and shared what they got with the poor. Perhaps she lived in a forest, in a cave, with good thieves, of course, and cooked for them and guarded the gold they'd stolen. Or perhaps she was wandering over the earth counting her treasures, like the Robber Princess Yengalycheva, together with the Holy Virgin, who no doubt was continually exhorting her as she exhorted the Robber Princess:

It is not for you, greedy slave,
To gather all earth's gold and silver.
It is not for you, hungry soul,
To conceal your bareness with the earth's goodness. . . .

94

And mother would reply in the words of the Robber Princess:

> Most holy virgin, pardon me,
> Have pity on my sinful soul.
> I did not plunder for my own sake,
> But for my one and only son!

And the Virgin, who was kind, like Grandmother, pardoned her and said:

> Oh, Varyushka, of Tartar blood,
> Oh, you evil unbeliever!
> Now, go your own way –
> And tread your own path of tears!
> Do not touch the Russian people
> But spy out the forest Mordvinian
> Or chase a Kalmuck over the steppes.

I was carried away into the world of dreams when I re-called these fairy tales, only to be woken up by the uproar and shouting downstairs in the entrance passage. As I leaned out of the window I could see Grandfather, Uncle Yakov and the pub landlord and the comical Cheremis Melyan pushing Uncle Mikhail through the gate out into the street. He put up some resistance, but they kept beating him on his arms, his back and neck, kicked him and finally sent him sprawling in the dust of the street. The gate banged to and the latch and bolt clattered as they were slammed shut. A crumpled cap was thrown over the gates; everything became quiet.

After lying still for a few moments my uncle got up. His clothes were all torn and dishevelled, and he picked up a stone and hurled it at the door. A hollow sound rang out, just like the bottom of an empty barrel. Some miserable-looking people crawled out of the pub, shouting and bellowing and waving their arms. Heads were poked out of the windows and the street became alive with laughing and shouting. All this seemed like a fairy tale – fascinating and exciting, but at the same time unpleasant and terrifying.

And suddenly everything vanished from my memory, as I am writing now, leaving silence and emptiness.

On the trunk by the door sat Grandmother, bent double, motionless and hardly breathing. I stood in front of her and stroked her warm, soft and wet cheeks. She didn't seem to notice and muttered gloomily: 'Good God, did your stock of common sense run out when it came to my sons? Lord, please help us.'

I imagine that Grandfather didn't live more than one year in that house in Polyevoi Street, from one spring to another, but during that time the house took on a new notoriety.

Almost every Sunday the street urchins would run up to the front door joyfully announcing to everyone in the street:

'There's another fight at the Kashirins!'

Usually Uncle Mikhail appeared in the evening and kept the house under siege and in a state of terror the whole night. Sometimes he brought two or three assistants – scruffy louts from the Kunavino quarter. They used to climb up from the gully into the garden and give full vent to their drunken ecstasy, pulling up the raspberry and blackcurrant bushes. On one occasion they smashed up the bath house and broke everything that could be broken – shelves, benches, kettles. They even tore the stove up from the floor, smashed some of the floorboards and ripped the door out of its frame.

Grandfather stood by the window, a threatening, speechless figure, and listened to them smashing his house up. Hidden in the darkness, Grandmother ran round the yard pleading:

'Misha, what are you doing!'

And she was answered by a string of obscene and idiotic Russian oaths, whose meanings must have been incomprehensible even to the animals that spewed them up.

There was no chance of being with Grandmother at a time like this, and without her I was terrified. I went down to Grandfather's room, only to be greeted with a hoarse shout:

'Clear off, blast you!'

I fled up to the attic and stared out through the window into the murky garden and yard, trying not to let my grandmother out of sight: I was terrified they might kill her, and I cried out and called to her. She did not come, but my drunken uncle heard me and started abusing Grandmother with foul language.

One evening, which was very much like this in many respects, Grandfather was ill, and lay in bed rolling his head, which had a towel tied round it, from side to side and grumbling:

'Is this what I've lived and slaved for, sinned for? If it weren't for the shame of it, I'd call the police and have them up before the Governor in the morning. ... What a disgrace! But how can a father set the police on his own sons? You've said enough, old man, so lie still.' Suddenly he jumped out of bed and staggered to the window. Grandmother caught hold of him under the arms and asked:

'Where do you think you're going?'

'Light a candle,' he ordered, gulping noisily for breath.

When Grandmother had lit the candle, he took the candlestick and, holding it out in front like a rifle, shouted through the window in a loud, mocking voice:

'Ah, Mishka, thief in the night, you mangy hound!'

Just then the uppermost pane in the window was shattered and half a brick landed on the table near Grandmother.

'Missed!' roared Grandfather, and I wasn't sure whether he was laughing or crying. Grandmother caught him up in her arms, just like me, and carried him to the bed, murmuring in a voice full of fear and trembling: 'What you going on about, eh? If you went to the police it would be Siberia for him. Surely he understands that, mad though he is!'

Grandfather twitched his legs and sobbed hoarsely:

'I hope they kill him!'

From outside came the sound of roaring and banging. I took the brick and ran to the window; Grandmother managed to catch me and fling me into a corner:

'Little idiot!' she hissed.

On another occasion my uncle, armed with a thick stake, broke into the house from the yard and stood on the steps of the dark porch, beating on the door, behind which waited Grandfather with a stick in his hands, two lodgers with clubs, and the innkeeper's wife, a tall woman with a rolling pin. Grandmother stamped about and pleaded:

'Let me go and speak to him. Just one word.'

Grandfather stood up, sticking his leg out like the peasant carrying the spear in a painting called 'The Bear Hunt'; when

97

Grandmother approached him, he silently shoved her away with his elbow and leg. All four stood there, terrified and expecting the worst. Above them burnt a lamp which hung from the wall and flickered, casting a dim, feeble light on their heads. I watched all this from the attic ladder and I felt like carrying Grandmother up with me.

Uncle was furiously breaking down the door, and now it was hanging perilously, ready at any moment to come away at the top hinge – the lower was already broken off and made a horrible grating noise. Grandfather urged on his helpers in a voice that grated as well:

'Hit him on the arms and legs, mind, but not on the head.'

By the side of the door was a small window – just big enough to get your head through. Uncle had already broken the glass in it and now it had turned black, like a socket without the eye, with bits of splintered glass sticking out all round the edges.

Grandmother rushed up to it, thrust her arm through it and waved it around:

'Misha, for God's sake go away!' she shouted. 'You'll be crippled for life. Get out of here!'

He hit her on the arm with his stake. I could see something very broad-looking flash across the window, immediately after which Grandmother slumped down to the floor on her back, just managing to cry out:

'Misha, get out of here . . . run . . .'

'Was that you, Mother?' wailed Grandfather, frightening me out of my wits.

The door burst open and my uncle jumped through the black opening only to be thrown backwards off the porch like a shovelful of earth.

The innkeeper's wife took Grandmother to Grandfather's room. He soon followed her there, gloomily went up to her and said:

'Any bones broken?'

'Yes, I think so,' she replied without opening her eyes. 'What have you done with him?'

'Leave off, won't you!' snapped Grandfather. 'Do you think I'm a wild animal or something? He's lying tied up in the barn. I doused him with some water. ... Swine. ... Which one of us does he take after then?'

Grandmother groaned.

'I've sent for the bonesetter ... so be patient for a bit,' said Grandfather, moving close to her on the bed. 'They'll be the death of us both – they'll send us to our graves before our time.'

'Let them have all the money.'

'And Varvara?'

They talked for a long time – Grandmother softly and plaintively, Grandfather angrily and noisily.

Then a little hunchbacked old woman came in. Her lower jaw trembled, her mouth was wide open, like a fish, and her sharp nose curved round into it over her upper lip. I couldn't see that she had any eyes and she could hardly shuffle along, scraping her crutches along the floor. In her hand was a bundle which jingled as she walked.

I thought that this was Death in person who'd come for my Grandmother. I leaped over to her and shouted at the top of my voice:

'Get out!'

Grandfather roughly caught hold of me and hauled me off to my attic without any further ceremony.

Chapter 7

IT did not take me long to understand that Grandfather and
Grandmother worshipped different Gods.

Grandmother would wake up and sit for a long time on the
edge of the bed combing her wonderfully long hair. With her
teeth clenched she would twitch her head and tear out whole
plaits of long black silky hair and curse, under her breath, so
as not to wake me:

'To hell with this hair, all matted into one lump*! I can't
do a thing with it.'

When she had somehow managed to disentangle her hair,
she would quickly plait it into thick strands, hurriedly wash
herself, snorting angrily, and then stand before her icons,
without having succeeded in washing away the irritation from
her large face, all wrinkled with sleep. And now would begin
the real morning ablution which straight away completely
refreshed her. She would straighten her stooping back, throw
her head back and gaze lovingly at the round face of the Virgin
of Kazan, throw her arms out wide, cross herself fervently
and whisper noisily in a heated voice:

'Blessed Virgin, remember us in times of trouble!'

She would bow down to the floor, slowly unbend and then
whisper again ardently:

'Source of all joys, purest beauty, flowering apple tree. . . .'

Almost every morning she would find some new words of
praise, which made me listen to her prayers with even greater
attention.

'Dearest heart of heaven. My refuge and protection,
Golden Sun, Mother of God, save us from evil, grant we
offend no one, and that I in turn be not offended without just
cause!'

Her dark eyes smiled and she seemed to grow younger

* *Translator's Note:* Gorky's grandmother apparently suffered from a
scalp disease (*plica polonica*) where the hairs become matted together from
a sticky secretion. For some reason this was common in Poland and the
marshy parts of Russia.

again as she crossed herself again with slow movements of her heavy hand.

'Jesus Christ, Son of God, be merciful to me, poor sinner, for Thine own Mother's sake.'

Her prayers were always a service of sincere praise that came straight from her heart.

She didn't pray long in the mornings, as the samovar had to be got ready – Grandfather didn't keep any servants and if Grandmother was late with the morning tea, which had to be served exactly on time, he would curse her long and angrily.

Sometimes he would wake earlier than Grandmother, climb up to the attic, and, catching her at her prayers, would listen to her whispering for some time, disdainfully twist his thin, dark lips and growl at her later when they were having tea:

'How many times, blockhead, have I taught you how to pray, and still you mutter in your own sweet way, like a heretic. God will lose his patience one day!'

'Don't worry, He'll understand,' answered Grandmother convincingly. 'He can understand whatever you say to Him.'

'Blasted Chuvash!'

Her God was with her all day, and she even talked about him to animals. It was plain that it was easy for everything to submit to this God: people, dogs, birds, bees, even herbs. He bestowed his kindness on all earthly creatures without distinction, and was close to all things. One day the cat belonging to the innkeeper's wife – a spoilt, cunning, fawning creature with a sweet tooth, smoky-coloured fur and golden eyes, and the favourite of everyone in the yard – dragged a starling in from the garden. Grandmother took the tortured bird away and started scolding the cat:

'You've no fear of God, you miserable wretch!'

The innkeeper's wife and the man who looked after the yard both laughed at this, but Grandmother shouted furiously at them:

'You think that animals don't know about God? Every living thing knows about God just as much as you; don't you feel any pity?'

As she harnessed the plump, mournful Sharap, she chatted to him:

'Why are you so down in the dumps, my servant of God? Getting old, aren't you?'

The horse would sigh and shake his head.

All the same, she didn't mention God by name as often as Grandfather did. Grandmother's God I could understand, and he didn't terrify me, yet it was impossible to tell a lie in his presence – that would have been shameful. All he aroused in me was a feeling of overwhelming guilt and I never lied to Grandmother. It was simply impossible to hide anything from this benevolent God and I had no wish to do so either. One day the innkeeper's wife, after a quarrel with Grandfather, let Grandmother have the full force of her tongue – though Grandmother had nothing to do with it – and even threw a carrot at her.

'You idiot!' my grandmother said calmly. But I was deeply hurt and decided to take revenge on the evil woman.

For a long time I tried to think up a way of inflicting the greatest possible pain on that red-headed fat woman with her double chin and eyeless face. From my observations of the civil wars waged by the neighbours I discovered that they took revenge on each other by chopping off cats' tails, poisoning dogs, and killing cocks and hens, or by creeping into the enemy's cellar at night, pouring kerosene into barrels of pickled cabbage and cucumbers, or emptying casks of kvass. But none of these was drastic enough for me – something far more impressive and terrifying was needed.

And this is what I thought up:

I waited until the innkeeper's wife had gone down to the cellar, and then shut the hatch and locked it over her, danced a dance of revenge over it, flung the key on to the roof and rushed as fast as my legs could take me to the kitchen, where Grandmother happened to be doing the washing. It took her some time to find out why I was so delighted, and when she did, she gave me a smack in the right place, dragged me outside and sent me up on the roof after the key. Amazed at this reception, I silently retrieved the key and then ran off to one corner of the yard, from where I could see Grandmother freeing the captive innkeeper's wife. Then both of them, laughing all over their faces, came towards me across the yard.

'You'll get it from me!' said the innkeeper's wife, threatening me with her plump fist, but still smiling benevolently with that eyeless face of hers. Grandmother took hold of me by the scruff of the neck and hauled me off to the kitchen, where she asked me: 'What did you do that for?'

'She threw a carrot at you. . . .'

'So you did it for me? Well! What a nerve! I've a good mind to put you under the stove to keep the mice company. Perhaps that will knock some sense into you! A fine protector! If I told your grandfather, he'd flay you alive. Off to the attic and learn your lessons for tomorrow. . . .'

The whole of that day she didn't say one word to me, except in the evening, when before saying her prayers she sat down on my bed and told me, in these memorable words:

'Listen, angel, and don't you forget: don't meddle with things that don't concern you. Grown-ups are soiled by life; they have already been put to the test by God. But you haven't, and you have a child's way of looking at things. Wait until God puts you on trial, touches your heart, shows you your appointed task and the path you must tread. Understand? And it's not for you to decide who should be punished. God will judge and give punishment where it's due. That's his business, not ours.'

For a moment she was silent, then she took her snuff, blinked her right eye and added:

'Sometimes even God can't tell who's guilty.'

'But doesn't God know everything?' I asked in astonishment. She answered in a calm, sad voice:

'If He knew everything, then people wouldn't do a lot of things. He looks down on us from Heaven, and at times He has such fits of crying and sobbing: "My people, my dear people, I'm so sorry for you!"'

She began to cry herself and without pausing to wipe her wet cheeks went off to a corner to pray. From that time onwards the God she worshipped became closer to me and I understood him better. Grandfather used to teach me that God was all-seeing, all-knowing and present everywhere, that he was a help to people in their daily lives. But he didn't pray like Grandmother.

In the morning, before standing in front of the icons, he would spend a long time washing himself. Then, when he was neatly dressed, he would carefully comb his red hair, put his beard straight, and after inspecting himself in the mirror, tucking his shirt in, and tying a black kerchief round his waistcoat, would carefully, almost stealthily, approach the icons. He always stood on the same knot in the floorboards, which looked like a horse's eye, and he stayed there for about a minute, his head lowered and his arms stiffened against his sides, like a soldier. Then, keeping his trim figure upright, he would say in an inspired voice: 'In the name of the Father, the Son and the Holy Ghost!'

I thought that the room became especially quiet after these words – even the flies seemed to buzz with more restraint.

Then he would stand, his head thrown back, his raised eyebrows bristling, and his golden beard stuck out at right angles to his face. In a firm voice he would read the prayers, just as if he were reciting a lesson, and his voice had an urgent, very distinct ring.

'For the day of judgement cometh when every man's deeds shall be made known.'

He beat himself gently on the chest with his fist and asked insistently:

'Against Thee, the one God, have I sinned. . . . Turn away Thy face from my sins.'

He rolled out every syllable quite distinctly as he read the Creed. His right leg twitched, just as though he were beating time to the prayer. His whole body strained towards the icons, he seemed to grow taller, and at the same time thinner, slimmer, neat and spruce – and compelling.

'Thou who didst bear the Great Healer, heal the long continued terrors of my soul. I bring Thee the groaning of my heart: have mercy, O Mother of God.'

Here he would utter a loud invocation, the tears welling up in his green eyes.

'Let my faith be counted to me for good, O my God, and

visit not upon me those works which find no favour in Thy sight.'

Now he continually crossed himself, convulsively, and nodded his head like a butting ram. His voice reached a high pitch and was heavy with sobbing. Long afterwards, when I visited synagogues, I realized that Grandfather prayed just like a Jew.

The samovar had long been puffing away on the table and a smell of hot rye cakes and curds wafted through the room – this made me feel very hungry! Grandmother gloomily leaned against the lintel of the door, her eyes cast down, and sighed. The cheerful sun looked through the garden window, dew sparkled like pearls on the trees, the morning air smelled delightfully of fennel, currants and ripening apples, but Grandfather took no notice and still stood there praying, rocking and shrieking.

'Quench the fire of my passion, for I am base and accursed!'

I knew all his morning and night prayers off by heart and followed every word to see if he made a mistake or left out something. This happened extremely rarely, but when it did, I felt a malicious joy. His prayers finished, Grandfather would say to Grandmother and myself:

'Good morning!'

We used to bow to each other and finally we sat down at the table. At this point I would say to Grandfather: 'You left out "sufficient" this morning!'

'Are you telling me the truth?' he would ask nervously and apprehensively.

'Of course you did. You ought to have said: "And may my faith be sufficient unto my need" but you left out "sufficient".'

'Well I never!' he would exclaim with a guilty wink.

Later he would find some way of getting his own back, but until then I sat there triumphantly, revelling in his embarrassment.

Once Grandmother said jokingly:

'Goodness gracious, God must be bored stiff hearing your prayers, same old thing again and again.'

'What?' he said in a menacing voice. 'What are you babbling about?'

'You never say anything that comes from your own heart when you speak to God, however hard I listen.'

He turned purple, shook all over, jumped up on a chair and threw a saucer at her head, screeching like a saw cutting through a knot: 'Get out of here, you old witch!'

In his stories about God's invincible strength he always made a special point of emphasizing His cruelty: some people sinned and were drowned, others sinned and were burnt, and their towns razed to the ground. God punished with famine and pestilence and he was always a sword over the land, a scourge to sinners.

'All who violate God's laws by disobedience will be punished by ruin and affliction,' he drummed into me, tapping the table with his bony fingers.

I found it hard to believe that God was so cruel. I suspected that Grandfather had made it all up on purpose, to make me frightened of *him*, and not God. I asked him outright:

'Are you telling me this just to make me obey you?'

'Of course! And if you didn't?'

'And what about Grandmother?'

'Don't believe anything that old fool says!' he said sternly. 'From the time she was a little girl she's been nothing else but stupid, illiterate and crazy. It's more than her life's worth if she starts trying to tell you about such important things again. Tell me: how many ranks of angels are there?'

I answered, and then I asked:

'And what are civil servants?'

'Want to know everything, don't you?' he said, smirking, lowering his eyes and chewing his lips. With reluctance he explained:

'That's nothing to do with God – civil servants are humans! A civil servant feeds on regulations, he eats them the whole time.'

'What are regulations?'

'Regulations? The same as habits,' he answered more readily and cheerfully, his clever, piercing eyes twinkling. 'People live together and make agreements between themselves. For example, they say: "This is better than anything else, so we'll make it a custom, a regulation, a law!' It's like when the boys in the street have a game, and they decide on the rules, and how they're going to play. And what they agree on is the law!'

'And civil servants?'

'Troublemakers who come and break all the laws.'

'Why?'

'That's something you won't understand,' he said with a stern frown. Then he continued his sermon:

'God stands above all earthly dealings! Men want one thing, and he wants something else. Everything that's human perishes. God has only to breathe and everything's turned at once to ashes, dust.'

I had plenty of reasons for wanting to know all about civil servants, and persevered.

'Uncle Yakov often sings:

> "Bright angels are God's servants,
> But civil servants – serfs of the devil." '

Grandfather raised his beard with the palm of his hand, put it in his mouth and closed his eyes. His cheeks quivered. I could see he was laughing inside.

'I'll have to tie up your legs with Yashka's and fling you both in the river. He's no business singing such songs, and you shouldn't listen to them either. Those are heretical jokes, the work of dissenters and unbelievers.' After a moment's reflection he looked at me piercingly and said softly: 'Ah, what a lot they are!'

While he elevated God to an awe-inspiring position above men, like Grandmother he brought him into all his business – and countless numbers of saints as well. Grandmother didn't seem to recognize any of the saints except Nicholas, Uri, Frol and Lavr, although they were very kind and close to people, passing through villages and towns, influencing their lives, and generally behaving just as they did. Grandfather's saints were almost all martyrs, who had broken idols, or quarrelled with the Roman emperors, for which they had been tortured, burnt and flayed. Sometimes Grandfather would say dreamily:

'I wish God would help me sell this house, so I could make five hundred roubles. Then I'd say Mass for Nikolai the Saint!'

Grandmother laughed and said to me:

'The old fool. As if St Nikolai had nothing better to do!'

For a long time I kept Grandfather's church calendar, which had several things written in the margins. Opposite St Joachim and St Anne's day, he'd written in bright red ink and upright characters: 'Saved from trouble by their goodness.'

I remember that word 'trouble': worried about supporting his sons, who'd turned out failures, he'd gone in for money-lending, and had secretly taken several articles as security. Someone reported him, and one night the police came round to search the house. There was a terrible to-do, but everything ended happily. Grandfather prayed until dawn and in the morning, with me looking on, he wrote those words in the calendar.

Before supper he would read the Psalter with me, or the prayer book, or that ponderous volume of Efrema Sirin's Prayers and Hymns. When we'd finished eating he would begin his prayers again and in the quietness of the evening the sad, penitential words would ring out:

'What can I bring Thee or what shall I give Thee, Thou Immortal King who hast all great gifts? ... And guard our thoughts from straying. ... Lord, preserve me from mine enemies. ... Give me to weep and to remember the hour of my death....'

Often Grandmother used to say:

'I've never felt so tired! Too tired to say my prayers before I go to sleep.'

Grandfather used to take me to church: on Saturdays, we went to vespers, and on high holidays to late mass. Even in church I could tell which God the people were praying to: the ones who were reading like the priest and deacon prayed to Grandfather's God, but the choir always sang in praise of Grandmother's.

Of course, I've described rather crudely the distinction made by a child between these two Gods, which, I remember quite clearly, confused and deeply troubled my divided self. But Grandfather's God did arouse fear and hostility in me.

He loved no one, watched everything with a stern eye, and above all else saw in men nothing but what was foul, evil and sinful. Clearly he didn't trust men, was perpetually waiting for them to repent, and loved punishing people.

In these days my thoughts and feelings about God were the principal food for my soul, the most beautiful thing in life, and all other impressions only repelled me by their cruelty and nastiness, awakening disgust, and sadness. God was the best and brightest of all that surrounded me: this, of course, was Grandmother's God, a dear friend to everything that lived. Naturally, I wasn't troubled at all by the question: Why can't Grandfather see that God is good?

I wasn't allowed to play in the streets, because it made me too excited. Its effect on me was almost intoxicating, and nearly every time I went out to play I became the scapegoat for any mischief or disturbance.

I didn't have many friends and the neighbours' children were hostile towards me. I didn't like being called Kashirin, and as a result they shouted the name to each other even more: 'Here comes old skinflint Kashirin's son. Biff him one.'

And battle would commence.

I was strong for my years and a very nimble fighter. Even my enemies recognized this and always attacked me in a gang. All the same, the street always defeated me, and I would return home usually with a bloody nose, torn lips, bruised face, my clothes in shreds, and covered in dust. A frightened Grandmother would meet me and say sympathetically:

'What, fighting again, turnip-head? What you got to say for yourself? I just don't know where to start . . .'

She would wash my face, press spongilla, copper coins against the bruises, or dab me with goulard, and scold me:

'Why are you always fighting? At home you're quiet enough, but as soon as you get out there you're a different person! Shame on you. I'm going to tell Grandfather not to let you out any more!'

Grandfather would inspect my bruises, but he never shouted at me, but only used to mutter and sighed:

'Medals again? Well, my brave warrior, don't you dare go out in the street again, d'you hear?'

The street had no attraction for me if it was quiet, but whenever I heard children laughing and making a noise I disobeyed Grandfather. A few bruises and scratches didn't worry me, but the cruelty of street sports never failed to shock me – a cruelty which had become only too familiar and which drove me to desperation. I couldn't bear to see the boys making cocks or dogs fight each other, torture cats, chase goats that belonged to Jews, or make fun of drunken beggars and especially the religious fanatic Igosha, who was called 'Death in the Pocket'.

He was a tall, thin, smoke-blackened man with a heavy sheepskin coat and a dense beard on his bony, rusty-looking face. He walked round the streets bent double, swaying to and fro and silently staring at the ground beneath his feet. His face of cast-iron with its sad little eyes inspired a timid respect in me and I thought this man was occupied with some very important business, that he was searching for something and must not be disturbed.

The boys used to run after him and throw stones at his hunched back. For a long time he would make out as if nothing was going on and pretended not to feel any pain. Then he would suddenly stop dead, throw back his head, straighten his hairy cap with a convulsive movement and look around as if he had just woken up.

'Igosha, Death in the Pocket! Igosha, where are you off to? Look, you've got death in your pocket!'

He would clutch his pocket and then, bending down quickly, would pick up a stone, a small lump of wood or a clod of dried earth, and wave his long arm, clumsily, muttering curses under his breath. Whenever he swore, he used the same three filthy words and in this respect the boys' store of obscenities was immeasurably richer than his. At times he would limp after them in futile pursuit. His long coat got in his way and he would fall down on his knees and lift himself up with his black arms that resembled two thin branches. The boys would hurl stones at his back and sides, and the more daring ones used to run right up to him, empty a handful of dust over his head and leap away.

An even more distressing sight that the street had to offer

110

was our foreman, Grigory Ivanovich. He'd gone quite blind and now wandered about begging, a tall, silent, handsome figure. His guide was a little, grey old woman who would stop at every window and say in a squeaky voice, her eyes perpetually on the look-out for food:

'Help a poor blind beggar, for Christ's sake. . . .'

Grigory never said anything. He would stare through his small black glasses straight at the walls of houses, at windows or passers-by, and gently stroke his beard with his dye-stained hand. His lips were always firmly closed. I often watched him but never heard any sound from those closely shut lips and this silence I found more painful than anything else. I couldn't bring myself to go up close to him and whenever I saw him, I used to run off home and say to Grandmother:

'Grigory's coming!'

'What's that?' she would say nervously, in a pained voice. 'Run after him and give him this!'

Stubbornly and angrily I would refuse to go. Then she would go herself and stand for a long time talking to him on the pavement. He would laugh, shake his beard, but say very little, in words of one syllable.

Sometimes Grandmother would take him into the kitchen and give him tea and food. Once he asked where I was. Grandmother called me, but I ran away and hid among the firewood. I couldn't bear to be near him and felt terribly ashamed in his presence. And I knew that Grandmother felt ashamed as well. One day we had a talk about Grigory. After she'd seen him out of the gate she walked quietly round the yard and cried, her head bowed. I went up to her and took her hand.

'What's this, why do you run away from him?' she asked softly. 'He loves you . . . he's a good man. . . .'

'Why doesn't Grandfather give him anything to eat?' I asked.

'Grandfather?'

She stopped, pressed me to her and in an almost prophetic voice whispered: 'Remember what I'm telling you: the Lord will send us bitter punishment for the way we've treated this man. Yes, bitter punishment.'

She wasn't wrong. Ten years later, when Grandmother had gone to eternal rest, Grandfather himself was wandering around the streets, penniless and demented, pitifully calling out at windows: 'Give me just a small piece of pie ... that's all I want! Ah, what people!' The only thing left from the Grandfather of before was this plaintive, bitter, disturbing: 'Ah, what people!'

Besides Igosha and Grigory Ivanovich there was a dissolute old woman, Veronikha, the sight of whom made me run from the street. She turned up on Sundays, huge, dishevelled, and drunk. She had a special way of walking, and didn't seem to move her feet, or even touch the ground, but floated along like a storm cloud, bellowing coarse songs. Everyone who came across her hid from her behind doors, round corners, or ran into shops. She literally swept the street. Her face was almost blue, swollen like a bladder, and there was a terrifying mockery in the stare of her great grey eyes. Sometimes she howled and cried:

'My little children, where are you?'

I asked Grandmother what she meant.

'That's no business of yours,' she answered gloomily, but all the same told me: 'This woman had a husband, Voronov, who was a civil servant, and wanted promotion. So he sold his wife to his superior, who took her away somewhere, and she didn't come back for two years. When she returned, her children – a boy and a girl – had both died, her husband had gambled with government money and was in prison. So she took to drink to drown her sorrows, and lived a dissolute, drunken life. Every Sunday evening the police would pick her up. . . .'

No, it was far better to be at home than out in the street. I particularly enjoyed the time after supper, when Grandfather went to Uncle Yakov's workshop and Grandmother would sit by the window and tell me interesting tales, and talked about my father.

She cut off the broken wing of the starling that had been rescued from the cat and in its place expertly attached a tiny piece of wood. When the wound had healed up and the bird had recovered, she taught it to speak. She would stand for a whole hour by the cage which hung by the window and in a deep voice repeat over and over again to that clever, coal-black creature – it really was a fine, large bird:

'Come on. Say: "Tweety wants some porridge!" '

The starling would cock its bright, round, comical eye at her, bang its stick on the thin floor of the cage, puff out its beak and whistle like an oriole, imitate a jay, a cuckoo, and try to miaow like a cat, howl like a dog. But it could never copy the human voice.

'Enough of your nonsense!' Grandmother would say seriously. 'Say: "Tweety wants porridge!" '

That black feathered 'monkey' would screech deafeningly something vaguely resembling my grandmother's words, and she would laugh with joy, give the bird some millet with her finger, and say:

'I know you, you crafty old devil! You're pretending you can't do it, but I know you can if you want to!'

And in the end she taught the bird to speak. After a short while it could ask for porridge, quite clearly, and when it saw my grandfather would say something that sounded like 'Hello'.

At first it was kept in Grandfather's room, but it was soon consigned to our attic, because it had learned to mimic Grandfather. Grandfather would say his prayers, pronouncing every word in that distinct way of his, and the bird would poke its yellow, waxen beak through the bars of the cage and whistle:

'Thou, thou, thee, thou . . .'

This annoyed Grandfather very much. Once he stopped in the middle of his prayers, stamped his foot and shouted savagely, 'Take that devil out of here or I'll kill it.'

Much of what happened in our house was interesting and amusing, but at times I felt weighed down by a sadness impossible to overcome. It was as though I had been filled up with something very heavy and for a long time I lived at the bottom of a deep and dark pit, without sight or hearing, or any kind of feeling, blind and half dead. . . .

Chapter 8

QUITE unexpectedly Grandfather sold the house to the publican and bought another in Kanatny Street. Unpaved and overgrown with grass, clean and quiet, this street led straight out to open fields and was made up of small, brightly painted houses.

The new house was smarter and more pleasant than our old one. Its front was painted warm, restful, raspberry-red; the light-blue shutters on the three ground-floor windows and the lattice shutter of the attic window stood out brightly. The left side of the roof was attractively covered with the thick foliage of an elm and a lime tree. In the yard and garden there were many comfortable little nooks, which seemed to have been specially made for hide-and-seek. The garden was particularly fine, not very large – a pleasant wilderness. In one corner was the small bath house, just like a toy. In another was a large, fairly deep pit, overgrown with grass. The charred remains of the former bath house, which had been burnt down, stuck out from it. On the left the garden was bounded by Colonel Ovsyannikov's stables, and on the right by the Betlengs' outhouses. Right at the bottom it adjoined the estate belonging to Petrovna, who owned a dairy farm. She was a plump, handsome-looking woman, noisy, and shaped like a bell. Her little house, dark and ramshackle, had settled into the earth and was covered all over with moss. Its two windows looked out benignly on to the fields, which were disfigured by deep gullies. In the distance was the huge, dense blue mass of the forest. All day long soldiers moved and ran through the fields. Their bayonet blades flashed like white lightning in the slanting rays of the autumn sun.

The whole house was crammed with people I'd never seen before. The front part was occupied by a Tartar soldier and his little round wife. From morning till night she shouted and laughed and played on a richly decorated guitar, and the song she sang most often, in her high, sonorous voice was:

Not to love one alone,
But to seek another
Try to seek her out,
And rich reward awaits you
On the only true path!
O, swe-eet re-ward. . . .

The soldier, who was as round as a ball, would sit by the window, blow out his blue cheeks, goggle his twinkling, brownish eyes, and puff endlessly at his pipe, with a strange, barking cough: 'Vookh. Vookh.'

In the warm annexe over the storehouse and stables lived two draymen, a small grey-looking man called Uncle Peter, and his dumb nephew Stepa, a smooth, well-built young man with a face like a brass tray. And there was Valei, a tall, gloomy Tartar orderly. All these were new people, unfamiliar in every way.

But the lodger who had an irresistible attraction was 'Just the Job'. He'd taken a room at the back of the house next to the kitchen. It was long and had windows that looked out on to the garden and the yard.

He was a thin, stooping man with a white face and a black, forked beard. His eyes were kind, and he wore spectacles. He wasn't given to saying much, kept to himself, and when he was invited to dinner or tea, always answered: 'Just the job!'

And Grandmother began to call him Just the Job when he called on us and behind his back as well. 'Lenka, go and tell Just the Job to come and have tea with us!' 'Just the Job, you're not eating very much!'

The whole of his room was stuffed with piles of boxes, thick books in the new typography, which was all Greek to me; everywhere were bottles of different-coloured liquids, pieces of copper and iron, and bars of lead. From morning until evening, dressed in his reddish-brown leather jacket and grey check trousers which were soiled all over with paint and had a nasty smell, he would stand there, a dishevelled, awkward figure, melting lead, soldering copper, weighing something on a small pair of scales, calling out aloud, burning his fingers and hastily blowing on them, stumbling over to sketches on the wall and wiping his spectacles before he sniffed at them, so close he almost touched the paper with his straight, strangely pale nose. And sometimes he suddenly stopped in the middle of the room, or by the window, and stood stock-still for a long time, silent and mesmerized, his eyes closed, his face turned upwards.

I used to climb out on the roof of the barn and watch him across the yard through an open window. I could see the blue flame of the spirit lamp on the table and a dark figure. He would usually be writing something in a tattered notebook; his spectacles glinted coldly, like icebergs. The magic wrought by this man kept me up on the roof for hours on end, and kindled my curiosity until it became unbearable.

Sometimes, standing there framed by the window, he looked straight at the roof, with his hands clasped behind him, but he didn't seem to see me, and this I found very annoying. Then he'd suddenly jump back to the table, and, bent almost double, would start rummaging around.

I think I'd have been afraid of him if he'd been better dressed, and richer, but he was poor. The dirty, crumpled collar of his shirt stuck out of his leather jacket, his trousers were patched and stained, and he had well-worn slippers on his bare feet. Poor people weren't frightening, but harmless: this opinion was strengthened by the kindness with which Grandmother treated them and the contempt Grandfather had for them.

Nobody in the house liked Just the Job. He was spoken about with ridicule, the soldier's gay wife called him 'Chalky Nose', Uncle Peter, 'Apothecary' and 'Wizard', and Grandfather, a 'worker in black magic' and 'freemason'.

'What does he do?' I asked Grandmother. She replied sharply:

'That's nothing to do with you. Just keep your mouth shut. . . .'

Once, having summoned up my courage, I went up to his window, and asked him, barely concealing my excitement: 'What are you doing?'

He shuddered, stared at me for a long time over his spectacles, stretched out his hand, covered in sores and scars, and said:

'Climb up.'

His invitation to climb in through the window and not through the door raised him even higher in my estimation. He sat down on one of the boxes, put me in front of him, moved me away, then brought me back again and finally asked in a low voice:

'Where are you from?'

It was very strange: four times a day I sat down at the same kitchen table with him, and he didn't seem to know me. I replied: 'I'm the grandson. . . .'

'Oh, of course,' he said, inspecting his finger, and then fell silent. I decided I must explain everything to him:

'I'm not a Kashirin, but a Peshkóv.'

'Péshkov?' he repeated, stressing the wrong syllable. 'Just the job!' He made me move to one side, got up, went over to the table and said:

'Sit there and don't move.'

I can't remember how long I sat there watching him scraping with a rasp a piece of copper fixed in a vice. The gold dust of the filings fell on to a piece of cardboard under the vice. Then he gathered them together into one handful, emptied them into the thick cup, added some white dust like salt which he took from a jar, poured something over them from a black bottle which made everything in the cup hiss and smoke, and give off a sharp, acrid smell which filled my nostrils and made me cough and shake my head. The sorcerer asked boastfully:

'Nasty smell, isn't it?'

'Yes.'

'Good, that's very good!'

'What's he boasting about?' I thought and said in a stern voice:

'If it smells nasty, it can't be any good.'

'Well,' he exclaimed, winking, 'that's not always so! Do you like playing knucklebones?'

'You mean fivestones?'

'Fivestones then!'

'Yes, I do.'

'Would you like me to make a throwing cockle for you?'

'Yes.'

'Give me the knucklebone then.'

He came up to me once more, holding the smoking cup in his hand, and glancing at it with one eye.

'I'll make it, but if I do, you must never come here again.'

This hurt me deeply.

'Don't worry, I'll never show my face here again. . . .'

I strode off angrily to the garden. Grandfather was busily manuring the roots of an apple tree. It was autumn, and the leaves had been falling for quite a few weeks.

'As you are here you can prune the raspberry bushes,' he said, handing me the shears.

I asked: 'What's Just the Job making?'

'He's ruining that room,' he answered angrily. 'He's burnt the floor, stained the wallpaper, and torn it. It's no good, he'll have to clear out.'

'Of course,' I agreed, beginning to clip the dry branches of the raspberry bush as fast as I could.

When it rained in the evenings – and if Grandfather was out – Grandmother used to hold very interesting meetings in the kitchen and invite all the lodgers, which included the draymen, the orderly, and the lively Petrovna, who used to come very often, and sometimes a gay woman lodger would turn up. In one corner by the stove Just the Job was always to be found sitting silent and motionless. The dumb Stepa would play cards with the Tartar, Valei, who used to snap them under his wide nose and say:

'You devil!'

Uncle Peter would bring an enormous crust of white bread and a large earthenware jar of home-made jam. He would slice the bread, smear it liberally with jam, and hold out the tasty slices in the palms of his hands as he offered them to the guests with a low bow.

'Please do have some,' he said invitingly, and whenever anybody took a slice he would look closely at his palm, and lick any drops of jam there were left there.

Petrovna would bring a cherry liqueur in a bottle and the gay young lady handed out nuts and sweets. A sumptuous banquet would then follow and this was my grandmother's favourite form of enjoyment.

Not long after Just the Job had bribed me to stay away from his room, Grandmother gave a party like the one I've just described.

A dreary autumnal rain splashed down, the wind moaned, the trees scratched against the kitchen walls. It was warm and cosy in the kitchen. Everyone sat close to each other and was quiet and friendly. Grandmother told her stories without a break, each story better than the other. On this occasion Grandmother gave everyone the full benefit of the enormous number of stories she knew – and this was very rare for her. She sat on the edge of the stove, her feet resting on the step, and leant towards her audience, whose faces were lit up by the small tin lamp. When she was in the mood, she always liked to sit up on the stove.

She explained this by saying:

'I must be high up when I recite, it's much better up there.'

I sat at her feet, on the wide step, almost directly above the head of Just the Job. Grandmother started telling the story of Ivan the Warrior and Miron the Hermit; the precise sonorous words would flow rhythmically:

> Once there was an evil warrior, Gordion,
> Black of soul, stony of heart;
> He hated truth, and was cruel to men,
> And lived like an owl in an oak's hollow;
> The one this Gordion hated most of all
> Was old Miron, who lived as a hermit,
> One of truth's silent defenders,
> An unswerving champion of peace.
> Now Gordion summoned his faithful warrior,
> The Brave Ivanushka by name:
> 'Go now, Ivanko, and kill the old man,
> Too long he's held his head so high!
> Go and cut it off
> By holding on to his grey beard,
> And bring it back for my hounds to eat.'
> Ivan, obedient, followed the command,
> Bitterly thinking to himself:

'I go not of my own free will
But this is my master's decree.'
He hid his sword under the ground
And greeted the hermit with a bow.
'How are you, old man?
Is God being kind to you?'
At this the far-seeing sage laughed
And said with those wise lips of his:
' 'Tis time you stopped deceiving me,
All is known to God.
Good and evil are in his hands!
I know very well your reason for coming.'

Ivanka felt ashamed before the hermit,
And feared disobedience's reward,
He took his sword from its leather sheath
And brandished the cold steel on high.
'I should like to have done with thee
Without your seeing the weapon.
Come now, make your prayers,
Pray to God the last time,
For yourself, me, and all mankind,
And then I'll cut your head off!'
Miron went down on his knees,
Down by the oak sapling,
Which bowed its leaves before him.
The old man said with a smile:
'Look, Ivan; long must you wait!
Prayers for mankind are long,
Better kill me at once,
And the less tiring it will be for you.'
Ivan angrily frowned,
And boasted stupidly:
'What has been agreed, remains so:
On with your prayers, though a century they may last!'

The hermit prayed until nightfall,
And from night until the next dawn,
And from dawn again till night,
And from summer on to autumn,
Year after year Miron prayed
And the young oak grew to the clouds,
And a thick forest grew from the acorns,

And still no end was there to his holy prayer!
And there they are to this day:
The old man still weeps for man
In earnest plea for help,
And for the Blessed Virgin's smile.

And nearby stands the warrior Ivan,
His sword has long gone to dust
And his fine trappings rotted away.
Summer and winter he stands naked,
Burnt by the heat, yet never quite consumed;
Gnawed at by worms – but never devoured;
Untouched by wolves or bears,
Or frosts or storms.
He is powerless to move from there,
Nor raise a hand or say a word.
This is his punishment
For following that evil command;
And hiding behind another's conscience!
And the old man's prayers for us poor sinners
Even now flow up to God,
Like a bright river to the ocean-sea!

At the very beginning of Grandmother's story I noticed
that Just the Job was greatly disturbed: he kept on moving
his hands with strange jerky movements, taking off his
glasses and putting them on again, waving them in time to the
beat of the musical words, nodding his head, rubbing his eyes
hard, and continually wiping his forehead and cheeks as
though he'd broken out into a heavy sweat. When any of the
audience moved or coughed or shuffled his feet, our lodger
would hiss menacingly:

'Ssh!'

When Grandmother had finished he sprang to his feet and
started spinning round and round, making wild, unnatural
flourishes. Then he muttered:

'That's marvellous, it should be written down. It's all so
true and really Russian. . . .'

I could now see he was crying and his eyes were filled with
tears, which welled out in a veritable flood. It was a strange
and very touching sight. He ran round the kitchen, with

clumsy, comical hops, waving his glasses in front of his nose as he tried to put them on. But he didn't manage to hook them behind his ears. Uncle Peter laughed at him, but everyone else sat in mute astonishment. Grandmother said hastily:

'Write it down then, there's nothing wrong in that. I know lots of others as well. . . .'

'No, it's this one I like. It's so very Russian,' the lodger shouted excitedly. He suddenly stopped still in the middle of the kitchen, shouted out loud, and began swishing his right arm through the air while his glasses trembled in his left hand. He kept on talking feverishly, shrieking and stamping his feet, repeating the same words over and over again:

'You mustn't let someone else be your conscience. Never!'

Suddenly his voice broke off. He gave everyone a rapid glance, then slunk off quietly and guiltily, his head hanging down. Everyone laughed and looked at each other in embarrassment, and Grandmother moved into the deep shadows at the back of the stove and sat there heavily sighing.

'What's bitten him?' asked Petrovna, wiping her thick, red lips.

'Nothing,' answered Uncle Peter. 'He's like that. . . .'

Grandmother climbed down from the stove and silently began to warm the samovar while Uncle Peter said slowly:

'It's the same with all the gentry. Moody lot!'

Valei chipped in, gloomily:

'Can't expect anything else from bachelors!'

Everyone laughed, and Uncle Peter drawled:

'It made him cry.'

I felt bored. My heart was heavy with sadness. Just the Job had amazed me. I felt sorry for him, and could not forget his tear-filled eyes.

He didn't spend the nights at home and would return for dinner the next day, subdued, dishevelled, and clearly embarrassed in front of everyone.

'I made a bit of a scene yesterday,' he said to Grandmother like a guilty schoolboy. 'I hope you're not angry.'

'Why should I be?'

'Because I interrupted you, and talked too much.'

'You didn't offend anyone.'

I felt that Grandmother was afraid of him. She didn't look him in the face and spoke to him in a soft voice which was very unusual for her. He went over to her and in a forthright way that amazed me by its frankness, said:

'I'm all alone, I've no one at all! If you have no one to speak to, then suddenly everything boils up inside you and overflows. . . . Then you can't keep silent any more and you feel like talking to a tree or a stone. . . .'

Grandmother moved away from him.

'You should get married.'

'Ah!' he exclaimed, frowning all over his face and he walked out waving his arm.

Grandmother scowled as she watched him go, then took a pinch of snuff and said to me in her commanding voice:

'You keep away from him. God alone knows what kind of a man he is.'

But again I felt drawn towards him.

I saw how his face had changed when he said 'all alone'. In those words there was something I could understand, which touched my heart, and I went to see him.

I looked through the window of his room. It was empty and resembled an attic into which a lot of useless things had been thrown hastily and untidily – things as useless and as strange as their owner. I went into the garden and found him in the pit. He was sitting there all hunched up and uncomfortable on the end of a charred beam, with his elbows on his knees and his hands on the back of his head. The beam was covered with earth, and one end, shiny as coal, stuck up in the air above the rank wormwood, nettles and burdock. The sight of him sitting there so uncomfortably made me want all the more to be kind to him.

For a long time he didn't see me, but looked straight past me with the unseeing eyes of a brown owl; then he asked with a note of annoyance in his voice:

'Looking for me?'

'No.'

'What do you want then?'

'Nothing.'

He took his glasses off, wiped them with his handkerchief which was covered with black and red stains, and said:

'Come down here.'

When I sat at his side he hugged me tight.

'Sit still. We're just going to sit here without speaking to each other. Agreed? Like this. You're quite a stubborn chap, aren't you?'

'Yes.'

'Well, it doesn't matter!'

We sat silently for a long while. It was a mild, quiet evening, one of those sad evenings in late summer when all the flowers are visibly fading and turning pale with every hour of the day, and when all the heady scents of summer are drained from the earth, leaving only a cold, damp smell. The sky at this time has a strange transparence and the jackdaws arouse melancholy thoughts with their restless flashing through the pinkish sky. Everything is still and quiet. Every sound – the rustle of a bird or of a leaf falling – becomes magnified and makes you shudder apprehensively, and then you are swallowed up again by the silence that holds the whole earth in its grip and fills the heart.

At such moments thoughts are born which are particularly pure and light, but also as evanescent and gossamer-like as a spider's web and too elusive to be captured in words. They flare up and fade away with the speed of falling stars, setting the soul on fire with sadness, caressing it, disturbing it, making it boil up, melt into a mould from which it takes its life pattern and crystallizes into what is called character.

As I pressed against our lodger's warm side I looked with him through the black branches of the apple trees at the crimson sky and watched the flight of the busy linnets. I saw the goldfinches stripping the crowns of the dried-up rape plants, picking out the sour seeds, and the shaggy grey clouds with purple edges spreading from the fields, while below them crows wearily flew off to their nests in the cemetery. Everything seemed good, unusually easy to understand, and close to me. Sometimes Just the Job would ask with a deep sigh:

'Marvellous, isn't it? But don't you feel the cold and dampness?'

And when the sky had darkened and everything around seemed to swell out with the moistness that came with twilight, he said: 'That's enough. Let's go home.'

He stopped when we reached the wicket gate into the garden and said softly: 'You have a fine grandmother. What a world this is. . . .'

He closed his eyes and smiled and said in a low voice, very distinctly, as if he were reading from a book:

> 'This is his punishment
> For following that evil command
> And hiding behind another's conscience!

Don't ever forget that!'

Pushing me on, he asked:

'Can you write?'

'No.'

'You must learn. And when you've done that, write down your grandmother's stories . . . it's really worth the trouble.'

We became firm friends. From that day I went to see Just the Job when I felt like it and would sit on one of the boxes filled with rags, quite free to watch him melt the lead or heat the copper without anyone interfering. He would make the iron red-hot and forge it into sheets on his anvil with a small hammer which had a beautiful handle. He'd weigh everything on a delicate pair of copper scales and pour different liquids into fat white jars and watch them smoke and fill the room with an acrid smell. Then he'd frown, peer into a thick book and grunt as he bit his red lips or softly drawled in his hoarse voice: 'Ah, rose of Sharon.'

'What are you making?'

'Something, my friend.'

'What?'

'If I told you, you wouldn't understand.'

'Grandfather says that you forge money. . . .'

'Grandfather? That's a load of nonsense! Money is rubbish!'

'How can you buy bread without it?'

'Yes, true enough, you need money to buy bread –'

'And meat as well. Do you see?'

'Yes, meat as well.'

He laughed ever so softly in the most endearing way, tickled me behind the ear as if I were a kitten and said:

'You win when it comes to arguments. Beat me every time. So let's be quiet for a moment.'

Sometimes he stopped working, sat down beside me, and we would both look through the window at the rain falling on the roofs, at the yard, now overgrown with grass, or at the apple trees gradually losing their leaves. Just the Job was given to few words, but only used those necessary to make his point. More often, when he wanted to draw my attention to something, he would gently nudge me and point it out by winking and moving his eyes.

I could see nothing remarkable in the yard outside, but those nudges with the elbow and brief words of his made everything become important, significant, so they became firmly entrenched in my mind.

A cat ran across the yard and stopped to look at its reflection in a shining puddle and raised its soft paw to stroke it. Just the Job said softly:

'Cats are proud and mistrustful creatures.'

Mamai, our reddish-gold cock, fluttered up on the garden fence, flapped its wings, nearly fell off, and in its annoyance started crowing angrily as it stretched out its neck.

'The General's important, but not very clever,' he said.

The clumsy Valei stumbled through the mud like an old horse; his face, with its large cheekbones, was puffed out and he blinked at the sky. A white ray from the autumn sun struck him right on the chest and made one of his brass buttons glint. The Tartar stopped and touched it with his crooked fingers.

'Anyone'd think he'd just won a medal. . . .'

My attachment to Just the Job grew stronger and stronger and I became completely dependent on him, not only when I'd suffered cruel insults and beatings, but in happy times as well. A quiet person, he never stopped me when I blurted out everything that came into my head, whereas Grandfather always rudely interrupted with an expression like: 'Stop your gabbling, gas-bag.' Grandmother was so occupied with her own thoughts she never listened to or took in what anybody else had to say. Just the Job always listened attentively to my chatter and often used to say with a smile:

'That's not true, my friend, you made it up!'

These blunt remarks of his were always apt and timely, and he had a knack of seeing right through me and knowing what I was thinking or feeling. If I was about to say something that wasn't to the point, or untrue, he would see this at once and stop me short with a curt but well-meant 'You're lying, friend' even before I had time to open my mouth. Often I tried to put this magical power of his to the test by inventing some story or other, but he'd see at once I wasn't telling the truth and would shake his head before I'd gone very far and say, 'You're lying, my friend.'

'How do you know?'

'I can tell.'

Grandmother would often take me with her when she went to the Sennaya Square for water, and once we saw five townsmen beating a peasant. They threw him down and started tearing at him like a pack of dogs. Grandmother took the pails from the yoke and, swinging them round and round, rushed at the men.

'Run away,' she shouted to me.

But I panicked, ran after her and began throwing stones and pebbles at the men, while Grandmother bravely set about them with her yoke, beating them on the shoulders and face. Some other people arrived on the scene and the men fled. Grandmother washed the victim. His face had been trodden on and it still makes me feel sick to think of him pressing his dirty fingers to his torn nostril and howling and coughing, while the blood spurted into Grandmother's face and on to her breast. She shouted as well and was shaking all over. As soon as I got home I ran to the lodger and began telling him about all that had happened. He stopped working and stood before me holding up a long file, like a sword. Then he interrupted me and said in an unusually convincing voice:

'Wonderful, that's exactly how it happened. Marvellous!'

I was so struck by what I'd seen that his words did not

startle me, and I carried on, but he hugged me and started stumbling round the room.

'That's quite enough! You've described it perfectly, understand? Perfectly!'

This remark infuriated me and I broke off. But then I realized – and I can still recall how startled I was – that he'd stopped me at the right time: I had, in fact, told him everything.

'It's best not to think about such things – it's horrible turning them over in your mind.'

Sometimes he would say things, quite out of the blue, that have stayed with me all my life. Once I told him about my enemy Klyushnikov, a bully from Novaya Street, a fat boy with a large head. Neither of us could get the better of each other when we fought. Just the Job listened carefully to my tale of woe and said:

'That's all nonsense. It's not a question of strength. Real strength is speed of movement. The quicker you are, the stronger, understand?'

The following Sunday I tried moving my fists quicker and easily vanquished Klyushnikov. This made me value our lodger's words even more.

'You must learn how to take hold of things, understand? And that's very difficult.'

I didn't understand but couldn't help remembering these words and others like them, chiefly because there was something in their simplicity that was annoyingly mysterious: surely getting hold of a stone, a piece of bread or a cup or a hammer didn't require any special skill?

At home Just the Job was more and more disliked. Even the friendly cat belonging to our gay lady lodger wouldn't climb up on his knees as it did with everyone else, and didn't come when he called. For this I would beat it, pull its ears and was almost reduced to tears in my efforts to persuade it not to be frightened of him.

'My clothes smell of acid, that's why it won't come,' he explained, but I knew that everyone else, even Grandmother, had a different explanation, which showed their hostility – unjustified and insulting though it was.

'What do you hang round him for?' Grandmother would ask angrily. 'Take care he doesn't teach you something else. . . .'

Grandfather, that old red stoat, cruelly beat me for each visit he found out about.

Of course, I didn't let Just the Job know that I was forbidden to see him, but I told him outright what everyone thought of him.

'Grandmother's afraid of you: she says you're an expert in black magic and Grandfather says the same, and that you're one of God's enemies and a dangerous person.'

He twitched his head as though driving away a fly. His chalky face reddened into a smile that made my heart jump and everything turn green before my eyes.

'You don't have to tell me, friend,' he said softly. 'It's all very depressing, isn't it?'

'Yes.'

'Very depressing.'

In the end they got rid of him. One morning after breakfast I went to visit him and found him sitting on the floor packing his things into the boxes and quietly singing about the Rose of Sharon.

'Goodbye, my friend, I'm leaving now.'

'Why?'

He stared at me and said:

'Don't you know? Your mother wants the room.'

'Who said that?'

'Grandfather!'

'He's lying.'

Just the Job drew me close to him and when I'd sat down beside him on the floor he said:

'No need to get angry now. I thought you knew and didn't want to tell me. It's not very pleasant, I thought to myself. . . .'

For some reason I felt irritated and annoyed with him.

'Listen,' he said almost in a whisper, smiling at the same time. 'Remember when I said to you: don't visit me?'

I nodded.

'You were angry with me?'

'Yes.'

'I didn't want to offend you, but I knew very well that if we became friends you'd get it properly in the neck.'

He spoke like someone of my own age, and his words made me feel terribly happy. I even thought that I'd understood him all along, and said: 'I knew all the time!'

'Well, there you are. That's the position then, my dear friend.'

I felt a terrible aching in my heart.

'Why doesn't anyone like you?'

He hugged me, pressed me to him, and answered with a wink:

'Because I'm a stranger, understand? That's the whole trouble. . . .'

I tugged at his sleeve, unable to say anything.

'Don't be angry,' he said once more and whispered into my ear: 'Don't cry either.'

But tears were flowing down his cheeks from under his clouded spectacles. Then we sat for a long time in silence – as we'd grown used to doing – only occasionally saying a few brief words to each other.

That same evening he left after hugging me tightly and saying a warm farewell to everyone. I walked through the gates and watched him jerking up and down in the cart as its wheels crunched over little mounds of frozen mud. As soon as he'd gone Grandmother started scrubbing and cleaning out the dirty room while I went from corner to corner trying to get in her way.

'Go away!' she shouted as she bumped into me.

'Why did you make him leave?'

'Nothing to do with you!'

'You're a lot of fools!'

She laid about me with a wet rag, at the same time crying: 'Have you gone mad, or what?'

'I don't mean you, but everybody else,' I said correcting myself, but this didn't calm her down.

At supper Grandfather said:

'Thank God that's the last of him! Every time I saw him I felt a terrible pain. We had to get rid of him.'

Just out of malice I broke a spoon and was duly punished.

And this was the end of my first friendship with one of that innumerable company of people who are foreigners in their own country, but who are in reality its finest sons. . . .

Chapter 9

IN recalling my childhood I like to picture myself as a beehive to which various simple obscure people brought the honey of their knowledge and thoughts on life, generously enriching my character with their own experience. Often this honey was dirty and bitter, but every scrap of knowledge was honey all the same.

After Just the Job had left I became friendly with Uncle Peter. He was like Grandfather, being thin, neat and clean, but was shorter and more slightly built. He was like an adolescent boy who'd dressed up as an old man for fun. His face seemed to be woven, like a sieve, from fine leather bands, among which his comical, lively eyes with their yellowish whites darted about like caged siskins. His bluish-grey hair was curly and his beard made into ringlets. He smoked a pipe and its smoke, the same colour as his hair, curled as well. Even his florid speech, which abounded in puns and comical phrases, seemed curly. He had a buzzing voice that might have been warm and affectionate but for the fact that it gave me the impression he was laughing at everyone.

'When I was a young boy the Countess Tatyana Alexeyevna told me: "Be a blacksmith," but then she changed her mind and said: "Help the gardener." Fair enough. Another time she said: "Have a go at fishing, Petrushka." It's all the same to me and off I went fishing. But as soon as I became mad on it – good-bye fish, thank you very much! So I'm sent to town as a cab driver, and forced to turn most of my earnings over to her Ladyship. All right then, if it's a cabman she wanted, I didn't mind – it was up to her. But before she got a chance to change her mind again, along came the emancipation and I was left with a horse, which I now have instead of a countess.'

The horse was old and white and looked as if a drunken house-painter had started slopping different colours on it and got tired in the middle. Its legs seemed all out of joint and the creature looked like a heap of rags sewn up to resemble a horse. Its bony head with its dull, dim eyes drooped mournfully and appeared to be loosely tacked on to the body by swollen veins and ancient, worn-out hides. Uncle Peter treated it with respect, never beat it and called it 'Tanka'.

'Why do you give that nag of yours a Christian name?' Grandfather said to him once.

'You're wrong, Vassily Vassilyevich, with due respect. Tanka's not a Christian name. You're thinking of Tatyana!'

Uncle Peter was literate and extremely well read in the Bible. He was always arguing with Grandfather about which saint was holier than the other. They vied in the severity of their judgements on the great sinners of ancient times. Absalom came in for most criticism. Sometimes arguments took a purely grammatical form, my grandfather arguing that certain words ended in 'khom' while Uncle Peter insisted they should end in 'sha'.

'You've got your own way and I've mine,' retorted Grandfather, going red in the face. 'All these "shas" of yours!' he said teasingly.

But Uncle Peter, looking out from behind a thick cloud of smoke, would spitefully ask: 'And how are your "khoms", any better? They mean nothing to God, who's more than likely saying to himself, "Though the prayer's well meant, it's not worth a cent!"'

'Get out of here, Alexei,' Grandfather would shout at me, his green eyes sparkling.

Peter was a great one for cleanliness and tidiness. If he happened to be walking through the yard he would kick any woodshavings, old bits of crockery or bones to one side and, what's more, would mutter threateningly:

'Useless rubbish. It only clutters the place up.'

He was very talkative, good-natured and cheerful, but at times his eyes turned bloodshot, clouded over and became as still as a dead man's. He used to find a place for himself in a corner of the room and sit there in the darkness, hunched up, sullen and silent like his nephew.

'What's the matter, Uncle Peter?'

'Go away,' he would answer sternly, in an empty voice.

In one of the houses in our street a gentleman took up

residence. He had a bump on his forehead and a very strange habit: on Sundays he would sit by the window and spray gunshot at dogs, cats, chickens, crows – even passers-by he took a dislike to. Once he caught Just the Job with a broad-side of duckshot. The pellets didn't go through his leather jacket, but some of them landed in his pocket. I remember the lodger examining the grey pellets closely, through his spectacles. Grandfather advised him to complain to the police but he threw the pellets into one corner of the kitchen.

'It's not worth it,' he said.

On another, later, occasion the marksman put some pellets into my grandfather's leg. He was furious, reported it to the police and got some witnesses together, former victims and onlookers; but suddenly the gentleman disappeared.

Every time shots rang out in the street, Uncle Peter, if he happened to be home, would hurriedly cover his grey head with the faded cap with the large peak he wore on Sundays and rush outside. There he would hide his hands under the back of his long coat, which he made to stick up, like a cock's tail, stretch his belly out and stride along the pavement past the marksman. He used to walk past him, then back again. The whole household would stand at the gates to see the blue face of the soldier, and above it, his wife's blond head would be staring out of the window. Some neighbours came from the Betlengs' yard as well, and only Ovsyannikov's grey house didn't show any sign of life.

Sometimes Uncle Peter's excursions into the street ended in failure – the hunter, evidently, didn't consider him game worth firing at; but occasionally the double–barrelled rifle went off, 'Bang, bang.' Without quickening his steps Uncle Peter would come up to us and say in a very satisfied voice:

'Hit me in the lapels.'

Once he was hit in the neck and shoulder. As she picked the shot out with a needle, Grandmother said:

'What do you have to encourage that raving lunatic for? He'll have your eyes out next!'

'Don't worry yourself, Akulina Ivanovna,' Uncle Peter said contemptuously. 'He's hopeless with a rifle.'

'But why egg him on?'

'You think I'm egging him on? I only want to tease him.'

As he scrutinized in the palm of his hands the pellets that Grandmother had taken out, he said:

'What a hopeless shot! Now the Countess Tatyana Alexey-evna, who was married for a short time – she changed husbands like they were footmen – had an officer living with her called Mamont Iliich. How that man could shoot! The things he could do with bullets! He'd get Ignashka the fool to stand a good forty paces away and tie a bottle to his belt so it hung down between his legs. Ignashka would open his legs wide and laugh like the idiot he was. Mamont Iliich would aim his pistol and bang! The bottle went crunch. Once, however, a horsefly bit Ignashka and made him jump, so the bullet hit him on the knee cap. They called a doctor, and off came the leg before you could say knife. They buried the leg. . . .'

'And the idiot?'

'Oh, he was all right. An idiot doesn't need legs or arms and lives through his stupidity. Nobody minds an idiot, they're quite harmless. You know the saying, "From a fool there's no offence".'

Grandmother wasn't at all surprised by these stories – she knew dozens like them – but I felt rather ill at ease and used to ask Peter:

'Could a gentleman beat someone to death?'

'Why not? Of course he could. They even killed each other. One day a lancer came to see Tatyana Alexeyevna and had a row with Mamont. Straight away they got their pistols, went off the the park, near the pond, on the path, and bang! the lancer shot Mamont in the liver. Mamont went to the church-yard and the lancer to the Caucasus . . . and it was their own doing! As far as peasants and suchlike are concerned, they kill them like flies. But not so in the old days, when they weren't cruel towards the peasants – they were their property! Now they don't care.'

'Then they didn't worry themselves too much either,' said Grandmother.

Uncle Peter agreed.

'True. One's own property – but not worth much!'

He was kind to me and spoke more warmly to me than the grown-ups, and although he wasn't afraid of looking you straight in the face, there was something I didn't like about him. When he invited everyone to eat his favourite jam, he would spread my slice the thickest and bring me some ginger-bread and poppy seeds, chatting seriously and quietly the whole time.

'Well, sir, what are you going to be when you grow up? A soldier or a government clerk?'

'A soldier.'

'That's good. It's easy to get into the army these days. The church is quite good too, you just go around shouting "God have mercy!" A priest's life is easier than a soldier's but easiest of all is a fisherman's. He doesn't have to do anything at all – just learns as he goes along.'

Very amusingly he showed how the fish swim round the bait and how perch, mullet and bream struggle when they're hooked.

'You get angry when Grandfather beats you,' he said con-solingly, 'but you shouldn't. It's only to make you learn and what you get is really nothing at all. Take my Countess Tatyana. She was famous for her floggings. She employed a man especially for the job, Christopher he was called. Such an expert he was, people from neighbouring estates used to ask if they could borrow him: "Let's borrow him," they'd say. "Some of the servants need flogging." And she'd lend him out.'

He described coolly, and in great detail, how the Countess, in her white muslin skirt and gossamer-like scarf coloured like the sky, would sit by the portico in front of her house in a red armchair while Christopher dealt out whippings to men and women, right under her nose. 'And what's more, sir, this Christopher was from Ryazan – just like a gipsy or Ukrainian, with moustaches right round to his ears, and when he shaved off his beard, his face was blue all over. And he could act stupid when he wanted his own way. He used to fill a cup with water in the kitchen, catch a fly, or a cockroach, or some sort of beetle, and then hold it down with a small twig for a long time if need be, until it drowned. Sometimes he'd get a louse or something which he found under his collar and drown that. . . .'

These stories were already very familiar, as I'd heard Grandmother or Grandfather tell many like them. Different from each other in their own little ways, there was something they all had in common. In each one a man was tortured, ridiculed or persecuted. I was tired of stories like these and didn't want to hear any more.

'Tell me another,' I asked the cabman.

He'd pucker all his wrinkles round his mouth, make them run up to his eyes, and oblige me with another story.

'All right then, you glutton, here's another. We once had a cook . . .'

'Who had?'

'Why, the Countess Tatyan.'

'Why do you call her Tatyan, like a man, and not Tatyana? She's not a man, is she?'

He laughed delicately.

'Of course she was a woman, but she had a small moustache. Black it was. She was a black German originally and they're very like Negroes. Well, as I was saying, this cook – it's so funny, this story. . . .'

The funny story related how the cook spoiled a fish and cabbage pie, and they made him eat it all at once, which he did and it made him ill.

'I don't think that's funny,' I said petulantly.

'What is, then? Let's hear something from you.'

'I don't know any . . .'

'Then shut up.'

And once more he began spinning his boring yarns.

Sometimes, on high holidays, my cousins would come and visit us. There was the sad-looking, lazy Sasha (Uncle Mikhail's boy) and the spruce Sasha, son of my other uncle, who knew everything. Once when we were all climbing over the roofs of the outhouses, we caught sight of a gentleman in the Betlengs' yard wearing a green fur-lined frock coat. He was sitting on a pile of firewood and playing with some of the puppies. His small, bald, yellow head wasn't covered. One of the cousins suggested stealing one of the pups and an ingenious plan was hatched on the spot: the cousins would immediately go out into the street and up to the gate of the house, while I frightened the gentleman. As he ran away, my cousins would rush into the yard and seize one of the puppies.

'What can I do to frighten him?'

'Spit on his bald head!'

Was it a great crime to spit on a man's head? Often I had heard about, and seen, men treated far worse than that, and so I honourably did my duty. There was a terrible row afterwards. A whole army of men and women from the Betlengs' house marched into our yard, led by a young, handsome officer, and because, at the time of the crime, my cousins were peacefully playing in the street – knowing nothing, of course, about the wild mischief I was up to – I was the one Grandfather thrashed – a thrashing which satisfied to a high degree the whole Betleng household.

When I was lying half slaughtered on the kitchen bench, in came cheerful Uncle Peter, all dressed in his Sunday best.

'A clever idea of yours, sir,' he whispered. 'Just what he deserved, that old goat. As far as I'm concerned, you can spit on the lot of them! You should have thrown a brick at his rotten old head!'

I could see the round, hairless, childlike face of that man as he squealed softly, and pitifully, just like one of the puppies, and wiped his yellow bald head with his little hands, and I felt terribly ashamed and hostile towards my cousins. But now all was forgotten in a flash, as I peered into the cabman's wrinkled face which trembled in the same terrifying and repulsive way as my grandfather's when he beat me.

'Go away!' I shouted, pushing Peter away with my hands and feet. He tittered, winked and slid off the bunk. From then onwards I never felt any inclination to talk to him and I began avoiding him. At the same time I kept a close watch on him, vaguely expecting that something was going to happen.

The Betlengs' was a noisy, riotous household, made up of many beautiful young ladies who were visited by officers and students. They were always laughing, shouting and singing, and playing guitars. The house had a gay look, its windows sparkled and through them the bright green of potted plants could be clearly seen from outside. Grandfather didn't like the house at all. He would call its occupants 'Heretics, infidels!' When talking about the women there, he used some obscene word whose meaning was later explained to me by Uncle Peter by words even more malicious and filthy.

The stern, silent Ovsyannikov house inspired Grandfather with respect. It was high, although it only had one floor and was built out into a clean, deserted yard covered with green turf, in the middle of which was a well covered by a roof with two supporting columns. The house seemed to shrink back from the street as if trying to hide from it. Three of its windows, narrow and arched, stood high above the ground and the sun made their dull panes take on the colours of the rainbow. On the other side of the gates was a barn, which also had three windows, but imitation ones. They were made up of casings fixed to the grey wall, with the woodwork of the frame painted white. These blind windows were very unpleasant, and the whole barn seemed to say that the house wanted to hide itself away and live inconspicuously. This estate, with its deserted stables, and empty sheds with enormous gates, gave an impression of silent, injured pride.

Sometimes a clean-shaven, tall old man with white whiskers that stuck out like needles, would limp across the yard. And sometimes a second old man, with side whiskers and a crooked nose would lead a grey, long-necked horse from the stables. With its narrow chest and dainty legs it used to bow when it came out into the yard like a demure nun. The lame old man would slap it with his palm, whistle, breathe noisily, and then take the horse back to its dark stable. I thought the old man wanted to ride away but couldn't, because he was under a spell.

Three boys used to play almost every day in the yard, from noon to dusk; they were all dressed in grey jackets and trousers and their caps were the same. Their faces were round, they had grey eyes, and they resembled each other so much I could only distinguish them by their size.

I used to watch them through a chink in the fence, where they couldn't see me, although I wanted to be seen. I liked seeing them play unfamiliar games in such a friendly, happy way, and was impressed by their clothes and eager concern for each other – particularly noticeable in the way the older brothers treated the youngest – a comical, nimble pigmy of a boy. If he fell down they laughed, as boys usually do, but their laughter had no malice, and they rushed to help him at once. If he made his hands or knees dirty they wiped him clean with burdock leaves or used their handkerchiefs.

The second eldest would gently reprimand him with: 'You clumthy boy!' They never swore at each other or cheated. All three of them were strong and agile and there seemed to be no end to their energy.

Once I climbed up into a tree and whistled to them – this made them stop and quietly confer among themselves. I thought they might start throwing stones at me, so I clambered down, filled my pockets and shirt with ammunition and climbed up again. But by this time they had already moved off to another part of the yard and had evidently forgotten all about me. This was rather depressing, but I didn't want to be the first to open fire and soon someone called to them from a window: 'Children, come home, quick!' They went off without hurrying, meekly, like geese.

I often sat in the tree over the fence, hoping they would ask me to join in, but they never did. I used to imagine that I was playing with them and at times was so carried away that I shouted out loud and laughed. Then all three would look at me, quietly saying something to each other while I slid down the tree in embarrassment.

Once they began playing hide-and-seek and the second eldest was 'it'. He stood by a corner of the barn, keeping his hands over his eyes without cheating while his brothers ran off to hide.

The eldest nimbly and swiftly climbed into a wide sledge which was housed under the eaves of the barn, while the smallest, obviously at a loss where to hide, ran comically round the well.

'One,' shouted the eldest, 'two ...'

The small one jumped up on to the wooden rail of the well, seized the rope, and leaped into the empty bucket, which promptly disappeared, making a dull knocking sound against the sides.

The sight of the recently oiled wheel turning swiftly and smoothly filled me with horror, but I immediately realized that quick action was needed, and I jumped down into the yard and shouted: 'He's fallen into the well!'

The second brother reached the edge of the well at the same time as me and clutched the rope, which jerked him off his feet and burnt his hands. But I'd already managed to get a hold on the rope and now the eldest brother came running up. As he helped me haul the bucket up he said:

'Gently, please!'

Quickly we hauled the little boy up: he was in a terrified state. Blood dripped from the fingers of his right hand and his cheek was badly scratched. He was drenched up to the waist, deathly pale, but all the same managed to smile as he stood there shivering with his eyes opened wide:

'Wha-a-t a long way d-o-o-wn!'

'Cwaythy, that's what you are,' lisped the second brother, putting his arm round him and wiping the blood off his face with a handkerchief, while the eldest frowned and said:

'We might as well go home. They're bound to find out.'

'Will you get a good hiding?' I asked.

He nodded, held out his hand to me and said:

'You must have run very fast!'

I was overjoyed at this praise, but before I could shake his hand he was talking to the second brother again.

'Get a move on or he'll catch cold. We'll say he fell down. No need to mention the well.'

'All right, then,' agreed the little one, still shivering. 'I'll say I fell in a puddle.'

They all went off.

Everything had happened so quickly that when I looked up at my branch, it was still shaking, throwing down yellow leaves.

For a week or so the brothers didn't come to the yard, but when they did turn up at last, they were noisier than ever. When the eldest saw me up in the tree he shouted in a friendly voice:

'Come and play with us!'

We climbed into the old sledge under the barn's over-hanging roof and had a long chat and a good look at each other.

'Did you get a beating?' I asked.

'Not half,' answered the eldest.

It was hard to believe that these boys, like myself, also came in for beatings and I felt a sense of outrage on their behalf.

'Why do you trap birds?' asked the smallest.

'They've got nice voices.'

'You mustn't do that, they're better off free, so they can fly where they want. . . .'

'I won't do it any more then!'

'Before you stop, catch one for me.'

'For you? What kind'

'A cheerful one, to put in a cage.'

'You'll want a siskin.'

'The cat'll get it,' said the second brother, 'and Papa won't allow it.'

The eldest agreed.

'Do you have a mother?'

'No,' said the eldest, but was soon corrected by the second brother.

'We do have one, only she's not our real mother. She's dead.'

'You mean she's a stepmother,' I said. The eldest nodded.

All three suddenly became pensive and sad. From Grand-mother's stories I knew what a stepmother was, and I could appreciate their silence. They sat there, tightly pressed against each other, alike as peas. And I recalled the step-mother who was a witch, and who by her cunning and deceit-fulness took the place of a real mother.

'Don't worry – she'll come back one day,' I said encour-agingly.

The eldest shook his shoulders:

'How can she, if she's dead. That's impossible.'

Impossible? But how many times had the dead come back to life – even when they'd been hacked to pieces – if they were sprinkled with water from a spring. How many times had a death turned out to be unnatural, not caused by God, but brought about by witches and sorcerers!

Excitedly I started telling them Grandmother's stories, but no sooner had I begun than the eldest laughed sneeringly and said:

'We know all those – they're just fairy tales.'

His brothers listened in silence; the smallest pouted, while the second eldest leant towards me with his elbow on one knee and bent his other arm round his little brother's neck. It had already grown quite late, and reddish clouds hung low over the roofs when the old man with his white whiskers appeared again in a long brown robe like a priest's and a shaggy fur cap.

'Who's that?' he asked, pointing his finger at me.

The eldest brother got up and nodded towards Grandfather's house.

'He's from over there.'

'Who told him to come here?'

The three brothers all got up silently from the sledge and went home, putting me in mind once more of obedient geese.

The old man took me firmly by the shoulder and led me through the yard up to the gates. He made me feel so frightened that I was near to tears, but he strode along so quickly that I was out in the street before I had time to burst into tears. He stopped by the gate, shook his finger threateningly at me and said:

'Don't ever let me find you in here again!'

This made me very angry.

'As if I wanted to see you, you old devil!'

With his long hand he seized me once again and led me along the pavement, his questions raining on my head like hammer blows.

'Is your grandfather at home?'

As luck would have it, he was. He faced the terrifying old man, his head thrown back, his beard sticking out in front and he said hurriedly, looking into those eyes which were as round and lustreless as copeck pieces:

'His mother's away, and I'm a very busy man. There's no

one here to keep an eye on him all the time. Please forgive me, Colonel!'

The Colonel roared so loud, he could be heard all over the house. Then he turned round, like a wooden post, and left. Soon afterwards I was thrown out into Uncle Peter's cart which was waiting in the yard.

'In trouble again?' he asked, unharnessing the horse. 'What for this time?'

When I told him he flared up and hissed:

'What you want to make friends with that lot for? They're noblemen's sons, the little vipers! And look where it landed you! You must get your own back!'

He went on hissing for a long time. Enraged by the beatings I'd suffered, I agreed with everything he said, but then his wrinkled face quivered more unpleasantly, and made me think that the brothers wouldn't escape a beating either, and that as far as I was concerned they weren't to blame.

'I like them, so why should I get mixed up in a fight? You're lying to me the whole time.'

He glanced at me, then suddenly shouted:

'Get out of my cart!'

'You old fool!' I cried as I jumped out.

He started chasing me through the yard, but I was too quick for him and he ran after me shouting like a maniac.

'So I'm a fool? A liar? I'll show you. . . .'

Grandmother came out on to the kitchen steps and I threw myself towards her. He started complaining to her. 'This brat won't let me have a moment's peace! I'm five times his age and he calls me a liar and uses disgusting language.'

When someone lied to my face it left me helpless with amazement. I stood there gaping, but Grandmother said in a firm voice:

'You're the one who's lying, Peter – that boy would never call you dirty names.'

Grandfather would have believed the cabman.

From that day onwards a silent, malicious war was born between us: he tried to find every conceivable opportunity of bumping into me by accident, or hitting me with the reins. He let my birds out of their cages, and once even set the cat on them. For the least reason he complained to Grandfather about me, always exaggerating everything. I came to look on him more and more as a child, just like myself, but dressed up as a grown-up. I would undo his sandals, untie and cut into the laces, so they broke when he put them on. Once I put pepper in his cap and he sneezed for a whole hour. I did everything I could to equal him in cunning and strength. He used to spend all Sunday tracking me and more than once caught me with the brothers, which was strictly forbidden, and he'd haul me off straight away to my grandfather and tell him what I'd been doing. My friendship with the boys continued, and gave me more and more pleasure. In the small narrow passage between the wall of Grandfather's house and the Ovsyannikovs' fence grew an elm, a lime tree, and a thick clump of elderberry. Underneath this bush I'd cut a semi-circular opening in the fence and the brothers would come singly or in twos and we'd sit there quietly talking, squatting on our heels or kneeling. One of us always kept watch in case the Colonel should come and catch us.

They told me about the dull life they led, which made me feel very sad, and about the birds I'd caught for them, and all the things young boys talk about. But never once did they mention their father or stepmother, at least, I can't remember if they did. Most often they simply asked me to tell stories and I conscientiously repeated Grandmother's tales. If I forgot anything I asked them to wait while I ran off and made Grandmother jog my memory. And this pleased her no end.

I told them a great deal about Grandmother, and once the eldest said with a deep sigh: 'All grandmothers are good . . . we used to have a good one. . . .'

So often, and so sadly did he say 'used to be', 'was', 'had been', you would have thought he had been on this earth for a hundred years and not eleven. I remember he had narrow knees, delicate fingers. He was slim and fragile-looking, but his eyes were bright and gentle as church lamps. His brothers were also very charming, and inspired complete confidence in me, and made me want to do things to please them. But I liked the eldest most of all. I would become so carried away by our conversations that frequently I didn't see Uncle Peter coming. He would chase us away, drawling in his heavy voice: 'What, not again?' I could see he was becoming more and more the victim of fits of melancholy, and I even learned to guess what mood he was in when he came home from work. Usually he opened the gates without hurrying, and I could hear the hinges make a long, lazy squeaking noise. But if he was in a bad mood, the hinges would grate sharply, as if groaning with pain.

His dumb nephew had gone off to the country to get married. Peter now lived alone above the stables, in a small, wretched room with a tiny window. The place was filled with the oppressive smell of fusty leather, tar, sweat and tobacco. Because of these smells I could never bring myself to visit him. He would go to sleep with the lamp still burning, which made Grandfather very angry.

'You'll set the whole place on fire, Peter!'

'Don't worry. I always stand the lamp in a cup full of water,' he would reply, looking to one side.

At this time looking out of the corner of his eyes had become a habit with him, and he'd long stopped going to Grandmother's 'evenings'. He didn't give me any more of his jam, his face seemed to have dried up, the wrinkles become deeper, and he tottered about like a sick man.

One morning in the week I was helping Grandfather scrape away the snow in the yard – there had been a heavy fall during the night – when suddenly there was the unmistakable loud click of the wicket latch and in came a policeman. He shoved the gate to with his back and signalled to Grandfather with a fat grey finger. When Grandfather had gone up to him, the policeman leant towards him with his big nose until he almost chipped Grandfather's forehead with it, and said something I couldn't hear, to which Grandfather hastily replied:

'Here? When? My memory's not so good. . . .'

Suddenly he jumped up comically and shouted:

'Good God! It can't be true!'

'Quiet,' the policeman said sternly.

Grandfather looked round and saw me.

'Put the spades away and go back to the house.'

I hid round a corner and saw them enter the cabman's

lodgings. The policeman took his right-hand glove off and started slapping his left with it.

'He knows we're after him. He's abandoned the horse and gone into hiding.'

I ran into the kitchen to tell everything to Grandmother. She was kneading dough in the trough and her flour-covered head rocked from side to side. When she heard what I had to say she replied calmly:

'Looks like he's stolen something. ... Go and play now, it's none of your business.'

When I went back to the yard Grandfather was standing by the gates, with his cap off, crossing himself and looking up at the sky. His face was angry and bristling and one leg was quivering.

'I thought I told you to go into the house,' he shouted, stamping his foot.

This time he followed me into the kitchen and called out: 'Mother, come here!'

They went into the next room and stayed there a long time whispering to each other, and when Grandmother came back into the kitchen I could see from her face that something terrible had happened.

'What's the matter?' I asked.

'You be quiet,' she answered softly.

For the whole of the day it was dreadful and terrifying to be in that house. Grandfather and Grandmother kept looking at each other in horror. They lowered their voices and used short words that I couldn't understand, and this heightened the terror even more.

'Mother, go and light all the lamps,' ordered Grandfather with a slight cough.

Reluctantly, and without any hurry, they sat down to supper just as if they were expecting something to happen any minute. Grandfather wearily puffed out his cheeks, sighed and grumbled:

'Man has no chance against the power of the devil. A pious, church-going man, and look what's happened. What do you make of it?'

Grandmother sighed.

The winter day, coloured like dull silver, dragged on endlessly, and the atmosphere in the house grew more oppressive and uneasy. Towards evening another policeman came in. This one was red-headed and plump. He sat on the kitchen bench dozing, giving little snorts, and he bowed when Grandmother asked him:

'How did they find out?'

The policeman took his time answering and then said in a husky voice:

'Don't worry, we always find out everything.'

I remember sitting by the window and warming an old coin in my mouth so I could make an impression of St. George killing the Dragon on the icy window pane.

Suddenly there was a loud noise in the hall and the door burst wide open. Petrovna stood at the door and shouted deafeningly:

'Come and see what's out *there* at the back. . . .'

Seeing the policeman she dashed back towards the hall, but he caught her by the skirt and roared:

'Not so fast. Who are you? *What's* out there?'

He was scared out of his wits.

She collided with the door, fell on to her knees and started shouting, choked with words and tears.

'I'm going out to milk the cows when all of a sudden I sees what looks like a pair of boots in the Kashirins' garden.'

At this point Grandfather stamped with rage and bellowed furiously:

'Idiot, you're lying! How could you see anything in our garden – the fence is too high for one thing and there's no holes in it. You're lying. There's nothing there!'

'Good God,' moaned Petrovna, holding out one hand to him and clutching her head with the other. 'He's right when he says I'm lying. I'm walking along, and I sees tracks leading to your fence, in one place the snow all trodden down, so I goes and looks over the fence and there he was lying there . . .'

'Whooooo?' roared Grandfather.

This shout was terrifyingly long-drawn-out and no one could make out what Grandfather was trying to say. Then

148

suddenly everyone seemed to go mad and ran into the garden, pushing each other in their frantic rush. There, in the pit, covered with soft snow, lay Uncle Peter, his back propped up against a charred beam and his head slumped on his chest. Below his right ear was a deep gash, all red, and just like a mouth. Bluish, jagged pieces of flesh stuck out of the wound like teeth. I closed my eyes in terror and through my eyelashes could see the familiar saddler's knife on Uncle Peter's knees and next to it the blackened, twisted fingers of his right hand. His left hand was flung to one side and half buried in the snow, which had melted beneath him and his slight body had sunk deep into the soft bright down, looking more like a child's than ever. On the right of the body there was a strange red pattern in the snow, just like a bird makes, on the other side it was undisturbed, smooth and dazzling white. His humbly lowered head pressed his chin against his chest, crushing his thick curly beard, and a large bronze cross lay on his bare chest, surrounded by red streams of congealed blood. The noise from everyone shouting made my head spin. Petrovna didn't stop shouting for one second, then the policeman shouted to Valei to go somewhere, and Grandfather joined in with:

'Don't tread on the tracks!'

Suddenly he frowned, looked down at his feet and said to the policeman in a loud, commanding voice:

'It's no use shouting your head off, officer. This is God's will, God's judgement, so you can keep your meddling noses out of it.'

All at once everyone stopped shouting and stared at the dead man, sighing and crossing themselves.

Some people ran into the garden, climbing over Petrovna's fence, falling over, cursing, but made comparatively little noise until Grandfather, after a look around him, cried out loud in despair:

'Neighbours, you've broken all the raspberry bushes. You should be ashamed of yourselves!'

My sobbing grandmother took me by the hand and led me into the house.

'What did he do?' I asked.

'Got a pair of eyes, haven't you?' she answered.

All that evening, until far into the night, strange people stamped about and shouted in the kitchen and the room next to it. The police shouted orders and someone who looked like a priest was writing notes down and asking questions in a quacking voice, like a duck:

'What? What?'

Grandmother was serving everyone with tea in the kitchen and a round-shaped, pock-marked man with whiskers and a squeaky voice was saying:

'We don't know his real name, only that he's related to the Elatmas. As for the dumb boy, he's no more dumb than you or I. Confessed everything. And the third one – yes, there's a third mixed up in it – confessed. They robbed some churches a long time ago – it's their speciality.'

'God help us!' sighed Petrovna, her face red and wet with tears.

I lay on the stove bench and as I looked down, everyone seemed small, fat and hideous. . . .

Chapter 10

ONE Saturday, early in the morning I went off to Petrovna's kitchen garden to catch some bullfinches. I tried for a long time, but the red-breasted, proud birds evaded my traps. Showing off their beautiful plumage, they would skip over the chased-silver snow crust, fly on to the shrubbery with its warm coat of hoar frost and sway on the branches like bright flowers, scattering bluish sparks of snow. It was so pretty that my failure to trap the birds didn't worry me. I wasn't what you might call a passionate hunter and in this case trying to catch them always gave me greater pleasure than solid results. I loved watching the habits of small birds, and thinking about them.

It's wonderful to sit alone at the verge of a field of snow and listen to the birds twittering in the crystalline silence of a frosty day, while somewhere far off the bells of a passing troika – sad herald of the Russian winter – sing out.

Chilled by the snow and feeling that my ears were frozen, I collected my traps and cages, clambered over the fence into Grandfather's garden and went home. The front gates were open and a huge peasant was leading out three horses harnessed to a large closed sleigh. Thick clouds of steam rose from them and the peasant whistled cheerfully. My heart jumped.

'Who did you bring?'

He turned round, looked at me from under his arms, jumped up on the driving seat and said:

'The priest!'

I felt relieved: if it was the priest, he was probably visiting one of the lodgers.

'Come on, me hearties,' the driver shouted as he tugged the reins, breaking the silence with his gay whistling. The horses tore away together and I watched them go and closed the gates.

When I got into the empty kitchen I could hear my mother's powerful voice in the next room. Every word rang out distinctly:

'What now! You want to do away with me?'

Without stopping to take my coat off I threw down the cages and leaped into the hall, where I bumped into Grandfather. He seized me by the shoulders, stared wildly into my face and with great difficulty gulped something down and said hoarsely:

'Your mother's back. Get a move on. Go on! No, wait a minute. . . .' He shook me so hard that I could hardly stand up, and shoved me towards the door. 'Go on, go on . . .'

I pushed at the door, which was padded with felt and buckram, and was a long time finding the handle. My fumbling fingers twitched with cold and excitement. Finally I managed to open the door, very quietly, and then I stood blindly on the threshold.

'Here he is,' Mother said. 'How he's grown! What, don't you recognize me? Look what he's wearing! Really! His ears are white with cold. Mamma, give me some goose fat quick!'

She stood in the middle of the room, bent over me, and tore the clothes off me, turning me round and round like a ball. Her large body was wrapped up in a warm, soft, red dress, wide, like a man's cloak and with large black buttons running diagonally from one shoulder to the hem.

I'd never seen a dress like that. Her face seemed smaller than before – smaller and paler – and her eyes had grown larger and deeper, and her hair more golden. As she undressed me she threw my clothes towards the door, her crimson lips curling up in disgust. Her commanding voice kept ringing out:

'Why don't you say something? Glad to see me? Phooh, what a filthy shirt!'

Afterwards she rubbed my ears with goose grease. It stung, but it had a refreshing, appetizing smell which dulled the pain. I hugged her tight, and looked into her eyes, too paralysed to say anything. Through what she was saying I could hear Grandmother's soft, dejected voice: 'He pleases himself what he does . . . can't control him any more . . . not even afraid of his grandfather. . . . Ah, to think what we've come to, Varya!'

'Stop eating yourself up, Mother; everything's going to be all right.'

Compared with Mother, everything around me seemed small, wretched and old. Even *I* felt old, like my grandfather. Holding me tightly between her legs mother smoothed my hair with a heavy, warm hand.

'You need a haircut. And it's time you started school. Do you want to learn things?'

'I've learnt everything already.'

'There's just a little more you should know, dear. How strong you've grown!' Her rich laugh warmed my heart as she played with me. Grandfather came in, grey and bristling and his eyes reddened. Mother pushed me away with her hands and asked in a very loud voice:

'Well, Papa, what shall I do? Leave?'

He stopped by the window and scratched at the ice on the window with his nail. For a long time he said nothing, and everything in the room seemed to be on edge, tense, and as always in these strained moments, I felt my body had sprouted eyes and ears, that my chest had mysteriously widened, making me want to cry out.

'Leave the room, Alexei,' Grandfather said in an empty voice.

'Why?' my mother asked, drawing me to her once more. 'You're not to leave, I forbid it.'

Mother got up, sailed across the room like a cloud flushed by the sunset, and stood behind Grandfather.

'Papa, please listen!'

He turned to her and screeched:

'Shut up!'

'Well, I won't be shouted at,' she said softly.

Grandmother got up from the divan and pointed her finger menacingly.

'Varvara!'

Grandfather sat on a chair and muttered:

'Stop! Who do you think I am? What do you mean by it?'

And suddenly he roared in a voice that wasn't his:

'You've disgraced me, Varvara!'

'Go away,' ordered Grandmother. I went into the kitchen,

climbed up over the stove and for a long time lay there listening to them talking on the other side of the wall: they all spoke at once, interrupting each other, then there would be a complete silence, as if they'd all dropped off to sleep. They were discussing a baby that Mother had given away to someone, but I couldn't make out why Grandfather was so angry: because she'd had a baby without asking him, or because she hadn't brought the baby with her?

Then he went into the kitchen, all dishevelled, purple-faced and weary, and behind followed Grandmother wiping her tears with the hem of her woollen jacket. Grandfather seated himself on a bench and leant on it with his hands, bent double, shaking all over and biting his lips. Grandmother sank to her knees in front of him, quietly, without any fuss, then she said feverishly:

'Father, forgive her for Christ's sake! Even better people than us come to grief. Don't noblemen, merchants have the same trouble? You can see for yourself what a woman she is! Forgive her then, no one's perfect in this world. . . .'

Grandfather leant back against the wall, looked into her face and muttered with a twisted grin: 'Of course I will,' he sobbed. 'What else can I do? You'd forgive anybody. Ah!'

He leaned over to her, seized her by the shoulders and started shaking her. 'God forgives nothing,' he said in a quick whisper. 'Although we haven't got long, he's punishing us now, before we go to our graves. We'll never know any peace or joy in this world. Mark my words! We'll be beggars in the end, you see!'

Grandmother took his hands, sat next to him and gently laughed.

'And what of it? Frightened of being a beggar? Might as well get used to the idea. You'd sit at home while I went begging and I'd bring home food enough! So stop worrying!'

Suddenly he laughed, turned like a goat, seized Grandmother round the neck, hugged her, sobbing out loud:

'You dear, dear fool! My last hope! You don't regret anything and you understand nothing! Remember how we worked, how I sinned just for their sake. Don't we deserve just a little happiness in our old age!'

Unable to hold out any longer, I burst into tears, jumped down from the stove and rushed towards them, sobbing from the joy of hearing them – for the first time – speak so warmly to each other and from the sadness I felt for them in their grief. I sobbed for joy because Mother had returned and because they let me share in their sorrow, embracing me, hugging me and sprinkling me with their tears. Grandfather whispered into my ear: 'What are you doing here, you little devil! Now your mother's come back you'll stay with her and you won't want your wicked old grandfather any more, eh? And the same with your grandmother, who spoils you and takes your side every time.' He flung his arms out wide as if to tell us to go away, and then got up.

'Everyone's leaving ... at the least chance they're off ... everything's going to the dogs. Call her then! What you waiting for?' he said in a loud, angry voice. 'Let's get it over with.'

Grandmother left the kitchen. Grandfather bowed his head and went over to the corner: 'All-merciful God, see what's happening here in this house!' He struck himself hard with his fist on the chest. This I didn't like, neither did I like the way he talked to God, always showing off in front of him.

Mother came into the room and her red dress brought a splash of colour to the kitchen. She sat on the bench by the table, with Grandfather and Grandmother on either side, and the wide sleeves of her dress lay on their shoulders. She was telling them something in a subdued, serious voice and they listened silently, without interrupting her. Now they both seemed small and she looked as if she were their mother.

Worn out by the excitement, I fell asleep on the bunk.

In the evening the old people put their best clothes on and went to mass. Grandmother cheerily winked at Grandfather, who was wearing his freeman's uniform, and a coat made from raccoon fur and trousers outside his shoes. Then she winked at Mother and said to her:

'Just look at your father now, all spruced up like a young goat!'

Mother laughed gaily.

When we were left together in the room she sat down on the divan, with her legs drawn up under her, and slapped the side of the chair.

'Come over here. Well, how's life been treating you. Badly?'

'I don't know.'

'Does Grandfather still beat you?'

'Not so much now.'

'Really? Don't be afraid to tell me. . . . Well?'

I didn't feel like telling her about Grandfather and started talking about the very kind man who had lived in the room and whom nobody loved and who was thrown out by Grandfather. This story evidently didn't please her, and she said:

'Well, anything else?'

I told her about the three boys and about the colonel who chased me out of his yard. She pressed me close to her.

'What a terrible man. . . .'

And she fell silent, blinking at the floor and nodding her head. I asked her:

'Why was Grandfather so angry with you?'

'Because I did something wrong!'

'You should have brought the baby with you!'

She moved sharply away, frowning all over her face and biting her lips and then she burst out laughing.

'You horrible boy! Mind you don't say a word to anyone, do you hear. Keep your mouth shut – get it right out of your mind!'

She went on speaking in her soft but stern voice for a long time, saying something I couldn't make out, then she got up and started pacing up and down the room, tapping her chin and twitching her thick eyebrows.

A tallow candle was burning on the table, its guttering flame reflected in the emptiness of a mirror. Dirty-looking shadows crept over the floor. An icon lamp glimmered in one corner, and the icy window was silvery in the moon. Mother looked round the room, just as if she were searching for something on those bare walls, on the ceiling.

'When are you going to bed?'

'Fairly soon.'

'But you had a little sleep in the afternoon, didn't you?' she said with a sigh.

'Do you want to leave?' I asked.

'Where can I go?' she exclaimed in surprise. She raised my head and looked at me for a long time, so long that my eyes began to water.

'What's the matter?'

'My neck aches.'

And my heart ached too. I suddenly sensed that she wasn't going to stay in the house much longer. . . .

'You're going to be like your father when you grow older,' she said, pushing the mat aside with her feet. 'Has Grandmother told you anything about him?'

'Yes.'

'She loved Maxim very much. And he loved her. . . .'

'I know.'

Mother looked at the candle, frowned and snuffed it out.

'That's better!'

And in fact the room seemed fresher and cleaner without those dark, dirty shadows everywhere and bright blue pools of light appeared on the floor. The windows took fire with golden sparks.

'But where have you been living?'

She mentioned a few cities, just as if she were recalling something long forgotten, and still kept circling quickly round the room, without making any noise, just like a hawk.

'Where did you buy that dress?'

'Made it myself. I make all my own clothes.'

It was pleasant to think that she had nothing in common with anyone else I knew, but not to hear her say so little and leave my questions unanswered.

Afterwards she came and sat down by me on the divan and we stayed there not saying a word, hugging each other until the old people returned smelling of wax and incense and with a look of solemn peace on their warm faces.

Supper was a sedate affair, little was said and even that very cautiously, as if everyone was afraid of waking each other from a terrible dream.

Soon afterwards Mother, with great energy, set about driving the elements of 'secular' grammar into my head: for this she bought some books and with one of them, *Our Native Tongue*, I mastered in a few days the new reformed alphabet. Straight away Mother made me learn poetry by heart, and this was the start of a long period of mutual torment. The verses of one poem ran:

> O road, so big and straight,
> Much space you've taken from God.
> No axe or spade has levelled thee,
> Soft on hoof, and full of dust.

I read 'prostova' instead of 'prostora', 'rubili' instead of 'rovnyali', 'kopyta' instead of 'kopytu'.

'Think!' pleaded Mother. 'That's the genitive case of "prostoi" – prostova! Idiot! The word's "prostora" – understand?'

I understood, but still said 'prostova', amazing even myself.

She angrily called me stupid and obstinate. This distressed me very much and I concentrated all my efforts on memorizing those wretched lines. In my mind I could recite them without any mistake, but when it came to reading them out loud, I couldn't help mixing them up. I hated these elusive verses and from sheer spite started misquoting them on purpose, producing a whole string of absurdities concocted from similar-sounding words. I was delighted when I managed to deprive those bewitched lines of all meaning.

But this form of amusement had its reward: once, after a successful lesson, when Mother asked if I'd finally learned the poem, I couldn't stop myself saying:

> Road, toad, flowed, load . . .
> Hoofs, roofs. . . .

and so on. Too late I realized what I was doing. Mother suddenly got up and leaned her arms on the table and asked me, 'What does all that mean?' enunciating each word quite distinctly.

'I don't know,' I answered, horror-struck.

'Oh yes you do!'

'That's how it goes.'

'What?'

'A funny poem.'

'Stand in the corner.'

'Why?'

Quietly, but menacingly, she repeated: 'Into the corner!'

'Which one?'

Without answering she looked at me in such a way that I stood there at my wits' end trying to fathom what she wanted. There was a small round table in the corner where the icons were kept, with a vase full of heavily scented dried grasses and flowers standing on it. In the opposite corner stood a chest, covered with a carpet, and another corner was taken up by a bed. There wasn't a fourth as the door jamb came straight to the wall.

'I don't know what you want,' I said, despairing of understanding her.

She sank down on her chair, silently rubbing her forehead and cheeks, after which she asked:

'Did Grandfather make you stand in the corner?'

'When?'

'Any time!' she cried, banging her hand twice on the table.

'No. Not that I can remember.'

'You know that it's a punishment to stand in the corner?'

'No. Why a punishment?'

She sighed.

'Oooh! Come here.'

I went up to her and asked:

'Why do you shout at me?'

'And why do you mix up the poems on purpose?'

I explained as best I could that with my eyes closed I could remember them word for word but that they all came out differently when I tried reciting them.

'You're not pretending, are you?'

I said no, but was at once struck by the thought: 'Am I pretending after all?'

And suddenly, without hurrying, I recited all the poems without a single mistake. This astonished me, and at the same time destroyed me. I felt that my face had suddenly swollen up, and the blood ran to my ears, making them heavy. My head was filled with horrible noises, and there I stood before Mother, burning with shame, and through my tears I could see her face sadly darken, her lips tighten, and her eyebrows draw close together.

'How's that?' she said in a strange voice. 'You must have been pretending?'

'Don't know. I didn't want to . . .'

'You're a very difficult boy,' she said, and looked down at the floor. 'Go away.'

She made me apply myself more and more to learning poetry, and my memory took in less and less of those tedious lines, and as a result the irresistible urge to twist the words round, distort them, misquote and introduce variants of my own, grew stronger and stronger. This was an easy task: additional words came swarming to me and swiftly made nonsense of the texts. Often a whole line vanished from my mind, and however much honest effort I made to recapture them, I could never visually recall them again. The following wretched poem by Prince Vyazemski brought me much suffering:

> At evening time and early morn
> Old men, widows, orphans forlorn
> Are out begging for Christian charity.

And the third line:

> Beneath windows with bags they go . . .

I always managed to leave out in its entirety. My indignant mother would tell Grandfather about my performance, but he would reply in a threatening voice:

'He's too spoilt! He has a memory: knows his prayers better than me. He's always lying – he's got a memory like a stone: anything you engrave on it is there for ever! He needs a good beating!'

Grandmother would also testify:

'He remembers fairy tales and songs. But if he remembers songs, why not poetry: it's all the same, isn't it?'

All this was true and I felt very guilty, but as soon as I

embarked on a fresh poem, along would come creeping – like cockroaches – words which had no business to be there and which even formed lines of their own:

> At our gates
> Many old men and orphans
> Come and groan and ask for bread,
> Then they take it to Petrovna
> Sell it to her to feed her cows,
> And drink vodka down in the gully.

At night, when I lay with Grandmother in the bunk, I went through the wearisome ritual of repeating everything I remembered from books and everything I had invented myself; sometimes she laughed, but more often she scolded me.

'You can recite it after all! But you shouldn't make fun of beggars, God help them! Christ was a beggar – and all the saints as well.'

I murmured:

> I don't like beggars,
> Or Grandfather,
> What shall I do?
> Forgive me, God,
> Grandfather's always
> Looking for an excuse to beat me.

'What are you saying! May your tongue drop off!' said Grandmother angrily. 'Supposing Grandfather hears what you've been saying?'

'I don't care!'

'You're only making it worse for yourself by your monkey tricks and annoying your mother. Things are bad enough for her already,' she urged in a warm, thoughtful voice.

'Why are things bad for her?'

'Be quiet, can't you? You wouldn't understand. . . .'

'I know that Grandfather . . .'

'Be quiet now!'

Life was hard for me and I felt near to despair. But for some reason I didn't want them to know this, and I started making a real nuisance of myself. Mother's lessons became more frequent, more incomprehensible; I was quick at arithmetic, but couldn't bear writing and was hopeless at grammar.

But what oppressed me more than anything else was seeing my mother suffering so much in Grandfather's house. Her face had become a perpetual frown and she looked at everyone with the eyes of a stranger, sitting silently by the window for hours on end; she seemed to be completely fading away. The first days after her arrival she had looked agile, and fresh, and now she had rings under her eyes. For days she went about uncombed, in a crumpled dress and with her blouse unbuttoned. It shocked me to see her going to pieces. I wanted her to be always beautiful, stern and majestic, smartly dressed – better than anyone else! At lesson-time she looked right through me with far-away eyes, towards the wall or window, and would ask me questions in a tired voice, forget my answers and become more and more irritable. She shouted at me as well, and this shocked me: a mother should be more fair and just than anyone else, or so I'd learned from fairy tales. Sometimes I asked her:

'Don't you like it here?'

She would angrily retort: 'Mind your own business.'

I could see as well that Grandfather was cooking up things to scare Grandmother and Mother. Often he would shut himself in Mother's room and start screeching like that horrible wooden pipe used by the lame shepherd Nikanor. On one of these occasions Mother shouted fit to wake the whole house:

'No, never, never!'

The door slammed shut and Grandfather started howling.

That was in the evening. Grandmother, who was sitting at the kitchen table, was making a shirt for Grandfather and whispering to herself. When the door slammed she pricked up her ears and said:

'She's gone to the lodgers!'

Suddenly Grandfather leaped into the kitchen, ran up to Grandmother, hit her on the head and hissed, waving his bruised hand:

'When are you going to stop your prattling, you old witch!'

'You old fool,' Grandmother said calmly, putting her hair straight. 'You won't make me shut up. I'm going to tell her everything I know about your little tricks, you see!'

He flung himself on her and started raining blows on her enormous head. Grandmother put up no resistance and said:

'Beat me, beat me if you like! Go on!'

From my bunk I started hurling pillows, blankets, shoes at them, but my infuriated grandfather didn't notice. Grandmother fell on to the floor, where Grandfather kicked her on the head as she lay there. Finally he tripped and fell, upsetting a bucket of water. He jumped up, spitting and snorting, gave one wild look round the room and fled to his attic. Grandmother got to her feet, groaning terribly, sat on the bench and began tidying her hair. I jumped down from the bunk to be greeted with an angry: 'Pick the pillows up and put everything back by the stove! What got into *you*, flinging pillows around! You keep out of it in future! And that old devil, he's gone right out of his mind, the fool. . . .'

Suddenly she groaned and her face set in a deep frown. Then she lowered her head and called me over.

'Have a look here, where it hurts.'

I parted her thick hair and found a hairpin had gone deep into the skin. I pulled it out, found another, and my fingers went numb.

'I'd better call Mother. I'm frightened!'

She waved her hand.

'What's the matter with you? I'll give you call Mother! Thank God she didn't hear or see anything . . . and you want to call her? Get out, quick!' And with her nimble lace-maker's fingers she started ferreting around in her thick black mane. Summoning up my courage, I helped her pull out another two, thick bent hairpins.

'Does it hurt?'

'Not much, I'll have a hot bath tomorrow to ease the pain and wash the blood away.'

Then she asked me gently:

'And you, dear, don't breathe a word to your mother about your grandfather beating me. They've got their claws into each other as it is. Promise you won't tell.'

'Yes.'

'Good, and don't forget. Now let's get this room tidy. Is my face cut? No? Good, then they needn't ever find out. . . .'

She set about cleaning up the floor and these words poured straight out of my heart:

'You're . . . like a saint, you suffer and suffer and you never complain!'

'What rubbish are you talking now? A saint . . . why do you say that?'

For a long time she went on grumbling, hobbling about on all fours while I sat on the steps thinking up how to avenge her. It was the first time Grandfather had beaten Grandmother so cruelly and savagely in my presence. Before me, in the twilight, I could see his red face burning and his hair flopping about. The indignation in my heart welled up and I felt frustrated for not being clever enough to think up a way of properly paying him back.

But three days later, when I was fetching something from his attic, I came across him sitting on the floor in front of an open trunk and going through some papers in it. On one chair was his favourite church calendar – ten pages of thick grey paper, divided into squares for the days in the month, with figures of the appropriate saints in each square. Grandfather treasured this calendar, and allowed me to look at it on those rare occasions when for some reason he was particularly pleased with me. I would always look upon those small grey, endearing figures that crowded the pages with a feeling of deep emotion. I knew the lives of some of them – Kirik and Ulita, Varvara the Martyr, Pantaleimon, and many others; the sad life of that godly man, Alexei, particularly attracted me, as well as the beautiful verses about him that Grandmother often used to recite most touchingly. You would look at those hundreds of figures and take quiet consolation in the fact there always had been martyrs. Now, however, I resolved to cut the figures out of the calendar and when Grandfather had gone over to the window to read from a blue page covered with eagles, I grabbed a few pages, swiftly ran downstairs, stole the scissors from Grandmother's table, scrambled up on the bunk over the stove, and set about clipping off the saints' heads. After decapitating one row I began to feel sorry for those poor saints, and I started cutting along the lines dividing the squares. I hadn't time to cut through the second row when Grandfather appeared below me, got up on the ladder and asked:

'Who gave you permission to take the calendar?'

When he saw the little squares of paper scattered over the boards he seized them, brought them close to his face, threw them down, and picked them up again. His jaw went crooked, his beard jerked up and down and he breathed so hard that all the papers floated down on the floor again.

'What have you done?' he finally shouted, pulling me towards him by the leg. I somersaulted, and Grandmother caught me in her open arms.

'I'll kill you,' he roared, beating us both with his fists.

When Mother appeared I found myself in a corner by the stove and she protected me with her body, catching hold of Grandfather's hands as they flew at her face, and pushing them off.

'What a disgusting exhibition! Have you gone mad?' she said.

Grandfather sank down moaning on a bench by the window:

'They've killed me! Everyone's against me . . . aaa.'

'You should be ashamed of yourself!' my mother's empty voice rang out. 'Why do you always have to be pretending?'

Grandfather shouted, banged his feet on the bench and his beard comically poked upwards towards the ceiling. His eyes were shut tight. I thought that he felt very ashamed and that he really was pretending – that was why he closed his eyes.

'I'll paste the pieces on to a calico strip for you,' said Mother. 'It'll be better and stronger than before.' She went on as she inspected the fragments. 'They're all crumpled and shrivelled anyway . . . and falling to bits. . . .'

The way she spoke to him reminded me of lesson-time, when I understood nothing she was saying. Suddenly Grandfather got up, carefully adjusted his shirt and waistcoat in a businesslike way, cleared his throat and said:

'You can stick them on today. I'll bring the rest of the paper right away.'

He went to the door, but stopped and turned round and pointed at me with a crooked finger. 'He needs a good beating.'

'Yes, you're right,' agreed Mother as she turned to me: 'What did you do a thing like that for?'

'On purpose. If he touches Grandmother again, I'll cut his beard off. . . .'

Grandmother took off her creased jacket and said reproachfully:

'So you promised not to say anything! She spat on the floor. 'I hope your tongue swells up so big you can't wag it any more.'

Mother looked at her, crossed the kitchen and then came back to me.

'When did he beat her?'

'You ought to be ashamed of asking him that, Varvara. It's no business of yours,' Grandmother said angrily.

My mother put her arms round her. 'Ah, my dear mother!'

'A fine mother I am to you . . . go away. . . .'

They looked at each other in silence and moved apart. I could hear Grandfather stamping about in the hall.

During the first days after her arrival Mother had become friends with the gay wife of our military lodger and nearly every evening went to the front part of the house when people from the Betlengs – pretty girls, officers – used to come. Grandfather didn't take to this at all and more than once, when he was eating supper in the kitchen, would shake his spoon menacingly and growl:

'Another of their damn parties! I won't get any sleep now.'

Soon he asked the lodgers to clear out of the room and when they'd gone he brought some odd bits of furniture from somewhere or other, and put them in the front rooms which he locked with an enormous padlock. 'We don't need any lodgers – I'm going to do some entertaining myself.'

And on Sundays guests began to roll up. They included Grandmother's noisy sister, Matryena Ivanovna, a laundress, with a big nose. She used to wear a silk-striped dress and a gold-coloured head scarf. She would bring her two sons –

Vassily a cheerful and goodnatured draughtsman, with long hair, and dressed all in grey; and Victor, who had a horse-like head, a narrow face sprinkled with freckles, and clothes of varying colours. When he took his galoshes off in the hall he would sing in a mock soprano, like Petrushka the clown, 'Andrei-papa, Andrei-papa.'

This would both frighten and astonish me.

Uncle Yakov would turn up with his guitar, bringing with him a master watchmaker, bald, one-eyed, subdued, and looking like a monk in his long black jacket. He always sat smiling in a corner, his head to one side, mysteriously supported by one finger stuck into his clean-shaven double chin. He was a suspicious looking man, and his one eye stared at everyone with particular intensity; he said very little and often repeated the same phrase: 'Please don't trouble yourself, it doesn't matter. . . .' When I first saw him I suddenly remembered the time, long ago, when we were living in Novy Street and drums suddenly beat out, hollow-sounding and ominous. Then there came into view a large high black cart surrounded by soldiers and civilians. It was on its way from the prison to the main square and in it was a small man wearing a round cloth cap, with chains on his feet. A black board with white letters on it hung round his neck. The man bent his head down, as if he were trying to read what it said and the chains jangled as he bumped along. When Mother said to the watchmaker: 'This is my son', I drew back in horror, and hid my hands in my pockets.

'Don't trouble yourself,' he said, stretching his whole mouth towards his right ear in the most terrifying way. He caught hold of my belt and drew me towards him, quickly and swiftly turning me right round. Then he let me go, muttering approvingly:

'A strong boy.'

I climbed into a leather armchair in one corner of the room – so big, one could lie down in it, and which Grandfather was very proud of, calling it Prince Gruzinsky's chair. When I'd taken up my position I watched the grown-ups trying hard to show they weren't bored and the strange and suspicious way the watchmaker's face changed expression. It was oily, and seemed to run and flow like liquid. If he smiled, his thick lips moved towards his right cheek, and his small nose also travelled about, like a boiled meat dumpling on a plate. His large protruding ears moved very strangely. At times they rose with the eyebrow of his sound eye, and then dropped down towards his cheekbones: I thought that, if he'd wanted to, he could use them like hands and cover up his nose. Sometimes he would sigh, stick out his black tongue, round as a pestle, nimbly describe a perfect circle with it, and lick his thick greasy lips. All this was far from funny and only provided a source of amazement and kept my attention riveted to him the whole time he was there.

The guests were drinking tea mixed with rum – which smelled like burnt onions – and Grandmother's liqueurs, which were yellow and gold, or dark as tar, and some of them green. They were eating rich baked cream-and-honey cakes with poppy seeds. They sweated, puffed themselves out, and praised Grandmother's cooking. When they'd finished stuffing themselves and their faces were red and bloated, they solemnly settled into their chairs, and lazily asked Uncle Yakov to play.

He bent over his guitar, strummed away and sang in his unpleasant, tiresome voice:

> Ah we lived as best we could,
> Woke the town with our noise,
> And told the young lady from Kazan
> Everything we knew. . . .

I thought this was a very sad song but Grandmother said:

'Play something else, Yasha, a proper song. Remember the songs they used to sing in our days, Motrya?'

Smoothing her rustling dress, the laundress said convincingly:

'Fashions have changed, Mother.'

Uncle blinked at Grandmother, as if she were sitting a long way off, and obstinately continued his cheerless songs with their wearisome words. Grandfather was having a secret conversation with the watchmaker and was pointing out something to him with his finger. The watchmaker raised his eyebrows, looked towards my mother, nodded, and his liquid features became suddenly transformed again. Mother always sat among the Sergeyevs and would have a quiet serious chat with Vassily. He was in the habit of saying with a sigh: 'Yes, I must think about that.'

Victor would smile like a well-fed man, shuffle his feet and suddenly sing in his squeaky voice: 'Andrei-papa, Andrei-papa. . . .'

Everyone stopped talking on purpose and stared at him. The laundress said with a note of authority in her voice: 'He learned that from the theatre. . . .'

There were two or three such evenings, memorable chiefly for their crushing boredom. Afterwards the watchmaker would come every Sunday, in the afternoon, just after late mass. Once I was sitting in Mother's room helping her to unpick some old torn beaded embroidery, when the door suddenly half opened, Grandmother's frightened face appeared and just as quickly vanished. 'Varya, he's here,' she shouted. Mother didn't stir at all, and the door opened again to reveal Grandfather, who announced triumphantly: 'Get dressed, quickly Varvara. Hurry up!'

Without getting up or even giving him a look Mother asked: 'Where to?'

'Come along now and stop arguing. He's an honest man and master of his trade. He'll be a good father to Alexei.'

Grandfather's voice assumed an unusual note of authority; all the time he smoothed his sides with the palms of his hands and his elbows trembled behind his back, as if his arms wanted to stretch forwards and he was trying to stop them.

Mother calmly interrupted:

'I'm telling you I'm not interested.'

Grandfather, his hair bristling, strode up to her, stretched out his hands, groped and stooped like a blind man and said hoarsely:

'Come on, or else I'll have to make you. I'll drag you by the hair.'

'You'll make me, will you?' said Mother, rising to her feet. Her face had turned white, her eyes narrowed and she quickly started taking off her skirt and blouse, until she was left with

only her petticoat on; she went up to Grandfather and said:
'Take me then!'

Grandfather bared his teeth, and shook his fist at her:

'Varvara, get dressed!'

Mother pushed him away and caught hold of the door jamb.

'Let's go then,' she said.

'I'll put a curse on you!'

'I'm not frightened. Well?'

She opened the door but Grandfather seized the hem of her
blouse, fell down on his knees and whispered:

'Varvara, you'll come to a bad end, don't disgrace me now.
. . .' And he moaned pitifully, 'Mooother, Moother. . . .'

Grandmother had already barred Mother's way out; shaking her hands at her as if she were shooing a hen she drove her
back into the room.

'Varvara, you fool!' she muttered through her teeth. 'Go
back, you shameless bitch!'

She pushed her back in the room, bolted the door and
leaned over to Grandfather, helping him up with one hand
and threatening him with the other: 'You old devil, you
idiot!'

She sat him on the divan and he slumped down like a rag
doll, opened his mouth and shook his head. Grandmother
shouted out to Mother:

'Get dressed!'

Mother picked her dress up from the floor and said:

'I won't see him, do you hear?'

Grandmother pushed me off the divan: 'Get a jug of water
and quick about it!'

She spoke softly, almost in a whisper, with much com-
posure and authority. I ran into the hall and could hear,
heavy, measured footsteps in the front of the house. From
Mother's room came the cry: 'I'm leaving tomorrow!'

I went into the kitchen and sat by the window, as though
I was dreaming. Grandfather groaned and sobbed, Grandmother kept on complaining. Then the door slammed and
everything became quiet and sinister. I remembered the
errand I'd been sent on and I scooped up some water with the
copper jug and went back to the hall. Out of the front room

came the watchmaker, his head bowed. He was stroking his fur cap and sighing. Then came Grandmother with her hands pressed to her stomach, bowing behind him and saying softly: 'You must understand, we can't force her if she doesn't want to. . . .'

He tripped by the door and fell out into the yard while Grandmother crossed herself. She was shaking all over and I couldn't make out whether she was crying or laughing.

'What's wrong?' I asked, running up to her.

She snatched the jug from me, spilling water over my legs, and cried:

'Where've you been all this time. Shut the door!'

And she went into Mother's room while I went back to the kitchen, where I found them groaning, sighing and grumbling just as if they were trying to shift heavy furniture around.

It was a bright day; the slanting rays of the winter sun peered through the icy windows. On the table, laid for supper, dimly shone pewter cups, a decanter of golden kvass, and another of Grandfather's dark green vodka, distilled from cowslip and St John's wort. Through the thawed patches on the window I could see the dazzling white snow on the roofs, forming sparkling silver caps on the fences and starling-box. My birds played in sunlight-flooded cages which hung from the window joists. The gay, tame chaffinches twittered merrily, the bullfinches chirped, and the goldfinch was overflowing with song. But that silvery day, so bright and full of music, did not raise my spirits. I did not want that day or anything else. I suddenly decided to set all the birds free and was just taking the cages down when in ran Grandmother, slapping her sides and swearing as she rushed to the stove:

'Damn and blast all of you! You old fool, Akulina! . . .'

She rescued a pie from the oven, poked the crust with her finger and spat in anger.

'It's burnt. To hell with the whole damned lot of you. And what are you goggling about, you owl? I'd like to smash you all up, like cracked cups.'

And she burst out crying, turning the pie from side to side, sticking her fingers in its dry crusts; large tears slopped down on them.

Grandfather came with Mother into the kitchen. She flung the pie on the table, making the plates jump.

'All because of you! May you go penniless!'

My mother, gay and unperturbed, embraced her and tried to calm her down. My dishevelled and tired-looking grandfather sat at the table, tucked a serviette round his neck, blinked his swollen eyes in the sunlight, and muttered:

'What's all the fuss? We've had pies before. God's a miser – gives you minutes in return for years, and without any interest. Sit down, Varya, that's right.'

He seemed to have lost his reason, and throughout supper talked about God, about the impious Ahab, about a father's hard lot.

'Get on with your supper and stop talking so much!'

Mother was in a joking mood and her clear eyes sparkled.

'Were you frightened just now?' she said as she nudged me.

No, I wasn't frightened, but now I felt ill, on edge, and mystified by everything that had happened.

The meal, as usual on Sundays, was interminable and heavy, and my grandparents and mother didn't seem the same people who half an hour before had been shouting at each other, were at each other's throats and were all tears and sobbing. And I couldn't believe any longer that all this was in earnest and that tears came hard to them. All those tears and shouts, and all the suffering they inflicted on each other, all those conflicts that died away just as quickly as they flared up, had now become an accepted part of my life, disturbed me less and less, and hardly left any impression. Long afterwards I understood that to Russians, through the poverty and squalor of their lives, suffering comes as a diversion, is turned into a game and they play at it like children and rarely feel ashamed of their misfortune. In the monotony of everyday existence grief comes as a holiday, and a fire is an entertainment. A scratch embellishes an empty face.

Chapter 11

AFTER that episode Mother gained in strength, and dignity, and became the mistress of the house, while Grandfather receded into the background, and became pensive and quiet – not like his usual self at all. Now he hardly left the house and he'd taken to sitting by himself in the attic, reading a mysterious book called *Notes by My Father*. This book he kept locked up in a chest and often I used to see him wash his hands before taking it out. It was a small, thick book, bound in red leather. There was an inscription on the blue flyleaf, written in ornate, faded letters: 'To Vassily Kashirin with respect and fond memories.' It was signed with some strange name, a kind of flourish in the form of a bird in flight. When he'd carefully opened the heavy leather cover, Grandfather would put on his silver-framed spectacles and look at the inscription for a long time, twitching his nose to get his spectacles straight. More than once I asked him: 'What's that book?' and he would proudly answer: 'That's no business of yours. Just be patient for a little longer, until I'm dead, then I'll leave it to you. And my raccoon fur coat as well.'

His conversations with Mother became more restrained and less frequent, and he listened to what she had to say attentively. He would mutter to himself, make little flourishes with his arms and blink his eyes like Uncle Peter used to do.

His trunks were stuffed full of fantastic costumes: heavy silk skirts, satin jackets, silk sarafans woven with silver, women's head-dresses embroidered with pearls, brightly coloured scarves and kerchiefs, heavy Mordvinian necklaces, many with coloured stones in them. He would go into Mother's room carrying huge armfuls, lay all the clothes out on some chairs and tables for Mother to admire:

'In my days dresses were far richer and finer than they are today,' he would say. 'They spent more on dresses then, but lived more simply, peacefully. Those times will never return! Try this one on.'

Once Mother disappeared for a few moments in the next room and came out wearing a blue, gold-embroidered sarafan and a head-dress decorated with pearls. She curtsyed low to Grandfather and asked:

'Does it please your highness?'

Grandfather gave a loud sigh, beamed all over, walked round her, his arms flung out wide and fingers twitching, then he said indistinctly, as though in a dream: 'Ah, Varvara, if only you had more money and mixed with the right sort of people. . . .'

Mother lived in two rooms in the front of the house. She entertained quite a lot, and the most frequent guests were the Maximov brothers: Pyotr, a strong, handsome officer with a large bright beard and light blue eyes – Grandfather had beaten me in front of him after the spitting incident – and Yevgeny, tall like his brother, with skinny legs, a pale face and a small black pointed beard. His large eyes looked like plums, and he wore a greenish uniform with golden buttons and gold initials on his narrow shoulders. He was in the habit of tossing back his long wavy hair from his high, smooth forehead and smiling condescendingly; he'd always tell a story in a colourless voice, beginning with the same ingratiating words: 'If you ask me, how I look at it . . .'

Mother would listen to him with her eyes screwed up, laughing, often interrupting and saying: 'You're just like a child, Yevgeny, if I may say so!' The officer would slap his knee with his broad hand and shout: 'Yes, just like a child.'

Christmas was a noisy, gay time. Nearly every evening Mother's guests put on fancy dress – she would join in as well – and she always wore the best costume. Then they would all go out together. Every time she left with her gay crowd of friends, the house seemed to sink into the ground, and everything became dull and eerily silent. Grandmother would waddle through the rooms like an old goose, tidying everything up, and Grandfather would stand with his back to the warm stove, and say to himself:

'Fine, if that's how she wants it . . . we'll see what happens.'

After Christmas Mother took myself and Sasha, Uncle Mikhail's son Sasha, to school. Sasha's father had married again and right from the start his stepmother took a profound dislike to him. She started beating him and as a result Grandmother insisted that Grandfather took him in to live with us. We went to school for about a month. All I can remember having learnt during that time was how to answer when asked what my name was. I wasn't allowed to say simply 'Peshkov': one had to say: 'My name is Peshkov.' Also I couldn't say to the teacher:

'Stop shouting, old chap, I'm not frightened of you!'

I didn't like school from the start, but my cousin was very happy there to begin with, and made several friends, but once during lessons he fell asleep and suddenly shouted out loud:

'No, I won't!'

When he was woken up, he asked permission to leave the room, for which he was cruelly made fun of and the next day when we were crossing the gully in Sennii Square on the way to school, he stopped and said:

'You go on, I'm not coming. I think I'll go for a walk.'

He squatted down, carefully buried his bundle of books in the snow and went off. It was a fine January day, the silver sun shone everywhere and I felt very jealous of him. Reluctantly I continued my journey, as I didn't want to make Mother angry. Of course, the books buried by Sasha were never found, and next day he had a legitimate reason for not going to school. On the day after that Grandfather found out.

We were both brought up for trial in the kitchen, where we faced Grandfather, Grandmother and Mother, who sat at the table cross-examining us. I remember Sasha's comical answers to Grandfather's questions:

'Why were you absent from school?'

'I forgot where it was!'

'Forgot?'

'Yes, I kept on looking and looking . . .'

'You should have followed Alexei. He remembers!'

'I lost him.'

'Alexei?'

'Yes.'

'But how?'

Sasha pondered for a moment, then sighed and said:

'There was a snowstorm, you couldn't see a thing.'

Everyone burst out laughing as the weather had been clear and fine. Sasha smiled cautiously, but then Grandfather said spitefully, baring his teeth:

'You should have caught hold of his belt.'

'I did, but the wind tore me away,' explained Sasha.

He spoke lazily, despairingly, and I felt uncomfortable listening to his futile, clumsy lies. His obstinacy amazed me.

He got a thorough good hiding, and a retired fireman was hired as an escort – an old man with a crippled arm. His job was to follow us to make sure Sasha didn't stray off the path to knowledge. But this didn't help. The next day, when we reached the gully, my cousin suddenly bent down, took off a felt boot and flung it as hard as he could, and then did the same with the other, but in the opposite direction. Then he started running round the square in his socks. The old man, for some reason, was frightened of chasing after the boots and took me home, groaning all the way.

The whole day Grandfather, Grandmother and my mother searched the town for the runaway and it was evening by the time we found Sasha at Chirkov's inn near the monastery, where he was entertaining everyone by dancing. He was taken home, and not even beaten: they were too astounded at his obstinate silence. He lay beside me on the bunk over the stove cocking his legs up and kicking the soles against the ceiling.

'My stepmother doesn't love me,' he whispered, 'nor does my father, or Grandfather, so how can I live here? I'm going to ask Grandmother where the bandits hide out, so I can run away and join them, then you'll all be sorry. Will you come with me?'

I couldn't go with him, as I had my own ambition – to be an officer with a large, shining beard, and for this it was necessary to go to school. When I told this plan to my cousin he agreed with me, after a moment's reflection:

'Nothing wrong with that. When you're an officer, I shall

176

be a robber chief, and you'll have to capture me, and one of us will kill the other, or else take him prisoner. But I wouldn't kill you. . . .'

'I wouldn't kill you either.'

And so it was all decided.

Grandmother came into the room, climbed up on the stove, and after looking at us she said:

'Well, my little mice, my orphans, poor little waifs.'

After this show of pity she began cursing Sasha's stepmother, our fat aunt Nadezhda, an innkeeper's daughter. Then stepmothers and stepfathers in general came in for abuse. To illustrate her point she told us the story of the wise hermit Iona who, while still a boy, brought his stepmother to judgement before the heavenly courts. His father, a fisherman on Lake Byely, was, in the words of the legend:

Ruined by a young wife:
She got him drunk on home-made beer,
And with sleeping draught as well,
She put him, asleep, in an oaken chest, like a
          narrow coffin,
And taking the maple-wood oars
Rowed him out to the middle of the lake
Where the water was dark and deep, like a mill-pond,
– Lying ready to help in that shameless deed.
There she bent over, capsized the boat,
And over went the casket.
The husband sank like a stone
And she quickly swam to the bank
Where she fell on the ground
And began howling aloud,
Feigning her grief.
The good people believed her,
And joined her in her tears.
'Oh, alas, you young widow,
Great must be your woman's grief,
Our life is in God's hands,
And death is sent to us by God.'
Only the stepson, Ionushko,
Didn't believe her tears,
Put his hand on her heart

177

And said in gentle voice:
'O, destiny mine, O Stepmother,
O you bird of night so cunning,
I don't trust your tears.
Your sad heart really beats for joy.
Let us ask the heavenly judges,
And all the holy powers above:
Let someone take a Damascus sword
And hurl it into the sky.
If you are right – I shall be killed;
If I am right – it will fall on you!'
The stepmother looked at him
And her eyes filled with evil fire.
Firmly she rose to her feet
And began to argue:
'You stupid creature,
Cast out by nature,
What have you thought up here,
How can you say such things?'
People look on them and listen.
They see it's a dark affair.
Their faces downcast, they begin to think,
And take counsel among themselves.
Then the oldest fisherman came
And bowed to everyone,
And this was his decision:
'Place, O good people,
A Damascus sword in my right hand
And I shall hurl it in the air
And on the guilty head it will fall!'
The old man was handed the sword
And he threw it up in the air,
And it flew just like a bird in the clouds.
They waited and waited and still it flew.
The people look into the crystal vault,
Doff their hats and stand close together.
No word is said in the silent night –
And still the knife didn't fall.
The crimson dawn flared on the lake
The Stepmother is flushed by its light.
Mockingly she laughs.
And now the sword fell like a swallow
Straight into her heart.

All the good people went down on their knees
And prayed to God:
'Praise to Thee, for Thy true judgement!'
The old fisherman took Ionushko
To a distant hermitage
On the river Kerzhenets
Near the invisible city of Kitezh.

Next day I woke up covered in red spots: it was the beginning of smallpox. I was moved to the back room and for a long time I lay there without being able to see, my legs and arms firmly tied with wide bandages, and experiencing terrible nightmares, from one of which I nearly died. Only Grandmother came to see me, and she would feed me from a spoon, like a baby, and tell me endless, always new, stories. One evening, when I was getting better and the bandages had been taken off – only my fingers were still bandaged with mittens to stop me scratching my face – Grandmother was late for some reason and I was overcome by a feeling of terror: and suddenly I imagined I saw her, lying by the door, her face on the dusty attic floor and her arms thrown out wide. Her neck was almost in half, like Uncle Peter's, and a large cat with hungry, bulging green eyes was creeping towards her out of the corner.

I jumped out of bed, smashed the double-glazed windows with my legs and shoulders, and flung myself into a snowdrift in the yard. That evening Mother happened to be entertaining. No one heard the glass smash and I lay there a long time before anyone came. I hadn't broken anything, only dislocated my shoulder and cut myself badly on the glass. But I temporarily lost the use of my legs and I had to lie in bed for three months, unable to get up at all. I would lie there and listen to all the racket from downstairs – the slamming of doors and constant coming and going. That house was getting noisier every day.

Blizzards made a melancholy sound as they swept over the roof and just behind the attic door the wind raged and whistled, sounding a funereal note in the chimney and making the flue-dampers rattle. In the daytime I could hear ravens croaking, and on peaceful nights the mournful howling of wolves reached the house from the fields. To this music my soul matured. Then, timidly and imperceptibly at first, but growing warmer with each day, the shy face of spring peeped through the window with the radiant eye of a March sun. Cats began howling and singing on the roofs and the rustling sounds of spring penetrated the walls; icicles snapped, melted snow slid from the ridge of the roof, and bells rang out more sonorously than they did in winter.

Grandmother would come and see me. Her breath smelt more and more strongly of vodka, and then she began to bring with her a large white teapot, and hide it under my bed. She would wink and say:

'Don't tell the hearth goblins!'

'Why do you drink?'

'Ssh! You'll find out when you're older. . . .'

She'd take a swig through the spout, wipe her lips with her sleeve, smile sweetly and ask:

'Now tell me, sir, what was I telling you yesterday?'

'You were telling me about my father.'

'Where did I get to, then?'

I jogged her memory and the music of her words flowed on, like a stream.

She began telling me about my father and once, when she came to my room sober, looking sad and tired, she said:

'I dreamed about your father last night. He was walking through a field with a hazel stick in his hand and whistling to a spotted dog which ran after him wagging its tongue. I've been dreaming a lot about Maxim lately: looks like his restless soul can find no sanctuary. . . .'

Several evenings running she told me about my father – a narrative as interesting as any of her fairy stories. Father was the son of a soldier who became an officer and then was exiled to Siberia for cruelty to his subordinates. There, in Siberia, my father was born. He had a tough life, and when he was a young boy tried to run away. Once Grandfather hunted him with dogs in the forest, like a hare. Another time he caught him and gave him such a beating that the neighbours took the boy in and hid him.

'Are small boys *always* beaten?' I use to ask; Grandmother would calmly answer: 'Always!'

Father's mother died young, and when he was nine years old, my grandfather died, and Father was adopted by his godfather, who was a carpenter, apprenticed to the guild in Perm, where he started teaching him his own trade. But Father ran away, earned a living by leading blind beggars around the markets, and was sixteen when he came to Nizhny Novgorod. He started working for a firm of contract carpenters with Kolchin's steamboats. By the time he was twenty he was already skilled as a cabinet-maker, upholsterer and decorator. The workshop was next to my grandfather's house, in Kovalikha Street.

'They were a lively bunch, and their gardens had low fences,' Grandmother said laughing. 'There I was picking raspberries in the garden with Varya, when along comes your father, nips over the fence in a twinkling; scared out of my wits I was: there he was walking through the apples trees, a big strapping fellow in a white shirt and corduroy trousers, no hat, no shoes, and a leather band holding his long hair back. He'd come to propose to your mother! I'd seen him before, going past the window, and thought to myself: There's a fine chap! I asked him when he came up to us: "Lost your way again?" And he goes down on his knees, and says: "Akulina Ivanovna, here I am, all of me, body and soul. It's Varya I want. For God's sake help us, we want to get married." I was petrified, I don't mind telling you, and struck dumb. And then I saw your mother, the hussy, hiding behind the apple tree, her face as red as the raspberries, signalling to him, if you please, and her eyes all full of tears. So I said, "To hell with you! What have you been up to? Are you in your right mind, Varya? Young man, think what you're doing. Can you really support a wife and family?" – Grandfather at that time was a rich man, and the children hadn't been left anything yet. He had four houses, and money, and was a respected man. Not long before he'd been presented with a hat covered in gold braid and a uniform for nine years' service as works foreman without a break. So proud he was then! So I said what had to be said, shaking all over I was, and feeling really sorry for the two of them. You should have seen the look on their faces! Then your father said: "I know Vassily Vassilyev won't let me have Varya if he can help it, so I'm going to run away with her, but you must help us!" Asking *me* he was! I even tried to push him away, but he wouldn't budge. "I don't mind if you throw stones at me, only help me. I'm not giving in so easily." Varvara came up to him, put her hand on his shoulder and says: "We've been man and wife since May. All we need is a church wedding." I nearly fell through the floor, I did.'

Grandmother was shaking all over with laughter. She took some snuff, wiped the tears away and continued with a happy sigh:

'You're too young to understand the difference in being man and wife, and having a wedding in church. It's a terrifying thing, let me tell you, for a young girl to have a baby without being married. You remember that when you grow up, and don't you get young girls into trouble. You'd never live down the shame, and the girl would be unhappy, and there'd be a bastard child – just remember! You must always respect and love women and not just use them for a bit of fun. I know what I'm talking about!'

She pondered for a moment, rocking herself to and fro on the chair, then she gave a start and began again:

'Well, it was a problem, I can tell you. I gave Maxim one on the head, and pulled Varvara by the hair. Then Maxim says quite sensibly: "Fighting won't help!" And she says: "Yes, we should think first what we're going to do and then fight!" I asked him if he had any money. He replied: "I did have some, but I bought Varvara a ring with it." "How much did you pay for it – three hundred?" "No, about one hundred." In those days money was money. I looked at them both and thought what stupid children they were! Your mother said: "I hid the ring under the floorboards, so you wouldn't see it. We can sell it now!" Just like children! However, we all agreed the wedding would be in a week's time and I was to arrange things with the priest. But how my heart shuddered when I thought what Grandfather would say, and even Varvara was terrified. So it was all arranged. But your father had an enemy, a foreman or something, an evil man, and he'd guessed a long time ago what we'd been up to and had been watching us. Well, I dressed my little daughter up in the best I could afford, and led her out into the street. A troika was waiting round the corner. She got in, Maxim whistled and off they went. I was on my way back into the house, weeping buckets, when along came that swine I just told you about. "I'm an honest man," he says, "and I don't want to interfere in what's meant to be. Just give me fifty roubles and I won't say a thing." I didn't have any money, as I never liked it or saved any. Like a fool I says, "I haven't got any and I wouldn't give you any if I had." "You'd better promise to give me it later then," he says. But what was the use of promising if I had no hope of getting the money. "You have a rich husband, it shouldn't be difficult to steal from him." If I'd had any sense, I should have kept him talking for as long as I could, but stupid me spat right in his ugly mug and went home. He got to the yard before me and began stirring everyone up.'

She closed her eyes and said through her smile:

'It makes my flesh creep even now to think of the terrible things that went on then! Grandfather roared like a wild animal. It wasn't a joke as far as he was concerned. He used to look at Varvara and boast that she'd marry a nobleman, a gentleman. The Holy Virgin knows better than us who should be joined in wedlock. Anyway, Grandfather rushed around the yard as if it was on fire, called out Yasha and Mikhail, and that two-timing workman, and Klim the coachman. I saw him take an iron ball fastened to a strap and Mikhail grabbed a rifle. We had good, speedy horses, and a light droshky. They won't have much trouble catching them up, I thought. But just then Varvara's guardian angel put an idea into my head: I got a knife and hacked away the harness strap at the shaft, so it would break while they were on the way. And it did. The shaft slipped out, nearly killing your grandfather and Mikhail and Klim. But it held them up long enough, and by the time they got to the church Varvara and Maxim were already standing in the porch – married, thank God! They all went for Maxim, but he was very fit and exceptionally strong. He flung Mikhail out of the porch, breaking his arm, and hurt Klim as well, at which your grandfather, Yashka and the foreman panicked. Even though he was in a terrible temper your father kept his head and said to Grandfather, "Stop waving that strap about. I don't like fights. What I took, God gave to me and no one's going to take it away. I want nothing more from you." They fell back and Grandfather climbed into the droshky shouting: "Goodbye, Varvara, you're no daughter of mine. I never want to see you again. I don't care whether you starve now." He came back to the house and started beating me and cursing, but I didn't complain and just groaned a bit.

'I knew it would all blow over in time and that what was meant to be, would be. Then he said to me: "Well Akulina, now you've got no daughter, remember!" And I kept thinking to myself: "Lie as much as you like, you old red devil. Anger's like ice, and is very quick to melt." '

I listened attentively, hungrily. Some of the things in her story surprised me, for Grandfather had drawn a completely different picture of Mother's wedding. He was against it, and afterwards wouldn't allow Mother in his house. But she did in fact have a wedding, according to this version, not in secret, and Grandfather was in church with her. I didn't want to ask Grandmother which of them was more careful of the actual facts, because Grandmother's story was more beautiful and I liked it much more. When she was telling me all that happened she rocked to and fro, just as if she were in a boat. When she reached some very sad or terrifying incident, the rocking would become more violent, and she would stretch her arm out as though she were trying to hold something in mid-air. She would often close her eyes, and her wrinkled cheeks hid a kindly, fleeting smile. One could just detect the slightest trembling of her thick eyebrows. Sometimes her blind kindness, which accepted everything, good or bad, touched me deeply, but at other times I dearly wished she would curse out loud or make some sort of protest.

'For the first week or two I had no idea where Varvara and Maxim were, and then she sent a small, quick-witted boy to tell me where to find them. I waited until Saturday and made out I was going to late mass, but of course I went to see them! They'd taken a place a long way away, in Suyetinsky Street,

184

in the wing of a house. The yard was crowded with all kinds of workmen, and was dirty and noisy, but it didn't seem to worry them. They were just like a lively pair of kittens, the way they mewed and played. I took them what I could: tea, sugar, cereals, jam, flour, dried mushrooms, some money I managed to scrape together – I don't remember how much – but I took what I could get from Grandfather without him seeing: there's nothing wrong in stealing if you're doing it for other people! But your father wouldn't accept anything, and was very offended. "Do you think we're beggars?" he says. And Varvara took up the same tune: "What's that for, Mamma?" So I gave them a right telling-off. "Do you take me for a fool? I'm your own mother, idiot! When a mother is insulted here on earth our Heavenly Mother sheds bitter tears!"

'When I said this, Maxim seized my hand and started waltzing with me round the room – he was as strong as a bear! And there was Varvara putting on airs, just like a peacock, boasting about her husband, so you'd think he was a new doll, and telling all about how to run the house as though she'd been married sixty years. You would have died laughing! And those cheese cakes she served up with the tea – fit to break a wolf's teeth! And the cheese curds – like spreading gravel! And so it went on and on. You were just about to be born at this time. Grandfather didn't say a word, he was so obstinate! I used to creep off to see them – he knew this very well, but he didn't say anything. Nobody was allowed even to mention Varvara's name in the house, and everyone kept their mouths shut – at least I did. But I knew Grandfather couldn't go on very long like that, and he wasn't made of wood. Soon there was such a blizzard one night. The wind sounded like bears banging at the windows, and there was a terrible whistling in the chimneys, as if all Hell was let loose. There was I with Grandfather, neither of us able to sleep, so I said to him: "A rough night for beggars, even worse for those with uneasy consciences." Suddenly Grandfather asked: "How are they?" and I answered: "Fine, getting on quite well." And he said: "Who do you think I'm asking about?" "Varvara and Maxim." "And how did you guess?" "It's high time you stopped your game. It's not doing any good at all, is it?"

'Then he sighed and said: "You devils! Blue devils!" Then he asked: "What about that great big fool?" (meaning your father) "Am I right or aren't I?" I said: "A fool is someone who doesn't want to work and is a millstone round someone's neck. Just look at Yakov and Mikhail – aren't they fools? Who's the breadwinner in this house? You. And a fat lot of help you get from them!" At this he started swearing at me and calling me a fool and a vile woman, and a pimp, and God knows what else! So I kept my silence. "How could you be taken for a ride by someone you know nothing about, not even where he comes from?" he said. Still I said nothing, but when I saw he was getting tired, I told him: "I think you'd better go and see for yourself how they're getting on." To which he replied: "It'd be far better if they came here." This made me nearly weep with joy and he started undoing my hair (he loved playing with my hair) and mumbled: "Stop snivelling, idiot, don't you think I've a heart as well?" In those days your grandfather was a marvellous man, but as soon as he got it into his head that he was better than anyone else, then he became spiteful and stupid.

'Well, your father and mother came to see us in the end one Absolution Sunday, both looking very clean, smart, big and healthy. When Maxim stood by your grandfather, who only came up to his shoulder, he said: "Don't think for one moment, Vassily Vassilyevich, that I've come after a dowry. The reason for my visit is to pay my respects to my father-in-law." This pleased Grandfather and he laughed and said: "You're a fine fellow! Well, we've had enough of this playing around. You'd better come and live with us!" Maxim frowned and said: "Varvara can do what she likes, it's all the same to me!" Then they started having a real go at each other and I thought they'd never come to see eye to eye. I kept winking at your father and kicking him under the table, but he wouldn't give in! He had wonderful eyes: bright and pure, but his eyebrows were dark, and he had a habit of lowering them, so they hid his eyes, and his face turned to stone, the picture of obstinacy. Then he wouldn't listen to anyone except me. I loved him more than anything else, even my own sons, and he knew this and loved me as well! He'd hug me, or take me in his arms and pull me round the room. "You're my real mother!" he'd say, "like the earth, and I love you more than Varvara!" In those days your mother was a lively bundle of mischief and when he said things like that she used to rush at him and shout: "How dare you say such things, you great cauliflower-eared lout!" Then all three of us would fling ourselves about. Life was good then, my dear! Your father was a fine dancer and knew some lovely songs – he learnt them from blind tramps, and you know no one can sing better than them!

'So he set up house in the wing by the garden. That's where you were born, on the stroke of noon. Father had come home for his dinner – and there you were to meet him! He went mad with joy, and as for your mother, he embraced her so hard, you'd think she'd done something really impossible! He lifted me up on his shoulders, and carried me round the whole yard to tell Grandfather he'd got another grandson! Even Grandfather was tickled pink and burst out laughing. "What a lad you are, Maxim!" he said.

'But your uncles didn't like him – he never touched wine, had a quick tongue and was always up to all kinds of tricks. And later they made him pay dearly for it. Once, around Lent, the wind got up and suddenly the house was filled with a terrible moaning and howling. Everyone was scared out of his wits, thinking there were hundreds of ghosts running about wild. Grandfather panicked completely, ordered all the icon lamps to be lit and ran round shouting: "We must say a special mass at once!" Then suddenly all the noises stopped – which frightened everyone all the more. Uncle Yakov guessed that it was another piece of your father's work. And afterwards your father confessed that he'd put some bottles, all different sizes, in the window of the attic so the wind blew though their necks and made a different noise in each one. "Any more of these games and you'll find yourself back in Siberia," Grandfather warned him at the time.

'One year there was a severe frost and the wolves started

coming down from the fields, right into the yard. Sometimes they devoured one of the dogs, or frightened a horse or ate a drunken watchman. They made a lot of trouble! Your father would take his rifle, put his snow shoes on, and go out to the fields and bring back a wolf or two. He would skin them, stuff the heads and put glass eyes in, which he was very clever at. One night Uncle Mikhail went out to the lavatory and suddenly came running back, his hair on end, his eyes popping out, and too paralysed to say anything. His trousers were falling down and he got tangled up in them and tripped over. "A wolf!" he whispered. Everyone seized the first thing they could lay their hands on and rushed out to the lavatory with lighted torches. And sure enough there was a wolf poking its head out from the seat. They fired at it, beat it, but this didn't have the slightest effect. Then they took a closer look, and found a skin and an empty head, with the front legs nailed to the seat! Grandfather was mad with Maxim. And then Uncle Yakov started getting up to tricks. Maxim would glue together a cardboard head, paint in a nose, eyes and mouth, and use oakum for the hair. Then he'd walk along the street with Yakov, and poke the terrifying faces in at people's windows, making them cry out in fright. At night-time they'd dress themselves up in sheets, and frighten the priest, who once ran to tell the watchman, scaring him out of his wits and making him raise the alarm. That's only one of the things they got up to, and there wasn't any stopping them either. I tried to reason with them, so did Varvara, but you might have talked to the wall. Maxim would laugh and say: "It just chokes me how easily you can make people panic!" It was no use talking to him. . . .

'All this nearly brought him to an untimely end. Uncle Mikhail was just like Grandfather – quick to take offence, spiteful, and he'd made his mind up to get rid of your father. One day, at the beginning of winter, they were all four of them coming back from visiting some friends: Maxim, your uncles and a deacon (later he was defrocked for beating a cabman to death). They came down Yamsky Street and persuaded your father to go sliding with them on Dyukov pond, without skates, like little boys. Well, they got him there, and pushed him through a hole in the ice ... but you've already heard that story ...'

'Why were my uncles so wicked?'

'They weren't wicked,' answered Grandmother calmly, taking a pinch of snuff, 'just stupid. Mikhail's cunning, but stupid all the same and Yakov's just an idiot. As I was saying, they pushed him into the water and when he came up and tried to get a hold on the edge of the ice they began hitting his hands and stamping his fingers with their boots. Luckily for him he was sober, and they were drunk. With God's help he somehow managed to heave himself up above the ice and breathe by keeping his head above water and stay in the middle so they couldn't reach him. Then they started throwing pieces of ice at him and went off leaving him to drown on his own! But he climbed out, and ran to the police station – there's one in the square. The sergeant knew him and the whole family and asked what happened.'

Grandmother crossed herself and said gratefully: 'May the soul, O Lord, of Maxim Savvatyevich, find perfect rest with Thy saints, for he has earned it! He didn't say a thing to the police, and told them he'd got drunk and fallen into the pond without anyone's help. The sergeant said: "You don't drink. You're lying!" I don't know how long they kept him at the station. They dosed him with drink, gave him dry clothes to put on and wrapped a sheepskin coat round him, and the two policemen brought him home. Yasha and Mikhail hadn't arrived home yet, they were still crawling round the pubs, drinking their parents' health. Mother and I looked at Maxim, but we could hardly recognize him. He was blue all over, his fingers were cut, and bleeding, and there was snow on his temples, which didn't melt: the hair there had gone grey. Varvara cried out: "What have they done to you?" The sergeant started asking all sort of awkward questions, cross-examining everyone, and deep down in my heart I felt things were going badly. I set Varvara against the sergeant and started on Maxim myself. "What really happened?" I asked him. "Get Mikhail and Yakov before the police see them and let them say that we split up in Yamsky Street – they went on down Pokrovka, while I turned into Pryadilny Street. And

don't get it mixed up, or I'll be in trouble with the police!"
I went to Grandfather and said: "Go and have a word with
the sergeant while I wait for our sons by the gate." And I told
him the terrible thing that had happened. As he got dressed,
he was trembling all over, and he muttered to himself, "I
knew it would happen in the end. Just as I expected!" But he
was lying, as he didn't know anything. I gave each of the
children a good hard slap. Mikhail was so taken aback he
sobered up at once, but Yakov was so tipsy, all he could
mumble was: "I don't know anything, it's all Mikhail's work,
he's the eldest." We managed to pacify the sergeant, who
wasn't a bad sort, all in all. He said: "Mind how you go now.
If there's any more trouble, I'll know who it is!" With that he
left. Grandfather went up to Maxim and said: "Thanks.
Anybody else in your position would have acted quite differently. My daughter's brought a good man home!" He
could use fine words when he wanted to, your grandfather,
but later on in his life, out of stupidity and nothing more, he
locked up his heart. So the three of us were left there and
Maxim started crying and acting as if he were delirious. "Why
are they all against me? What have I done to them? Mamma,
tell me, what?" He used to call me mamma, not mamasha,
just like a little boy, which he really was. "Why?" he asked
again. What could I do but moan and sob? They were all my
children, after all, and I felt so sorry for them. Your mother
had pulled every button off her blouse and sat looking as if
she'd just been in a fight, all dishevelled she was. Then she
shouted: "Let's go away from here, Maxim! They're not your
brothers but enemies, and I'm so frightened!" I told her to
shut up and snapped: "Don't throw any more fuel on the
fire, there's enough smoke in the house already!" Then
Grandfather sent those two fools in to apologize, and your
mother jumped at Mikhail and slapped him hard on the face –
"There, I forgive you!" And your father started moaning:
"How could you do a thing like that, my own brothers? You
might have crippled me for life and how could I work without
fingers?" But somehow they made it up. Your father was
taken ill, and was laid up for seven weeks. Every minute he
kept saying: "Mamma, let's move to another town – I can't

stand it here any longer!" Soon afterwards he had to go to Astrakhan, where they were getting ready for the Tsar's visit in the summer and your father had to work on the new triumphal arch they were building. They took the first boat, and it broke my heart to see them go. Your father was really in the dumps and kept trying to persuade me to go with him. But Varvara was in high spirits and didn't even try to hide it, shameless bitch. . . . And so they went . . . that's all. . . .'

She gulped down a mouthful of vodka, took a pinch of snuff, and after a thoughtful look at the dark blue sky beyond the window, she said: 'Your father and I weren't blood relations, but we had the same heart. . . .'

Sometimes during her story Grandfather would come in, lift his polecat face up, sniff about with his sharp eagle-like nose, and watch Grandmother suspiciously, listening to what she was saying and muttering under his breath, 'You're lying, lying. . . .' He would ask unexpectedly: 'Alexei, has she been on the bottle again?'

'No.'

'You're lying. I can tell from the eyes.'

And he'd go away undecidedly. Grandmother would wink as she watched him go.

Once he stood in the middle of the room staring at the floor, and softly asked:

'Mother?'

'What?'

'You can see what's happening, can't you?'

'Yes.'

'What do you think, then?'

'It's fate! Remember, you were always talking about a gentleman.'

'Hm, yes. . . .'

'Well, this is him.'

'No money.'

'That's her affair.'

With this he went out. I sensed that all was not well, and asked Grandmother:

'What were you talking about?'

'You want to know everything, don't you?' she snarled, and

she massaged my legs. 'If you know everything when you're young, then there'll be nothing new to find out when you're an old man. . . .' She laughed and shook her head.

'Ah, poor Grandfather, you're a small speck in God's eye! Alexei, don't you say a word to anyone about this, mind, but Grandfather's lost every penny he had. He lent some man or other a lot of money – thousands – and the man's gone bankrupt. . . .'

Still smiling, she became lost in thought and sat there a long time without saying any more. Then her face clouded over, and turned wrinkled and sad.

'What are you thinking about?' I asked.

'Just another story to tell you,' she said with a start. 'Let's have the one about Yevstignei – all right? It goes like this!:

> Once upon a time there was a deacon Yevstignei,
> Who thought there was none cleverer than he,
> Neither among the clergy or the court,
> Nor all the old sages of the land.
> He'd strut about like a turkey
> And think he was lord of them all,
> And would teach all his neighbours
> That nothing for him was ever right.
> He'd look at a church – too low!
> And find a street was far too narrow.
> Any apple wasn't red enough,
> And the sun rose too early for him!
> He said the same about all he saw, this
> Yevstignei . . .

Here Grandmother puffed out her cheeks, rolled her eyes and her kind face became stupid and comical. In a lazy voice she went on:

> I could have built that better,
> I could have made a better job of it
> Only I haven't the time . . .

After a short silence she went on, speaking in a hushed voice with a smile on her face:

One night some devils came to see him.
'Don't you like it here, deacon!
Then come with us to hell,
The fires burn very hot there!'
Hardly had the deacon put on his hat
When the devils seized him with their claws,
Dragged him, tickled him, and howled,
And two sat on his shoulders
And pushed him into the fires of hell.
'Is everything all right, Yevstignei?'
The deacon roasted, his eyes rolled round,
And put his hands to his sides,
His lips pouted disdainfully:
'There's rather too much smoke here in hell.'

When she finished the fable in her rich, lazy voice, her expression changed and she explained to me with a gentle laugh:

'He didn't give in, Yevstignei, and wouldn't be budged in his opinions, just like your grandfather. Come, it's time you went to bed.'

Mother rarely came up to the attic, never stayed long and always spoke as if she were in a hurry. She'd become more beautiful, dressed better, and I could sense that a change had taken place in her and that the same had happened to Grandmother. I tried to guess what it was.

Grandmother's fairy tales interested me less and less, and even the stories about my father couldn't calm a vague feeling of alarm which grew stronger every day.

'Why is Father's soul troubled?' I would ask Grandmother.

'How should I know?' she'd answer, half closing her eyes. 'Only God knows that, it's not for us to know. . . .'

At nights, when I lay sleepless, gazing at the dark blue sky, and the trail of stars slowly sailing across the heavens, I used to invent sad stories, which centred on my father, who was always on the road alone, walking somewhere with a stick in his hand and a shaggy dog at his heels. . . .

Chapter 12

ONE day, towards evening, I fell asleep, and when I woke up I felt my legs had woken up too. But as soon as I lowered them over the side of the bed, they gave way again. All the same, I was convinced that my legs were sound and I would be able to walk again. I felt so overjoyed at this certainty that I cried out with joy, put the whole weight of my body on the floor and at once fell down. But I managed to crawl to the door and downstairs. I imagined the look of surprise on their faces when they saw me.

I don't remember how, but I ended up in Grandmother's lap in my mother's room. There were some people there I'd never seen before, and a dried-up looking woman in green was saying in a stern voice, which drowned everybody else's:

'Make him some raspberry tea and wrap him up from the head downwards.'

She was green all over – her dress, her hat and her face with a wart just under one eye. Even the small tuft of hair on the wart looked like grass. She dropped her lower lip, raised the upper, and looked at me with her green teeth, half covering her eyes with a hand in a black lace mitten.

'Who's that?' I asked timidly. Grandfather answered in an unpleasant voice:

'That's another grandmother for you.'

Mother laughed and pushed Yevgeny Maximov towards me. 'And this is your new father. . . .'

She started speaking very quickly, so I couldn't understand. Maximov blinked, leaned over to me and said: 'I'll buy you some paints. . . .'

The room was very bright, and on a table in the corner near the windows stood some silver candelabra, each with five lighted candles. Between them was Grandfather's favourite icon, 'Weep not for me, Mother!' The inlaid pearls glittered and melted in the candlelight, and flashes of fire came from the raspberry-coloured jewels set in the gold of the haloes. From outside in the street dim, round pancake faces pressed against the dark windows and flattened noses stuck to the glass. Everything around began to swim and the old woman in green felt around the back of my ears with her old fingers and said: 'By all means, by all means. . . .'

'He's fainted,' Grandmother said and carried me to the door. But I hadn't fainted, only closed my eyes – and when she was taking me upstairs I asked:

'Why didn't you tell me?'

'You keep quiet!'

'You're a lot of cheats. . . .'

When she'd put me on the bed, she buried her head in the pillow and broke into a convulsive sobbing. Her shoulders trembled violently as she said, choking with tears:

'Go on, you have a good cry as well.'

But I didn't want to. It was gloomy and dark in the attic and I was shivering. The bed shook and creaked, and the old woman in green seemed to be standing right in front of me. I pretended to be asleep and Grandmother left me.

Some uneventful days passed by in a thin stream of monotony.

After the engagement Mother went away somewhere and the house became depressingly quiet.

One morning Grandfather came in with a chisel, went up to the window, and started chipping away the putty from the outer window frame. Then Grandmother appeared with a bowl of water and some rags. Grandfather asked her in a quiet voice: 'Well, old woman?'

'Well what?'

'Are you pleased?'

In the same way as she spoke to me on the stairs she said: 'You keep quiet now!'

These simple words seemed to have a special meaning and concealed something very important and distressing which everyone knew about and didn't want to discuss.

When he'd carefully removed the frame Grandfather took it away and Grandmother flung open the windows. A starling whistled in the garden and the sparrows were chirping; the heady smell of thawed earth filled the room; at first I didn't recognize the bluish tiles in the stove, as they'd turned a faded white and it made me feel cold to look at them. I climbed out of bed.

'Don't walk about in your bare feet,' said Grandmother.

'I'm going into the garden.'

'It's not dry enough yet, you'll have to wait a few days.'

I didn't want to listen to her. Even the sight of grown-ups was unpleasant. The bright green needles of young grass had already pushed their way through the earth; buds swelled and burst open on the apple trees and the moss on Petrovna's roof had turned a lovely green. Everywhere there were birds.

These cheerful sounds and the fresh, fragrant air brought a pleasant dizziness to my head. In the pit where Uncle Peter had cut his throat lay a reddish-brown heap of high tangled grass, crushed by the snow. It was a nasty sight, and there was nothing springlike about the glossy black stumps of the charred beams. The whole pit was annoyingly out of place, serving no purpose at all. I felt a great longing to tear up the grass, drag out the pieces of brick, the beams, and to clear away everything that was dirty and useless and then build myself a neat little den where I could live in the summer without any grown-ups disturbing me. Immediately I got to work and at once completely forgot everything in the house. Although I was still smarting from the wrongs I'd suffered there, every day I thought less and less about them.

Now and again Grandmother or Mother would ask: 'What's all this sulking for?' It was an awkward question, as I wasn't really angry with them, only everything to do with the house had become so foreign to me. That old green woman would often join us for tea, supper and dinner, and she reminded me of a rotten post in a fence. Her eyes seemed sewn to her face by invisible threads. They rolled about easily and quickly in their bony sockets, seeing and taking note of everything, turning up to the ceiling when she talked about God and dropping towards her cheeks when the conversation was about more earthly matters, like the house. Her eyebrows looked as if they were made of bran which had been stuck on with glue. Her bare, wide teeth sank noiselessly into everything she shoved into her mouth with a hand comically bent and her little finger stuck out. Near her ears small bony lobes worked up and down, and the ears moved as well as the green hairs on her wart, which crept over her yellow, wrinkled and hideously clean skin. She was as immaculately clean as her son and I hated coming into physical contact with either of them. When she first came to the house she would press her dead hand against my lips. It smelled of yellow carbolic soap and incense, which made me jump back and run away. Often she said to her son: 'That boy needs educating, do you understand, Zhenya?'

He would obediently bow his head, frown and say nothing. That green woman made everyone frown.

I hated her and her son as well, so intensely that it brought me many a beating. Once over dinner she said, her eyes horribly protruding:

'Alexei, why do you bolt your food down. Such large mouthfuls. You'll choke yourself, dear.'

I took a piece of food from my mouth, stuck it on the tip of my fork and offered it to her. 'You can have it, if you want it so much.'

Mother hauled me away from the table and I was sent in disgrace to the attic, where Grandmother joined me later, roaring with laughter and holding her hand over her mouth. 'Heavens, what a sauce you've got!'

I didn't like to see her press her hand over her mouth, and I ran off, climbed up on the roof and sat for a long time by the chimney. Yes, I wanted to be rude and say spiteful things to everyone, and it was difficult to overcome this desire. But I had to keep up the struggle. Once I smeared my future father's and grandmother's chairs with cherry paste and they both got stuck. This was extremely funny, but when Grandfather had finished beating me, Mother came to the attic, drew me over to her, firmly held me between her knees and asked: 'Listen to me. Why are you so naughty? You don't know how hard it makes things for me!'

Her eyes filled with bright tears and she pressed my head to her cheek, which was so unbearable I'd rather she'd hit me. I promised never to insult the Maximovs again – at least, if she stopped crying.

'Yes, all right,' she said softly. 'But you mustn't be naughty.

We're going to be married soon, then we're going to Moscow and when we come back you're going to live with me. Yevgeny Vassilyevich is very kind and clever and you'll get on well together. You'll go to the high school and then you'll become a student – like he is now, and then a doctor, or anything you like. An educated man can be anything he wants. Go and play now.'

Those 'thens', strung out one after the other, seemed to form a ladder which led somewhere far away from me, into darkness and loneliness, and held out no happiness for me. I dearly wanted to tell her:

'Please don't get married, I'll look after you.'

But the words didn't come. My mother always aroused tender feelings of affection in me and I didn't feel ready to speak my mind.

My project in the garden was going very well. I'd pulled up and cut down all the grass with a scythe, and made a border round the pit, where the earth had fallen in, with pieces of brick. I'd made a wide seat which you could even lie on. I collected a lot of coloured glass and bits of broken crockery, smeared them with clay and set them in between the bricks. When the sun shone everything glittered with the rainbow colours of stained glass in a church.

'Very nice!' Grandfather said one day as he inspected my work. 'Only the grass will grow again if you don't get it out by the roots. Get me the spade and I'll dig them up for you!'

I fetched the iron spade, and he spat on his hands and with loud grunts started pushing the spade into the thick earth.

'You must get rid of those roots! Tomorrow I'll put some hollyhocks in and sunflowers – you see how pretty it'll look ... really pretty. ...'

Suddenly he bent over the spade and stopped talking. He stood quite still. I peered closely at him and could see small tears streaming down from his little, clever, doglike eyes.

'What's the matter?'

He started, wiped his face with the palm of his hand and looked vaguely at me.

'The sweat's just pouring off. So many worms!'

He set about with the spade again and suddenly said:

'You've wasted your time making all this. Just wasted it. I've got to sell the house soon. Probably towards the autumn. Mother needs the money for her dowry. Let *her* at least have a decent life. . . .'

He threw the spade down and, with a wave of his hand, went behind the bath house, in another corner of the garden, where his hot-beds were. I started digging again and right away cut my toe badly. As a result I couldn't go to the wedding and I just managed to walk to the gates and watched Mother walking arm in arm with Maximov down the street, her head bowed. Carefully she picked her way – just as if she were walking on sharp nails – over the grass which poked up between the pavement stones.

It was a quiet wedding. When they came back from church they all sat grimly drinking tea. Mother changed at once and went off to her room to pack, while my stepfather sat down beside me and said: 'I promised you a painting set, didn't I, but I couldn't find any good ones here. I'll send you one from Moscow.'

'And what do I need that for?'

'Don't you like painting?'

'I don't know how to.'

'In that case I'll send you something else.'

Mother came in.

'We'll be back soon. When your father's taken his examination and finished his course. . . .'

It was pleasant to hear them talking to me as though I were a grown-up, but it struck me as very strange that a man with a beard should still be a student.

'What are you studying?' I asked.

'Surveying.'

I felt too lazy to ask what that was. The house was filled with a weary silence and faint woolly rustling sounds. I prayed for night to come. Grandfather stood with his back to the stove and looked through the window with his eyes screwed up. The old green woman was helping Mother to pack and kept sighing and groaning. Grandmother, who had been drunk since midday, had been locked away in the attic so she wouldn't disgrace us.

Early next morning Mother left. She hugged me goodbye, lifted me high off the ground and stared into my eyes with a strange look. She kissed me and said: 'Goodbye, then. ...'

'Tell him to do as he's told,' said Grandfather sullenly, as he gazed at the sky, still tinted with pink.

'Do what Grandfather tells you,' Mother said as she made the sign of the Cross over me. I was expecting her to say something else and was furious with Grandfather for butting in. They got into the droshky. Mother's skirt caught on something and for a long time she sat there angrily trying to unhook it.

'Help her, or are you blind?' Grandfather said to me. But I didn't go, and felt bound down by heavy chains of despair.

Maximov carefully arranged his long legs with their narrow blue trousers in the carriage and Grandmother shoved some parcels into his hands, which he laid out on his knees and held with his chin. 'E-enough!' he drawled, nervously, wrinkling his pale face.

The old woman in green took her place in the other droshky with her elder son – the officer. She sat there stiff as a dummy, while he scratched his beard with the hilt of his sabre and yawned.

'So you're off to the wars?' Grandfather asked.

'Of course!'

'It's a good cause. We must beat the Turks.'

They drove off. Mother turned round several times, waving her handkerchief, and Grandmother leaned against the wall, shook her hand in the air and cried. Grandfather also brushed the tears away from his eyes and muttered short broken phrases: 'No good will come of it, no good. ...'

I sat on the kerb and watched the droshky bounce away: as it disappeared round the corner, something within me banged shut, closed up. ...

It was early. Windows were still shuttered and the street was deserted and dead – deserted as I'd never seen it before. In the distance came the tiresome sound of a shepherd's pipe.

'Let's go and have some tea,' said Grandfather as he took me by the shoulders. 'It looks like you're fated to live with me – you keep scraping against me like a match on a brick!'

From morning until night we both worked in the garden without saying a word to each other. Grandfather dug the flowerbeds, tied up the raspberry bushes, cut the lichen off the apple trees and squashed caterpillars, while I continued beautifying my sanctuary. Grandfather chopped off the ends of the charred beams, and put sticks in the earth for me to hang my bird cages on. I plaited together the dry grass and made a thick canopy which I hung over the seat I'd made, to keep off the sun and dew. Now it was a most delightful retreat.

Grandfather said: 'It's very useful if you know how to make things for yourself.'

I valued his words very much. Sometimes he would lie down on the seat I'd made and covered with turf, and slowly and deliberately, as if he had difficulty in getting the words out, would instruct me about life.

'Now you're a piece of flesh cut off from your mother. She'll have more children, and she'll love them more than you. As you see, your grandmother's started drinking again.' He'd stop for a long time, as though he were listening for something, then the heavy words would fall again from his grudging lips. 'That's the second time she's taken to drink. The first was when Mikhail was called up. And she persuaded me, the old fool, to buy him out. ... Perhaps he'd have turned out differently if he'd gone in. ... Ah, what's the use? ... And I haven't long now, which means you'll soon be left all alone. Understand? You must learn to be your own master and not work for anyone else! Live quietly, don't make any trouble, but be firm in all you do. Listen first to what people say, but then do what seems best to you. ...'

Excepting, of course, those days when the weather was bad, I lived in the garden the whole summer – even sleeping there on warm nights on a piece of sheep's-wool felt Grandmother had given me. Often she would sleep outside too: she'd bring an armful of hay and spread it near my bed, lie down, and for hours on end she'd tell me stories which she interspersed with sudden exclamations like:

'Look, there's a falling star! That's some poor lost soul

feeling homesick for mother earth. It means a good person's just been born somewhere.'

Or she'd point her finger and say: 'Look, there's a new star. Like a great big eye! Oh, dearest heaven, God's bright robe. . . .'

Grandfather would mumble: 'You fools'll be catching your death of cold or give yourselves a stroke. You'll get strangled by burglars!'

There were days when the sun would set and the sky overflowed with fiery rivers which would burn out, letting their golden-red ashes settle on the velvet green of the garden. Then one could feel everything grow darker, wider, and swell out, flooded by the warm darkness. Leaves heavy with sun would droop, the grass bent over to the ground and everything would grow softer, richer, and the air would be filled with light, caressing smells, just like music which floated in from the distant fields. Last post would sound from the camp. Then night approached and filled the breast with freshness and vigour, and like a fond mother's embrace, silence gently smoothed the heart with a warm, furry hand and erased everything from the memory that was best forgotten – all the corrosive, fine dust of the day. It was delightful lying face towards the sky; those great depths, receding further and further and revealing new constellations, imperceptibly lifted you from the earth and it was impossible to tell whether the whole earth had shrunk to your size, or if you had miraculously grown larger and swelled out until you mingled with all around you. Although it grew darker and quieter, invisible, sensitive strings would stretch out in all directions and each sound, whether a sleeping bird, a scuttling hedgehog or the soft sudden rise and fall of a human voice, had a sonority that wasn't heard during the day and was emphasized by that friendly, resonant silence.

A guitar being played, a woman's laughter, the clinking of a sword on the pavement, or a dog's bark – all these sounds were out of place here, and were only the last falling leaves of a faded day.

And there were nights when a sudden drunken shout in the street or the fields or the sound of someone running and tramping with heavy feet didn't seem at all out of the ordinary and aroused no interest in me at all.

Grandmother didn't sleep long and lay with her hands under her head. Holding back her excitement, she would tell me things, clearly not caring whether I listened or not. And always she managed to choose a story that gave the night even more meaning and beauty. The rhythmic flow of her words would send me off to sleep and I would awake to the sound of the birds. The sun would be looking into my face, the morning air would waft gently as it grew warmer, the leaves of the apple tree would shake off their dew and the moist green grass shine brighter and brighter until it became transparent like a crystal, while a thin vapour rose from it. The rays of the sun would fan out across the sky which grew a deeper and deeper lilac. Somewhere, unseen, high above, a lark would sing and every flower and sound seeped like dew into my heart, filling me with a calm joy and making me want to get up right away, start work and live in close friendship with every living thing.

This was the most peaceful and impressionable period of my life, and in that summer a feeling of confidence in my own powers was born in me and strengthened from day to day.

I ran wild and avoided people. I listened to the Ovsyanni-kovs' children shouting, but had no desire to go and play with them, and wasn't at all pleased to see the three brothers. On the contrary, I was worried in case they damaged my garden-sanctuary – my first independent creation.

In addition, Grandfather's sermons didn't hold my interest: they seemed to get emptier and were nothing more than a long string of petty complaints. He now had frequent arguments with Grandmother, chased her out of the house, so she'd go to Uncle Yakov's or Mikhail's. Sometimes she didn't come back for several days and Grandfather would do the cooking himself, burn his fingers, curse and shout, break the dishes and each day become more and more greedy.

At times he would come to my hut, sit himself comfortably on the turf, watch me for a long time without saying a word, then suddenly pop a question like:

'Why don't you say something?'

'What do you want me to say?'

Then he'd start his sermons all over again. 'You know we're not high-class people. Nobody's taught us anything, we've had to learn it all ourselves. Books have been written for other people to learn from, schools built, but we've had nothing like that. We've had to take everything we could get. . . .'

Then he'd lose himself in thought, dry up, and sit there motionless and dumb, making me feel very awkward.

In the autumn he sold the house and not long before it changed hands, one morning when we were having tea, he suddenly announced to Grandmother in a sullen, decisive voice:

'Well, I've kept you long enough. You must fend for yourself now.' This didn't surprise Grandmother at all, and she seemed to have known for a long time that it was coming. Slowly she took her snuff box out of her pocket, filled her spongy nostrils and said:

'All right then. What can't be cured must be endured!'

Grandfather took two dingy little rooms in the basement of an old house, in an alley at the foot of a hill. When they moved, Grandmother took hold of an old bast shoe, flung it into the fire, squatted and started invoking the hearth spirit. 'Hoblin goblin. Here's a sleigh for you. Come with us to our new home, where we hope we'll be happy.'

Grandfather stared through the window from the yard and shouted:

'Heretic! Just you try taking it with us! You'll bring shame on us all!'

'We'll have bad luck if we don't,' she warned seriously. But Grandfather flew into a temper and forbade her to bring the spirit.

The next three days he spent selling off our furniture and odds and ends to some Tartar secondhand dealers with whom he had angry arguments, while Grandmother looked out of the window, crying and laughing, and calling out softly: 'Take it all. Break it up!'

The thought of leaving my garden hide-out brought me near to tears. We went in two carts, and mine, which was crammed full with bits of furniture and crockery, shook so violently that it seemed to be doing its best to throw me off. And this feeling that someone was persistently trying to throw me off somewhere stayed with me for two years, right up to Mother's death.

Soon after Grandfather had settled in the basement, Mother arrived, all pale, much thinner and with enormous passionate eyes burning with surprise. She was continually staring at something and looked at her father and mother just as if she were seeing them for the first time. While she stood there without saying a word, my stepfather paced the room, whistling softly to himself, giving little coughs, and twiddling his fingers behind his back.

'Heavens, how you're growing!' Mother said to me, pressing my cheeks with her hot palms. She wore an ugly dress – broad and reddish and bulging out round her stomach. My stepfather offered his hand.

'Well, how are you? Eh?'

He sniffed and said: 'You know, it's very damp in here!'

They both seemed as if they'd been running about for a long time and in their creased, worn clothes looked worn out and ready to drop.

We had a boring tea. Grandfather watched the rain running down the windows and asked: 'Everything was lost in the fire then?'

'Everything,' my stepfather replied in a determined voice. 'We only just managed to escape ourselves.'

Mother leant on Grandmother's shoulder and whispered something into her ear, which made her blink as if blinded by the light. I felt more and more bored.

Suddenly Grandfather shouted out in a spiteful, but calm voice: 'It's come to my hearing, Yevgeny Vassilyev, sir, that there wasn't any fire at all and that you lost everything playing cards.'

The room become as silent as the grave. The samovar puffed, and the rain lashed against the windows. Then Mother said: 'Papa. . . .'

'What do you mean, *Papa*?' Grandfather shouted in a deafening voice. 'What's going to happen next? Didn't I tell you thirty and twenty don't go together. He's a fine one! Made you into a lady! Well, what have you got to say for yourself?'

All four started shouting, my stepfather loudest of all. I went outside and sat down on a pile of firewood, utterly stunned. Mother must have been changed for someone else, she looked so different.

In the room this was less noticeable, but here, in the dark, I could clearly remember exactly the way she looked before.

And then, quite mysteriously, I found myself in a house in Sormovo where everything was new and the walls bare of paper. The joints between the beams were lined with hemp and infested with cockroaches. Mother and my stepfather lived in two rooms facing the street, while I was with Grandmother in the kitchen, which had one window on to the roof. Beyond the roof, black factory chimneys stuck out obscenely towards the sky, belching out thick curly smoke, which the winter wind scattered all over the town. In our cold rooms there was always a strong smell of burning. Early in the mornings the factory howled like a wolf: 'Oooooo!'

If I stood on a bench I managed to see through the top windowpane and across the roofs to the factory gates, brightly lit by lamps and wide open, like the toothless black mouth of an old beggar. Into it poured a dense crowd of little people. At midday, the hooter sounded again, the black lips opened, revealing a deep hole through which the factory vomited up chewed-up people, who poured out into the street in a black stream. The snowy, rough wind swept down the street, driving the people into their houses. The sky was rarely to be seen above the town. Day in and day out another kind of roof, grey and flat, hung over the houses and the soot-stained snowdrifts. It weighed down on the mind and blinded the eyes with its wearying monotony.

In the evenings a dim red glow quivered over the factory. It lit up the tips of the chimneys, and it seemed that instead of having their foundations on solid ground, they were suspended from that smoky cloud, and pointed downwards towards the earth, breathing red flames, howling and screeching.

It made me unbearably sick to look at all this and an insidious boredom gnawed away at me. Grandmother took over the duties of cook – she got all the food ready, washed the floor, cut the firewood, fetched the water. She worked from morning till night, and went to bed moaning and groaning from exhaustion. Sometimes, when she'd done the cooking, she would put on her short, quilted jacket, tuck her skirt up high and go off to the town.

'Must see how the old man's getting on!'

'Take me with you!'

'You'll catch your death of cold. Just look at that blizzard!'

And she would walk about four miles along a road lost in fields of snow. Mother, her skin yellow from her pregnancy, would wrap herself round in a ragged grey frilled shawl to keep the cold out. I hated that shawl which destroyed the shape of her large, graceful body and detested the little tufts on the frill, and used to pull them off. And I hated the house, the factory and the village. Mother used to walk about coughing in tattered old felt boots, shaking her hideously large swollen belly. Her grey-blue eyes flashed angrily and would often stare emptily at the bare walls as though glued to them. Sometimes for hours on end she would look out into the street, which resembled a jaw in which some of the teeth had gone black, and twisted with age, while some had fallen out and had clumsily been replaced with new ones, which were too big.

'Why do we have to live here?' I asked.

Mother answered: 'Oh, shut up.'

She didn't say very much to me now, and only gave me orders: 'Get that, bring me this, fetch me some . . .'

They didn't let me go out very often, as each time I returned beaten up by the street urchins. But fighting was my only pleasure and I gave myself up to it body and soul.

Mother would flog me with a strap, but the punishment only put me in a worse rage and the next time I fought even more violently and as a result was punished more severely. And then I warned Mother that if she didn't stop beating me I would bite her hand and run away into the fields to freeze.

This made her push me from her in amazement, and she walked up and down the room, her breath coming in weary gasps, and said: 'Little beast!'

That living, throbbing gamut of feelings called love slowly faded in me and in its place there flared up, more and more often, smouldering blue fires of ill will against everyone. Discontent festered in my heart and a feeling of utter isolation in that grey, lifeless and ridiculous world dragged me down.

My stepfather was strict with me, said little to Mother and never stopped whistling or coughing. After dinner he used to stand in front of the mirror and carefully clean his teeth with a pick. His quarrels with Mother became more and more frequent and he talked to her as he would do to a stranger, which made me furious. During these quarrels he would shut the kitchen door tight, obviously not wanting me to hear what he was saying. All the same, I managed to hear his gruff, deep voice bawling away.

Once he stamped his foot and shouted out:

'Because of your blasted belly I can't invite anyone home, you old cow!'

In my astonishment and blind fury, I jumped up from the top of the stove so suddenly that I hit my head on the ceiling and bit my tongue so hard that it bled.

On Saturdays dozens of workers used to come to my stepfather to sell food coupons which they were meant to use in the factory shop. They were issued with these instead of wages and my stepfather bought them at half price. He would sit at the kitchen table, looking very stern and important as he took the coupons from them and said:

'One and a half roubles.'

'Yevgeny Vassilyev, for the love of God!'

'One and a half roubles.'

That senseless, obscure existence didn't go on for very long. Before Mother had her baby I was taken to Grandfather's. Now he was living in the Kunavino district, where he'd taken a tiny room with a stove and two windows looking on to a yard. The two-storeyed house was in Peschany Street, which ran downhill to the wall of the Napolyni church-yard.

'What?' he said with a squeaky laugh when he saw me. 'They used to say a boy's best friend is his mother, but now it looks like we'll have to say: not his mother, but his old devil of a grandfather. Ugh!'

I'd hardly had time to look round my new home before Mother and Grandmother arrived with the baby. My stepfather had been sacked by the factory for swindling the workers but he went off somewhere and managed to get a job as a ticket clerk in a station.

Many empty days passed and once again I was moved to the basement of a stone house where I lived with Mother again. She immediately sent me off to school. From the very first day it aroused nothing but loathing in me. I arrived wearing a pair of Mother's shoes, an overcoat made from Grandmother's jacket, a yellow shirt and long trousers, which right from the start made me the laughing-stock of the school. The yellow shirt earned me the nickname of 'ace of diamonds'. I soon hit it off with the other boys, but my teacher and the priest took an immediate dislike to me.

My teacher was bald, with a sallow complexion and his nose was continually bleeding. He would come into class with cotton wool stuffed up his nose, sit at his table, question us in a snuffling voice, and suddenly stop in the middle of a word to take out the cotton wool and inspect it, shaking his head all the time. His face was featureless, coppery, sour, and the wrinkles harboured a kind of green mould. Especially ugly were his leaden eyes, which didn't seem to deserve a place there at all, and they focused themselves so unpleasantly on me when he looked in my direction that I always wanted to wipe my cheek with the palm of my hand.

For a few days I sat in the front row, right in front of the teacher's desk. This I found unbearable. He seemed to see no one else except me, and kept on saying in his snuffling voice:

'Peshko-ov, change your shirt! Peshko-ov, keep your feet still! Peshko – o – v, your shoes have made a puddle again!'

I got my own back by the most daring tricks: once I laid my hands on half a frozen water-melon. I scooped it out and tied it to the top of the door in the dark vestibule. When the door opened the melon was lifted up and when my teacher shut it, it fell on his bald head just like a hat. The night porter hauled me off home with a note for my parents, and I paid for my mischief with a sound whipping.

Another time I sprinkled snuff in his drawer. He had such a fit of sneezing that he had to leave the room and sent as his deputy his son-in-law, who turned out to be an officer and made the whole class sing 'God Save the Tsar' and 'Ah Freedom, My Freedom'. Those who sang out of tune were rapped on the head with a ruler, in a way that didn't really hurt, but made a loud noise and which we found funny.

The teacher who took us for religious instruction was a handsome young priest with a thick growth of hair. He took a dislike to me because I didn't have a copy of *Sacred Stories from the Old and New Testaments* and because I mimicked the way he spoke.

When he came into the room the first thing he did was to ask:

'Peshkov, have you brought that book or not? Yes. The book?'

'No. I haven't. Yes.'

'What do you mean yes?'

'No.'

'Then go home. Yes. Home. I've got no time to waste on you. Yes. None at all.'

This didn't worry me too much, and I would stroll around the dirty streets of the quarter where we lived, closely observing its noisy life.

The priest had a fine, Christ-like face, warm feminine eyes and small hands, that seemed to fondle everything they touched. Whether it was a book, a ruler or a pen, he handled everything with loving care, as if what he touched was alive, and he was frightened of damaging it through carelessness. Even though he wasn't so gentle with children, they still loved him.

In spite of the fact I got on reasonably well in class I was soon told that I would be expelled for unsatisfactory behaviour. I became very depressed, as it threatened very unpleasant consequences: at home Mother was becoming more and more irritable and the beatings got more and more frequent.

But unexpected salvation appeared in the form of Bishop Chrysanth, a hunchback if I remember rightly, who once paid a visit to the school.* When that small man in his wide black robes sat at the table, pulled up his long sleeves to free his hands and said: 'Well, my children, let's have a little chat, shall we?' the atmosphere became suddenly relaxed and gay, and the whole room was filled with something strangely pleasant. After he'd talked to the others he called me out and asked seriously:

'You, how old are you? That all? Tall for your age, aren't you? Must have stood in the rain a long time, eh?'

He put one thin, skinny hand with its long, sharp nails on the table, ran his fingers through his thin beard with the other, stared at me with his kind eyes and suggested:

'Well now, tell me a story from the Bible – any one you like.'

When I told him I didn't have a book and couldn't learn anything from the Scriptures, he straightened his hood and asked:

'How's that? But you must learn the Bible. Perhaps you can recite something you've heard. The Psalms? That's fine. And your prayers. There, I said so! And the lives of the saints? In verse! So you're very learned after all!'

In came our priest, red-faced and breathless. The Bishop blessed him, but when the priest started telling him about me, he raised his hand and interrupted:

'If you don't mind, one moment. Come, tell us about that holy man Alexei.'

'Beautiful poetry, isn't it, my child,' he said when I stopped, having forgotten a line. 'Anything else? King David? I'd love to hear it!'

* *Author's Note:* Author of a well-known, three-volume work on *Religion in the Ancient World* and articles on 'Egyptian Metempsychosis' and 'Women and Marriage'. This last article, which I read in my youth, made a great impression on me. I think I may have got its title wrong. It was published in some religious journal of the '70s.

I could see he really was listening and that he liked poetry. He questioned me for a long time, then suddenly stopped, and inquired:

'Did you learn from the Psalter? Who taught you? Your good grandfather? Your wicked grandfather? Really now! I've heard you're a very mischievous boy.'

I could hardly get the words out, but I answered yes. The teacher and priest confirmed this confession in long wordy phrases. The bishop listened, his eyes downcast, then he said with a sigh:

'Did you hear what they said? Come here.'

He put his hand, which smelled of cypress wood, on my head.

'Why are you so naughty?' he asked.

'Learning from books is boring.'

'Boring? That's not so. If school were boring for you, then you'd be a bad pupil. But your teachers say you're good at learning things. It must be something else then.'

He took a small notebook from his breast pocket and wrote down.

'Peshkov, Alexei. Good. You'd better behave yourself in future and keep a tight hold on yourself and don't play about. A few pranks here and there don't matter, but all things in moderation. Otherwise you begin to upset people. Isn't that so, boys?'

A chorus of gay voices answered: 'Yes!'

'And of course you don't get up to mischief yourselves?'

The boys smiled and said:

'Oh yes we do! Lots and lots!'

The Bishop leaned back in his chair, drew me towards him and what he said came so much as a surprise that even the teacher and priest laughed: 'Don't think I didn't get into trouble when I was a boy! But what makes us misbehave?'

The children laughed, and he started cross-examining them, getting them to say what they didn't mean and contradict themselves, which made the atmosphere even gayer. Finally he stood up and said:

'I'm sorry to have to leave you rascals, but its time for me to go.'

He raised his arm, tossed back his sleeves to his shoulder, made the sign of the Cross in wide, sweeping movements and blessed us:

'In the name of the Father, the Son and the Holy Ghost, blessed be your labours. Goodbye.'

Everyone shouted: 'Goodbye, sir! Come and see us again.'

He nodded with his hood and said:

'Of course I'll come. Of course! I'll bring you some books!'

As he sailed out of the classroom he said to the teacher:

'Let them all have a half-holiday!'

Then he took me by the arm and led me into the hall, where he leaned over to me and said softly:

'Now don't forget, behave yourself. I know well enough why you get up to mischief! Goodbye!'

I was very disturbed by this remark and it left me feeling strange inside, as if something was boiling over. Even when the teacher had dismissed the class and kept me behind to tell me he expected me to be 'quieter than water' and 'lower than grass', I listened eagerly to every word he said.

In a kind, humming voice he said:

'Now you must come to my lessons. Yes. Without fail. And you must sit quietly. Yes. Quietly.'

After that things improved for me at school, but at home something very nasty happened. I stole a rouble from Mother. This was no premeditated crime: one evening she went out somewhere, leaving me at home with the baby. Out of sheer boredom I opened one of my stepfather's books – *Memoirs of a Doctor*, by Dumas Père – and between some pages discovered a ten-rouble and a one-rouble banknote. The book was too hard for me to follow, and as I closed it, the idea suddenly struck me that for one rouble I could buy not only *Stories from the Bible*, but *Robinson Crusoe* as well. I'd heard about this book not long before, at school. One frosty day, during break, I'd started telling the boys a fairy story when one of them suddenly said sneeringly:

'Fairy tales are rubbish! But *Robinson Crusoe* – there's a real story for you!'

Some of the others had also read *Robinson Crusoe* and found it very good, and I was very offended that Grandmother's story wasn't to their taste at all. There and then I decided to read *Robinson Crusoe*, just so I would be able to say, like them, 'That's rubbish!'

Next day I took with me to school the *Stories from the Bible* and two tattered little volumes of Andersen's *Fairy Tales*, three pounds of white bread and a pound of sausage. In a dim, tiny bookshop near St Vladimir's Church I found *Robinson Crusoe*, a thick book bound in yellow, with a picture of a bearded man in a fur cap and a wild animal's skin on his shoulders in the front. This I didn't like at all, but the fairy tales appealed to me at once, in spite of their tattered binding.

In the dinner-break I shared out the bread and sausage and we began reading that marvellous story *The Nightingale*, which had us all enthralled from the first page.

'In China all the people are Chinese, and the Emperor himself is a Chinaman.' I remember how that phrase enchanted me not only by its simple, laughing music but by something which was wonderful and good besides.

There was no time to finish *The Nightingale* in school-time and when I got home I found Mother frying eggs over the stove.

In a strange, faded voice she asked:

'Did you take that rouble?'

'Yes, I did. Look at these books.'

She gave me a thorough hammering with the frying pan, took away the volumes of Andersen and hid them away for good, which I found a lot more painful than the beating.

For some days I was away from school and during this time my stepfather must have told his friends at work about my exploit, and they in turn apparently told their children.

One of the boys carried the story to school and when I turned up for lessons I was welcomed with a new nickname – thief. It was a short and simple word, but unfair: after all, I hadn't

214

tried to cover up the theft. When I tried to explain this, nobody believed me, and this made me go home and tell Mother I'd never go to school again. A grey figure, with frenzied, tormented eyes, and once again heavy with child, she sat by the window feeding my brother Sasha and looking at me with her mouth opened wide, like a fish.

'You're lying,' she said. 'No one could have known you took the rouble.'

'Go and ask them.'

'You must have told them somehow. I want the truth. It *was* you, wasn't it? Tomorrow I'll find out who let the whole school know!'

I told her the boy's name. Her face wrinkled up in a pathetic frown and tears welled down her cheeks.

I went into the kitchen, lay down on my bed, made from some boxes over the stove, and listened to my mother quietly sobbing in the next room: 'My God, my God.'

I couldn't stand the foul smell of hot greasy rags round me any more and I got up and made for the yard. But my mother heard me and shouted:

'Where are you going? Come here!'

We sat down on the floor. Sasha lay in Mother's lap, pulling at the buttons on her dress and nodding his head backwards and forwards as though he were bowing.

'Bunnons,' he said, trying to pronounce 'buttons'.

I pressed close to Mother's side and she embraced me and said:

'We're very poor, and every copeck – every copeck. . . .'

But she never finished whatever she was saying and would squeeze me with her burning hands.

'That swine . . . that wicked swine. . . .' she said suddenly in words I'd already heard her say before.

'Sine. . . . ' repeated Sasha.

He was a strange child: clumsy and with a big head, he gazed at everything around him with beautiful blue eyes, showing by his gentle smile that he was waiting for something to happen. He started speaking very early, never cried, and lived in a perpetual state of quiet joy. He was very delicate, could hardly crawl, but always appeared very pleased when he saw me, made me take him in my arms, and loved to crumple my ears with his soft little fingers, which had a mysterious smell of violets. Quite suddenly he died, without having been ill at all. The day he died he was his normal happy self, but by the time evening came, when the bells were ringing for vespers, he was already laid out on the table. This happened soon after the second baby, Nikolai, was born.

Mother carried out her promise, and once more everything went smoothly at school.

But then they packed me off again to live with Grandfather. One evening when I was going from the yard to the kitchen for my tea, I heard my mother give a heart-rending scream:

'Yevgeny, I beg of you. I beg of you. ...'

'Nonsense,' my stepfather replied.

'But I know that you're seeing her. ...'

'Well, what of it?'

For a few seconds neither said anything, then Mother cleared her throat and said, 'You filthy scum.'

I heard him strike her and rushed into the room. Mother was on her knees propping herself up against a chair by her back and one elbow, her breast thrust out and her head thrown back; she was panting and her eyes shone with a terrifying light. And he was there, standing over her, in his bright, smart new uniform, kicking her on the breast with his long leg. I seized the bread knife with the ivory and silver handle which was lying on the table – the only thing of my father's left to her – and lunged at my stepfather's side as hard as I could.

Fortunately my mother managed to push him away so that the knife merely ripped open his coat and grazed his skin. With a loud groan he tore out of the room holding his side while Mother caught hold of me, lifted me up and with a shriek threw me down on the floor. My stepfather came back and took me away.

Late that evening, when he'd left the house, Mother came to my bed behind the stove and carefully hugged me and kissed me, and wept.

'Forgive me, I'm the guilty one. But darling, how could you? With a *knife*!'

Knowing full well what I was saying, I told her straight out that I was going to cut my stepfather's throat and then my own, and I really meant it. And I think I would have at least *tried* to do this. Even now I can see that hateful, long leg, with shining braid running down the middle of the trousers, dangling in the air, the tip of its boot kicking a woman's breast.

When I try to recall those vile abominations of that barbarous life in Russia, at times I find myself asking the question: is it worth while recording them? And with ever stronger conviction I find the answer is yes, because that was the real loathsome truth and to this day it is still valid.

It is that truth which must be known down to the very roots, so that by tearing them up it can be completely erased from the memory, from the soul of man, from our whole oppressive and shameful life. And there is still another, more positive reason which compels me to describe these horrible things. Although they arouse disgust in us, and crush the life out of many fine noble souls, the Russian man in the street is sufficiently healthy and young in spirit to overcome them — and overcome them he will.

Life is always surprising us — not by its rich, seething layer of bestial refuse — but by the bright, healthy and creative human powers of goodness that are for ever forcing their way up through it. It is those powers that awaken our indestructible hope that a brighter, better and more humane life will once again be reborn.

Chapter 13

AND once again I found myself with Grandfather.

When I turned up he banged his hand on the table and greeted me with the words:

'Well, you rascal, I'm not going to feed you any more. Let your grandmother look after you!'

'And so I will,' said Grandmother. 'Think of all the work!'

'Go and do it then,' he shouted. Then he suddenly calmed down, and explained to me: 'What I've got's nothing to do with her any more. Everything's separate now.'

Grandmother sat by the window swiftly making lace. The bobbins chattered merrily and the cushion stuck all over with brass pins shone like a golden hedgehog in the sun. Grandmother seemed to be moulded from brass, so little did she change. But Grandfather had grown thinner and more wrinkled, his red hair had turned grey and the calm authority of his movements had given way to a feverish restlessness. His green eyes surveyed everything with suspicion. Grandmother laughed as she told me how the property had been shared between her and Grandfather; he'd given her all the pots and pans and crockery and said:

'That's all you're getting from me!'

Then he took all her old-fashioned dresses, including a fox cape, and sold them for seven hundred roubles, lending out the money on interest to his godson, a converted Jew who dealt in fruit.

In the end he became a terrible miser and all self-respect was thrown to the wind. He began visiting old friends again who used to work with him in the guild work shops, and rich merchants, complaining that his children had ruined him, and begging for charity. Taking advantage of what respect they still had for him he wheedled a lot of money out of them and used to come home and wave bank notes under Grandmother's nose, boasting and teasing her, like a child. 'See that, you old fool. No one'd give you a fraction as much!'

He would lend the money to his new friend, a tall, bald

furrier nicknamed 'The Whip' and to his sister, a shopkeeper, fat, red-cheeked, with hazel eyes and as sweet and melting as syrup.

Everything in the household was very strictly shared out: one day Grandmother would get the dinner ready with food she'd bought, and the next day Grandfather bought the food – on those days dinner was invariably worse. Grandmother would buy good quality meat, but Grandfather was content with tripe, liver, lights, or stuffed pig's belly. They kept their own supplies of tea and sugar, but used the same pot for brewing up. When tea-time came Grandfather would ask her nervously: 'Wait a moment, not so fast. How much have you put in?' He would sprinkle the tealeaves in his hand, carefully count them and say:

'Your tealeaves are finer than mine, so I don't need to put so much in. Mine's much stronger!'

He would watch carefully while she poured the tea out in case his was weaker and she tried to do him out of a cup or two.

'One more cup?' she would ask before emptying the pot. Grandfather would peer into the teapot and say: 'Of course; there's another one there!'

They even bought their own oil for the icon lamps – and after fifty years of living and working together!

I found these quirks of Grandfather's both amusing and disgusting, but Grandmother only found them amusing. 'That's enough,' she used to say, trying to make me stop laughing. 'He's just getting a bit feeble-minded in his old age. He's over eighty – wait till you're as old as that! And it does no harm. Don't worry, I can always earn enough for a crust of bread!'

I too had started earning money. At weekends, early in the morning, I used to take a sack and go round the yards and streets collecting bones, rags, paper and nails. The rag-and-bone men gave twenty copecks for thirty-six pounds of rags and paper, the same for metal, and eight or ten copecks for the same weight in bones. I went round collecting after school as well, and on Saturdays sold about thirty or forty copecks' worth, and even more in a good week. Grandmother would take the money, hurriedly stuff it into her skirt pocket, and lower her eyes as she praised me: 'Thanks to you, dear, you and me won't starve. Not so hard, is it, after all!'

One day I found her looking at one of the coins and silently weeping. A single salty tear hung from the tip of her spongy nose.

More profitable than selling rags and bones was stealing logs and firewood from the timber yards along the Oka or at Peskii, an island where iron used to be sold in hastily constructed stalls during the fair. After the fair the stalls were taken down and the poles and planks from them were stacked on the island, where they were kept almost until the spring floods. Local landowners and landlords would pay ten copecks for a good plank and in one day it was possible to haul away two or three of them. But this we could do only in bad weather, when rain or snow drove the watchmen under cover.

We were a lively bunch: there was Sanka, 'the Dove', the ten-year-old son of a Mordvinian beggar woman – an endearing boy, very gentle and cheerful in his own quiet way. Then there was the orphan Kostroma, a boisterous, bony boy with huge black eyes who later, when he was about thirteen, hung himself in an approved school, where he'd been sent for stealing a pair of doves; and the Tartar, Habi, a strong boy of twelve, kind-hearted and simple; and the snubnosed Yaz, eight-year-old son of a gravedigger and night-watchman in a cemetery, who said as much as a fish and who suffered from the 'black sickness'. The eldest was Grishka Churka, son of a widowed dressmaker; he was a very reasonable, sensible person, and was passionately fond of boxing. We all came from the same street.

Stealing wasn't held as a crime in our district, as it was the habitual and almost the only way the half-starved small householders could survive. The fair only lasted for one and a half months, and this wasn't enough to feed the whole town. Many respectable citizens made a 'little something from the river' by fishing out logs and wood swept down by the floods and made small rafts out of them so they could be ferried away. Mostly, however, they stole from barges and other hunting grounds, 'monkeying it', as it was described, down the Volga and Oka, stealing any timber which wasn't properly secured. At the weekend the adults would boast about their hauls, and the children listened and learned.

In spring, during the feverish period of activity before the fair, the streets were overflowing with drunken workmen, cabmen and every other kind of labourer. The children would pick their pockets – a trade that was considered quite legitimate, and which was carried out fearlessly in front of the grown-ups. They stole tools from the carpenters, spanners from the cab drivers and coupling-pins from the carters, but our gang didn't go in for that game. One day Churka announced his decision: 'I'm not going to steal any more, Mamma won't let me.'

'And I'm too frightened,' said Habi.

Kostroma always felt aversion towards petty thieves and pronounced the word thief with special emphasis. When he saw strange boys robbing drunkards, he would chase them away and, if he managed to catch one, would give him a cruel beating. This morose boy with large eyes imagined himself as an adult, developed a special waddling walk, like a porter, and tried to speak in a deep, gruff voice. He was very stiff-looking, old, and unreal. The Dove was convinced that stealing was a sin.

But hauling logs from Peskii Island wasn't considered a sin; and not one of us was afraid. We worked out a routine that made our work considerably easier. In the evening, when it had got dark, or when the weather was bad, the Dove and Yaz went over the slushy, swollen back water ice to Peskii, quite openly, trying to attract the attention of the watchmen, while four of us crept up unnoticed from different directions. The watchmen, alarmed by Yaz and the Dove, would follow them. In the meantime, we assembled at a previously arranged meeting place among the piles of timber, chose our wood, and while our fleet-footed friends teased the watchmen, making them chase after them, we would make our way back.

Each of us had a piece of string with a big nail hooked at the end which we fastened on to the planks or poles and we dragged them over the ice and snow. The watchmen hardly ever saw us, and if they did, they never managed to catch up with us. We would divide the proceeds into six, which usually brought us about seven copecks each. On this amount one could eat very lavishly for one day, but the Dove's mother beat him if he didn't come home with a bottle of vodka. Kostroma saved his money, dreaming of the day when he would be able to go in for pigeon snaring. Churka's mother was a sick woman, and he tried to earn as much as he could. Habi was also saving up, so he could travel back to the town where he'd been born and from where he'd been brought up by his uncle, who was drowned soon after they arrived in Nizhny. Habi had forgotten the name of the town and all he could remember was that it was on the Kama, not far from the Volga.

For some reason this town became a subject of great amusement and we would tease our cross-eyed Tartar about it by singing:

> There's a town on the Kama,
> But where, we don't know,
> You can't touch it with your hands
> Or reach it on your feet!

At first Habi got very angry, but one day the Dove said to him in the cooing voice that justified his nickname:

'What's wrong with you? Angry with your own friends?'

This embarrassed the Tartar and he joined in the song about the town on the Kama himself.

All the same, we preferred collecting rags and bones to stealing timber. This was a particularly interesting occupation in springtime when the snows had melted and the rain had washed the paved streets of the deserted fair quite clean. In the gutters one could always find lots of nails, scraps of iron and often copper or silver coins. But we had to bribe the watchmen with four copeck pieces, or pacify them in some other way, or else they would chase us off or confiscate our sacks of loot. On the whole we had to work very hard for what money we managed to earn, but we all got on well together, and although we had our quarrels from time to time, I can't recall that we ever came to blows.

Our peacemaker was the Dove, who had a knack of saying

the right thing at the right time, and in simple, forthright language that never failed to startle and embarrass us. And the words that came out startled him as well. Yaz's spiteful sallies never offended or frightened him and everything that was bad he calmly, but convincingly, denied.

'What did you want to do that again for?' he would ask and we could see at once there was no reason.

He called his mother 'my Mordvinian', which we didn't find funny.

'Yesterday my Mordvinian rolled home dead drunk again,' he would tell us cheerfully, his round eyes sparkling like gold. 'She opened the front door and sat on the step singing like a hen!'

The serious Churka would ask: 'What – singing!'

The Dove would slap his knee and in a delicate voice begin to sing his mother's song:

> Oi, tap tap,
> The young shepherd knocks
> At the window with his crook,
> And off we run into the street!
> The shepherd Borka
> Sounds the evening call
> Upon his pipe,
> And everyone's quiet in the country.

He knew similarly vigorous songs and would sing them very well.

'As I was saying,' he continued, 'she fell asleep on the front doorstep and let all the cold in. I nearly froze, I'm telling you. Shivering all over I was, but she was too heavy for me to budge. So this morning I said to her: "Trying to kill yourself, with drink or something?" And she replied: "Don't worry, you won't have to put up with me for long – I'll be dead soon."'

Churka confirmed this in his solemn voice. 'Yes, you can see she hasn't got long, she's all swollen.'

'Will you be sorry?' I asked.

'What do you think?' the Dove said in suprise. 'She's been a good mother. . . . '

But although we all knew she continually beat the Dove, we believed this was true. On days when pickings were small, Churka would even say:

'Let's have a whip round for his mother to get some drink with, or else she'll start on him again. One copeck each!'

There were two of us who could read and write – Churka and myself. The Dove was extremely jealous of us and would pull at his pointed, mousey ear and say in his cooing voice:

'When I've buried my Mordvinian I'll go to school as well. I'll beg on my knees for the teacher to take me. When I've finished there I'll try and get a job as a gardener with the arch-bishop or even the Tsar!'

In the spring the Mordvinian, and an old man who was collecting money for a new church, and with a bottle of vodka in her pocket at the time, was crushed by a falling stack of logs. She was taken to hospital, and the practical Churka said to the Dove:

'Why don't you come and live with me? My mother'll teach you to read.'

And not long after that the Dove could be seen craning his neck to read shop signs: 'Grorecies.'

'Groceries, you nut,' corrected Churka.

'The leretts keep jumping about and changing places.'

'Letters.'

'They jump, just to show they're glad someone's reading them!'

His great love for trees and grass amazed us and was a constant source of amusement.

Our suburb, scattered as it was over sandy ground, was very sparsely vegetated, with only a few poor stumpy willows growing in the yards or stunted elder-bushes, and a few grey, dried-up blades of grass timidly hiding under the fences. If any of us happened to sit on that grass the Dove would angrily shout:

'What are you crushing the grass for? Can't you sit on the sand? Surely it doesn't make any difference?'

When he was there we felt awkward about breaking off a willow branch or cutting a willow twig on the banks of the

Oka, because he always looked at us in amazement, shrugged his shoulders, opened his arms out wide and said:

'What do you have to destroy everything for? You lousy lot!'

And his genuine indignation made us all feel ashamed.

Saturdays were spent in a high-spirited diversion and the whole week we prepared for it by collecting old bast sandals in the street and piling them up in hidden corners.

On Saturday evenings, when the bands of Tartar porters were making their way home from the Siberian wharf we would take up our positions at some cross-roads and fling the sandals at them. At first they were angry and swore and chased after us, but they soon got to like the game themselves. Knowing what was going to happen they would appear on the field of battle armed with copious supplies of sandals. What was more, they found out where we hid our ammunition and often stole from us. We complained about this:

'That's against the rules!'

Then they would share the sandals out, giving us half, and battle would commence. Usually they drew their ranks up on open ground while we ran round them screeching and hurling the sandals. They made hideous noises and deafened us with their laughter when a well-aimed missile knocked one of us flying face forward on to the sand.

The battles raged long and late, sometimes until it was dark, and then the people of the town would watch us from the cover of some street corner and shout for us to stop. The grey dusty sandals would fly through the air like crows and sometimes one of us was hit full in the face: but the pleasure of the game cancelled out the pain and sense of injury.

The Tartars became as excited as us. Often, when battle was done, we would go with them to their hostel, where they treated us to sweet horsemeat and a peculiar vegetable broth. After dinner we drank strong brick-tea, with little balls of sweet dough. We loved those huge men, each stronger than the other, and found something childlike in them, easy to understand. I was particularly impressed by their good-natured behaviour, their unwavering kindness, and their considerate and thoughtful attitude to each other.

Their laughter was fantastic and they almost choked themselves with tears in their fits of laughing. One of them, from Kasimov, who had a broken nose and fabulous strength, was said to have carried a bell weighing over eight hundredweight from a barge, far inland. He would howl with laughter and roar his rhymed nonsense.

'Vooo! Words are curds – money isn't honey!'

Once he put the Dove on the palm of his hand and lifted him high into the air.

'That's where a bird should live – up in the sky.'

When the weather was bad we went to the cemetery and met in the watchman's hut used by Yaz's father. He was a misshapen man, with long arms, dressed in rags, with filthy-looking tufts of hair growing on his grim face and small undersized head. In fact his head resembled a shrivelled-up burdock head and his long thin neck the stalk. He would blissfully half close his yellow eyes and mutter rapidly:

'May we all be blessed with sleep this night. Ooh!'

We bought a few ounces of tea, a little sugar, bread – and something that could on no account be forgotten – a small bottle of vodka for Yaz's father. Churka would order sternly:

'Put the samovar on, you filthy peasant.'

The gravedigger would laugh and put the tin samovar on to boil and while we waited for tea we would discuss the events of the day. He gave us good advice: 'Watch out, the day after tomorrow they come out of mourning at the Trusovs. They're making a big spread – there'll be lots of bones for you!'

'But the cook collects all the bones at the Trusovs,' remarked the omniscient Churka.

The Dove looked dreamily out of the window into the cemetery.

'It'll soon be warm enough to go into the forest!'

Yaz said very little and spent the time watching us closely with his sad eyes. Even when he showed us his toys – wooden soldiers, rescued from rubbish dumps, horses without legs, buttons and bits of brass – he kept silent. His father would put a whole selection of different cups and saucers on the table and bring in the samovar, and Kostroma poured the tea. The gravedigger drank his vodka, climbed up over the stove, stuck out his long neck, surveyed us with his owl-like eyes and growled:

'Perish the lot of you. Not like ordinary boys at all! A lot of thieves. God grant us sleep, ah!'

The Dove said to him: 'We're not thieves at all!'

If Yaz's father started boring us, Churka would silence him: 'Shut up, you filthy peasant!'

The Dove, Churka and I hated it when the gravedigger started enumerating the houses where there were sick people and guessing who was going to die next. He would speak about these things mercilessly, and with much relish, and when he saw we didn't like it he'd tease and torment us:

'Aha, so you're afraid. Of course you are. That fat one's going soon – and what a time it'll take him to rot!'

We tried to stop him but he wouldn't leave off:

'And you won't last much longer either, in those sewers of yours.'

'Then we'll die,' said the Dove, 'and we'll join the angels. . .'

'Y-you?' he said, breathless with amazement. 'You – angels?'

He guffawed, then started teasing us again with nasty stories about corpses. But sometimes he would tell us strange things in a subdued, gurgling voice.

'Listen, boys, and I'll tell you something! The day before yesterday a certain woman was buried. I knew all about her, and what do you suppose . . . ?'

He talked very often about women, always obscenely, but in his stories there was something provocative or pathetic and he seemed to be inviting us to enter into his thoughts, and we listened very carefully. He was a poor story-teller, nothing seemed to hang together, and often he interrupted himself to ask us questions. But his stories left disturbing fragments and splinters in the memory.

'They asked her: "Who caused the fire?" "I did." "And how, idiot? You were in hospital that night!" "I started the fire!" Why should she say a thing like that? God keep us from sleepless nights!'

He knew the life story of nearly everyone in the town whom

227

he'd buried in the sand of that depressing, bare cemetery. He seemed to open front doors for us and we would enter and see how people lived there, making us feel this was something important and significant. He would have gone on with his stories the whole night, but as soon as the windows of the hut grew dim with the approaching dusk, Churka would get up and say:

'If I don't go home Mamma will be frightened. Who's coming?'

We would all get up and leave. Yaz saw us to the fence, locked the gate, pressed his dark bony face to the grating and said: 'Goodbye!'

We shouted our goodbyes in turn, and always felt awkward leaving him there in the cemetery. Once Kostroma said as he looked back: 'One day we'll wake up and find he's died.'

'Yaz must have a worse life than anyone,' Churka often said, but the Dove always retorted: 'We don't have a bad life at all.'

In my opinion our life wasn't bad. The independent life in the streets was very much to my liking. I liked my friends as well and they inspired in me a feeling of restlessness, of always wanting to do them some good.

Things became difficult for me at school again and the boys laughed at me, calling me a rag-and-bone man, a tramp, and once, after a quarrel, they told the teacher I smelt of sewers and that it was impossible to sit next to me. I remember how deeply this hurt me and how hard it was to go to school after that. They invented the complaint just to spite me: every morning I used to wash myself thoroughly and never went to school in the clothes I wore for collecting rags.

But at last I passed into the third class and won some prizes: a *New Testament*, a bound Krilov's *Fables* and another book without a binding, with the mysterious title of *Fata Morgana*. I also got a good report. When I brought my prizes home Grandfather was very pleased and deeply touched, and announced that the books must be carefully put away in his own trunk. Grandmother had been ill for some days, and now had no money, and Grandfather moaned and roared at her: 'You'll eat and drink me out of house and home ... you lot. ... '

I took the books to a shop and sold them for fifty-five copecks, and gave the money to Grandmother. I scrawled all over the testimonial and gave it to Grandfather. He hid it away carefully without unrolling it or seeing that I'd ruined it.

I said farewell to school and settled down once more to street life, which now was more enjoyable. Spring was in full bloom, there was more money to be earned, and on Sundays we would all go out to the country, the fields and pine groves, and didn't return until late in the evening, pleasantly exhausted and firmer friends than ever.

But this kind of existence was short-lived: my stepfather got the sack and vanished again and Mother took my little brother Nikolai and went to live with Grandfather. As Grandmother had gone to live in the house of a rich merchant for whom she was embroidering a cover depicting the Body of Christ, I had to be nursemaid.

My mother, silent and wasted away, could barely move her legs, and looked at everything with terrifying eyes. My brother had scrofula, ulcers on his ankles, and was so weak he could only raise a feeble cry and moaned pitifully if he was hungry. When he'd been fed he would doze off and sigh strangely in his sleep, quietly purring like a kitten.

Grandfather felt him carefully all over and said:

'He needs proper food, but how can I feed all of you?'

Mother, who was sitting on the bed in a corner of the room, sighed hoarsely: 'He doesn't need much. . . . '

'A little is often a lot for others. . . . ' Grandfather waved his arm and turned to me:

'He needs to be free, out in the sun, on the sands. . . . '

I dragged home a sack of clean dry sand, heaped it in a sunny place by the window and buried my brother up to the neck, according to Grandfather's instructions. The baby liked sitting in the sand, sweetly blinking and looking at me with his strange shining eyes; they had no whites, only blue irises surrounded by a bright ring.

At once I became strongly attached to my brother. He seemed to understand everything I was thinking as I lay beside him in the sand by the window, through which would come Grandfather's squeaky voice:

'You don't have to be clever to die, but it's time you knew how to live.'

Mother would then have a long fit of coughing.

My brother would free his little arms and stretch out towards me, shaking his small white head; his thin hair was shot with grey and his face old and wise.

If a hen or a cat came near him, Nikolai would take a long close look, then turn to me with a faint smile, which disturbed me and made me think perhaps my brother sensed I was bored sitting there with him and really wanted to leave him and go out to play in the street.

We had a small yard crammed full with rubbish. Next to the gates were some ramshackle sheds, storehouses all made from odd bits of timber. These stretched away down to the bath house. The roofs were covered all over with bits of wood from boats, logs, planks, damp shavings, all fished out of the Oka during the spring floods. Ugly piles of wood cluttered up the yard, most of it still wet from the river, and lay there rotting in the sun, giving off a smell of decay.

Next door was a slaughterhouse for small livestock. Almost every morning we could hear the calves lowing and sheep bleating, and there was such a strong smell of blood that at times it seemed to hang in the air like a transparent purple net.

Whenever the animals bellowed, stunned by a blow with the back of an axe between the horns, Kolya, my brother, would screw up his eyes and puff out his cheeks in an effort, no doubt, to imitate them, but only succeeded in puffing out air: 'Phooooh.'

At midday Grandfather would stick his head out of the window and shout: 'Dinner!'

He fed the baby himself, holding him on his knees and chewing up bits of potato and bread, poking them into Nikolai's little mouth with his crooked finger, and getting the food all over his thin lips and little chin.

After he'd fed him for a little while, Grandfather would lift the child's vest, poke its swollen belly and say out loud:

'Do you think he's had enough? Should I give him some more?'

Mother's voice would come from the dim corner near the door:

'Can't you see he's reaching for the bread!'

'But babies are stupid! How can he know when he's had enough?'

And he continued shoving chewed-up food into Nikolai's mouth. It was intolerable and I felt a nauseating, stifling sensation down in my throat.

'That's enough now,' Grandfather said at last. 'Take him to his mother.'

When I lifted him up he would moan and reach out towards the table. Tall and thin like a fir stripped of its branches, Mother would force herself on to her feet and come to take the baby from me, stretching out her thin arms which hardly had any flesh on them.

It was as if she had been struck dumb. Whenever she spoke, which was very rarely, it was in a voice seething with emotion. and she stayed in her corner the whole day, just dying. I could feel that, and Grandfather was always talking about death, obsessively, particularly in the evenings when it grew dark outside and the warm smell of decay crept through the window, warm and stuffy, like a sheepskin.

Grandfather's bed stood in the front of the room, almost under the icons and he slept with his head towards them and the window. He would lie there muttering to himself for hours in the darkness.

'Now it's time for me to die. And how shall I look before my Maker? What shall I say? . . . My whole life's been spent running around after nothing. And what for? What does it all add up to?'

I slept on the floor between the stove and the window. This didn't leave much room for my legs, so I stetched them out under the stove, where I could feel the cockroaches tickling my toes. From this corner I could witness many events which filled me with malicious pleasure. When Grandfather was cooking he always managed to knock some of the windowpanes out with the end of the poker or oven fork. So strange and funny, that a clever man like him never thought of cutting down the handles.

Once, when something boiled over in one of the pots, he tugged so furiously at the oven fork that he smashed the window-frame and both panes of glass, upset the pot over the fireplace and broke it into the bargain. This incensed him so much that he sat on the floor and cried:

'My God, my God!'

During the day, when he'd gone, I took a bread knife and shortened the oven-fork handle by about three quarters. But when Grandfather saw my work he started cursing:

'Damn and blast you! You should have used a saw, a s-a-w! We could have made some rolling pins from the offcuts and got good money for them, you little devil!'

Waving his arms, he ran into the hall. Mother said: 'You shouldn't interfere. . . . '

She died in August, on a Sunday, about midday. My stepfather had just returned from his travels and had got another job somewhere in the town. Grandmother had taken Nikolai with her and gone to live in a clean little flat near the station; Mother was eventually going to join them there.

The morning of the day she died she'd said to me softly, but in a clearer, more carefree voice than usual:

'Go to Yevgeny Vassilyevich and tell him to come here!'

She lifted herself up on the bed, propping her hand against the wall, and sat up. 'Quick as you can!'

I thought she was smiling, and there was a new shining light in her eyes. My stepfather was at mass, and Grandmother sent me off to a Jewess (the wife of a policeman), who sold tobacco, for some snuff. She didn't have any ready and I had to wait while she rubbed the flakes.

When I got back to Grandfather's, Mother was sitting at the table, dressed in a clean, lilac-coloured dress. Her hair was beautifully combed and she looked commanding, just like she used to.

'Feel any better?' I asked, somewhat timidly.

She gave me a pained look and said: 'Come here! Where have you been all this time, eh?' I'd hardly time to answer when she seized me by the hair, took a long, supple knife made from a saw in her other hand and hit me several times with the flat side, lifting her hand high above her head. The knife flew out of her hand.

'Pick it up. Give it to me.'

I picked it up, threw it on the table and Mother pushed me away. I sat in front of the stove, terribly frightened, and watched every movement she made. She got up from the table and slowly made her way back to her corner, lay down on her bed and started wiping the sweat off her face with a handkerchief. Her hand shook, and twice dropped down to the pillow, which she wiped instead of her face.

'Bring me some water.'

I scooped a cupful from the bucket and she raised her head with difficulty, took a small sip, and a cold hand pushed mine away. She sighed deeply, looked at the corner where the icons were, then looked at me again.

What I thought was a smile flickered on her quivering lips. Gradually she lowered her eyelashes. Keeping her elbows pressed tightly against her side she moved her finger weakly while her hands crept slowly across the breast towards her throat. A shadow ran over her face, seemed to penetrate it, tightening her yellow skin and sharpening her nose. Her mouth opened as if in surprise, but I couldn't hear her breathe.

For what seemed an eternity I stood there with the cup in my hand and watched her face turn stiff, cold and grey.

When Grandfather came in I said:

'Mother's dead.'

He looked at the bed. 'Lying again, are you?'

He went over to the stove and made a deafening noise with the griddle and oven door as he drew out a pie. I looked at him, knowing full well Mother had died and wondering when it would sink in.

My stepfather arrived in a linen jacket and white cap. Without any noise he took a chair and carried it to Mother's bed, suddenly let it fall heavily on the floor and made a loud bellowing sound, like a trumpet:

'Yes, she's dead . . . look.'

Grandfather, with staring eyes, quietly shuffled away from the stove like a blind man, still carrying the griddle.

When the sand had been heaped over Mother's coffin Grandmother staggered about blindly among the graves and cut her face open on a cross. Yaz's father took her to his hut and while she was washing the wound offered her quiet words of consolation: 'Ah, God preserve us from sleepless nights! No point upsetting yourself like that! I'm right, aren't I? It comes to rich and poor alike, that's so, isn't it?'

He looked out of the window and suddenly leaped from the hut and came back with the bright and cheerful Dove.

'Look at this,' he said, holding out a broken spur to me. 'Lovely, isn't it? It's a present from me and the Dove. See that little wheel? Must have belonged to a Cossack. I wanted to buy it from the Dove, and offered him two copecks I did....'

'What lies!' the Dove said in a soft but angry voice.

Yaz's father jumped in front of me, winked at him and said: 'Can't take a joke, can he? To tell you the truth, it's a present from him, not from me....'

When Grandmother had washed she wrapped her blue, swollen face with a handkerchief and called out to me to go home, but I didn't want to, knowing there would be drinking and quarrelling at the funeral reception. While we were in the church Uncle Mikhail sighed and said to Yakov: 'Feel like a drink later?'

The Dove tried to make me laugh. He hung the spur on his chin and tried to reach it with his tongue. Yaz's father forced a loud laugh and shouted: 'Look at him!' but seeing I wasn't amused said seriously: 'You must try and pull yourself together. We all die, even birds. Would you like me to put turf round your mother's grave? Let's go now, you, the Dove, and me and we'll get some from the fields. Yaz'll come as well. You see, it'll look lovely with fresh turf all round....'

This idea pleased me and we all went off to the fields.

A few days after Mother's funeral Grandfather said:

'Alexei, you're not a medal, you're only hanging round my neck. There's no room for you here. You must go out into the world.'

And so I went out into the world.

Discover more about our forthcoming books through Penguin's FREE newspaper...

Penguin

Quarterly

It's packed with:

- exciting features
- author interviews
- previews & reviews
- books from your favourite films & TV series
- exclusive competitions & much, much more...

Write off for your free copy today to:
Dept JC
Penguin Books Ltd
FREEPOST
West Drayton
Middlesex
UB7 0BR
NO STAMP REQUIRED